DISRUPTING, DECENTRING AND DIVERSIFYING LANGUAGES AND CULTURES IN AUSTRALIAN UNIVERSITIES

DISRUPTING, DECENTRING AND DIVERSIFYING LANGUAGES AND CULTURES IN AUSTRALIAN UNIVERSITIES

EDITED BY ADRIANA DÍAZ,
BARBARA E. HANNA, SAMANTHA DISBRAY,
ANNA MIKHAYLOVA AND GRACE YUE QI

ANU PRESS

LCNAU STUDIES IN
LANGUAGES AND CULTURES

ANU PRESS

Published by ANU Press
The Australian National University
Canberra ACT 2600, Australia
Email: anupress@anu.edu.au

Available to download for free at press.anu.edu.au

ISBN (print): 9781760467074
ISBN (online): 9781760467081

WorldCat (print): 1529570519
WorldCat (online): 1529897506

DOI: 10.22459/DDDLCAU.2025

This title is published under a Creative Commons Attribution-NonCommercial-NoDerivatives 4.0 International (CC BY-NC-ND 4.0) licence.

The full licence terms are available at creativecommons.org/licenses/by-nc-nd/4.0/legalcode

Cover design and layout by ANU Press

This book is published under the aegis of the LCNAU Studies in Languages and Cultures editorial board of ANU Press.

This edition © 2025 ANU Press

Contents

List of illustrations	vii
Acronyms	ix
Editors and contributors	xi
1. Disrupting, decentring and diversifying languages and cultures in Australian higher education Adriana Díaz, Barbara E. Hanna, Samantha Disbray, Anna Mikhaylova and Grace Yue Qi	1
2. Slipping and sliding: Knowledge production, innovation and creativity from an Indigenous educational perspective Robyn Ober	19
3. Falling between the cracks: Learning and teaching Aboriginal languages in the adult education sector in South Australia Mary-Anne Gale and Rob Amery	41
4. Disrupting idealisations of communication in language learning pedagogy: Digital possibilities Levi Durbidge	63
5. In step: SOGIESC and language teaching, and learning and the linguistic diversification of gender justice Birgit Lang and Claire Maree	89
6. Diversifying language and culture through real-world connections: Virtual exchanges during the COVID-19 pandemic Matt Absalom and Roberta Trapè	115
7. Designing for adult language learning in a robot-assisted language learning context Grace Yue Qi, Yuping Wang and Nian-Shing Chen	147
8. 'It wasn't like getting up in front of the class to speak': Promoting L2 motivation and reducing L2 speaking anxiety through a podcasting project Riccardo Amorati, Elisabetta Ferrari and John Hajek	179

9. No tickets required! Interactive virtual tours and virtual environments in the study of Italian language and culture   201
   Elisabetta Ferrari and Mitch Buzza
10. Loosening the reins of teacher control: Empowering student writers through web-based tools   223
    Ana Maria Ducasse

Index   247

List of illustrations

Figures

Figure 1.1. Visual representation of disrupting, decentring and diversifying forces	8
Figure 1.2. Visualising the interplay of disrupting, decentring and diversifying forces	8
Figure 6.1. LGBTQI+ in Italy and Australia	130
Figure 6.2. The education of citizenship	131
Figure 6.3. Catcalling in Melbourne and Milan	132
Figure 7.1. A design pattern for teachers designing for adult language learning at university	157
Figure 7.2. An excerpt of learner-robot interactions	160
Figure 7.3. Making dumplings with a robot, a tablet and tangible objects (food ingredients and kitchenware)	164
Figure 7.4. Students' positive perceptions of statements incorporated in the post-study survey	165
Figure 7.5. The design team's immediate reflection, shared on the social media platform LINE	166
Figure 8.1. Factors contributing to students' motivation	187
Figure 8.2. The project as a challenging experience	189
Figure 8.3. The level of anxiety experienced in comparison to a class presentation	195
Figure 9.1. The beginning of the VR non-immersive video tour (Project 1)	209

Figure 9.2. Example of a virtual tour break and interactive links (Project 1) — 209

Figure 9.3. The voyage by sea of the two steamships, *Piemonte* and *Lombardo* (Project 2) — 211

Figure 9.4. 3D models of the expedition artefacts created with Sketchfab (Project 2) — 212

Figure 9.5. Virtual gallery of the three diarist-volunteers (Project 2) — 213

Figure 9.6. Video installation (Project 2) — 213

Tables

Table 3.1. Graduates of South Australian language training courses since 2011 — 48

Table 6.1. Virtual exchanges in 2021 — 124

Table 6.2. Virtual exchanges in 2022 — 127

Table 6.3. Italian students' comments — 134

Table 7.1. The task design process for making dumplings — 161

Table 8.1. The project as a rewarding experience and as an example of project-based learning — 190

Table 8.2. The use of language as part of the project and its link to the Italian presence in Melbourne — 192

Table 10.1. Template grading rubric — 232

Table 10.2. Student edits and sources table — 236

Table 10.3. Learner engagement as shown by LMS analytics — 238

Acronyms

AE	Aboriginal English
AfL	assessment for learning
AI	artificial intelligence
AILF	Australian Indigenous Languages Framework
AL	additional language
ASQA	Australian Skills Quality Authority
AWE	automated writing evaluation
CALL	computer-assisted language learning
CMC	computer-mediated communication
DBR	design-based research
ELT	English language teaching
ERT	emergency remote teaching
EUR	Esposizione Universale di Roma
IVEC	Introduction to Vocational Education Certificate
JML	Japanese men's language
JWL	Japanese women's language
KWP	Kaurna Warra Pintyanthi
L2	second language
LCNAU	Languages and Cultures Network for Australian Universities
LGBTQIA+	lesbian, gay, bisexual, transgender, queer, intersex and asexual
LMS	learning management system
MT	machine translation

NSW	New South Wales
NT	Northern Territory
OBL	object-based learning
OC	on-campus
OL	online
PBL	project-based learning
PISA	Programme for International Student Assessment
RALL	robot-assisted language learning
SA	South Australia
SACE	South Australian Certificate of Education
SAE	Standard Australian English
SAMR	substitution, augmentation, modification, redefinition
SGC	student-generated content
SOGIESC	sexual orientations, gender identities, expressions and sex characteristics
SSABSA	Senior Secondary Assessment Board of South Australia
TAE	Training and Education
TAFE	Technical and Further Education
TELL	technology-enhanced language learning
TPACK	technology, pedagogy and content knowledge
VET	Vocational Education and Training
VLE	virtual learning environments
VR	virtual reality
WA	Western Australia
WB	web-based

Editors and contributors

Matt Absalom is an award-winning educator who has held teaching and research positions in three Australian universities. His research interests cover aspects of teaching and learning, gender and languages education, applied linguistics and much more. Matt holds qualifications in music, education, languages and linguistics, and is a fierce advocate of multilingualism. His current position is in the Italian studies program at the University of Melbourne.

Rob Amery is a visiting associate professor of linguistics at the University of Adelaide. Rob completed a PhD in 1998 (published 2000, 2016) on Kaurna language reclamation. For more than 30 years he has worked closely with Kaurna people and their language, drawing on earlier experience in Central Australia and Arnhem Land to develop teaching programs and language resources, and implement strategies to reintroduce the awakening Kaurna language. Along with Kaurna Elders, he founded Kaurna Warra Pintyanthi (KWP) in 2002. He currently manages a small KWP team funded by the Commonwealth Indigenous Languages and the Arts program, which is producing electronic- and print-based Kaurna language resources.

Riccardo Amorati is a lecturer in the School of Languages and Linguistics at the University of Melbourne. Following his studies at the University of Bologna, Italy, he was awarded a PhD in applied linguistics from the University of Melbourne. His research focuses primarily on the psychological factors that influence second language learning (motivation, emotions, wellbeing) and on novel approaches to second language teaching. Other research interests include gender expansive language education and student recruitment and retention in language studies.

Mitch Buzza is an experienced digital producer within the higher education sector and is currently working in the Faculty of Arts at the University of Melbourne. During the 2000s, he coordinated part of a creative arts facility for Deakin University, specialising in imaging, digital darkroom printing and animation. From 2010, he has been supporting staff at the University of Melbourne with their learning management system platform and other related production work, such as small team video production, integrating edutech tools, and the production of virtual reality (VR) experiences and 360° 3D assets for classroom teaching. His current research and practice revolve around using social VR platforms and communities to 'world build' in low-code/no-code ways and exploring their possibilities for education.

Nian-Shing Chen is a chair professor at the Institute for Research Excellence in Learning Sciences at the National Taiwan Normal University. He is a three-time recipient of the National Outstanding Research Award from the National Science Council, Taiwan. He is ranked second among top authors in *Computers & Education* and fourth in educational technology for a publication in the *British Journal of Educational Technology*. His 2010 article in *Innovations in Education and Teaching International* was the most cited that year. According to the AD Scientific Index (2022), he ranks eighth in Education Research in Asia and was listed among the top 2 per cent of scientists globally in 2021. He currently serves as Editor-in-Chief of *Smart Learning Environments* and previously held the same role for *Educational Technology & Society*.

Adriana Díaz is a passionate languages and intercultural education scholar whose theoretical and empirical work centres on how insights from critical pedagogy and decolonial theories can help us un/relearn the ways in which we engage with the world. She is committed to creating innovative and inclusive liberatory learning experiences for language learners and fellow language educators to become critically aware of intersectional, power-bound dynamics in everyday interaction. This commitment is reflected in her scholarly publications and her work as a senior lecturer in Spanish and Latin American studies at the School of Languages and Cultures, University of Queensland.

Samantha Disbray is a senior lecturer in endangered languages and convenor of the Graduate Certificate in Indigenous Language Revitalisation at the University of Queensland. She lived and worked for many years in Central Australia as a community, education and research linguist. Her recent research focuses on language and the arts for language maintenance and revitalisation. With Pintupi–Luritja language specialists, she is co-curating the Wangka Walytja exhibition to showcase the illustrated literature of Papunya, opening in November 2024. Samantha is committed to promoting Indigenous language revitalisation through innovative community–university collaborations.

Ana Maria Ducasse is an associate professor that lectures in Spanish language, culture and sociolinguistics while publishing and supervising higher degree research in applied linguistics. She has investigated communication in IELTS (International English Language Testing System) speaking and compared TOEFL (Test of English as a Foreign Language) iBT (internet-based test)–speaking tasks with academic speaking. She has also investigated the differing interactional styles of Spanish and UK English speakers in persuasive entrepreneurial pitches and has been working on feedback on L2 writing tasks at RMIT University. In 2021, she joined Carmen Lopez Ferrero's team at Universitat Pompeu Fabra, Barcelona, on a four-year Spanish government-funded project, Inter_ECODAL, which examines interculturality and intercomprehension, and assesses plurilingual discourse competence feedback and the literacy of digital student feedback.

Levi Durbidge is a lecturer and coordinator of Japanese studies at the University of the Sunshine Coast. With more than two decades of experience in language education across Australia and Japan, his research explores the intersections and cultural politics of language learning, digital technology and international mobility. Levi's PhD thesis won the 2021 Michael Clyne Prize, and he received the MAK Halliday Award for Outstanding Research in Applied Linguistics in 2024. His book, *Language Learning, Digital Communications and Study Abroad: Identity and Belonging in Translocal Contexts*, was published by Multilingual Matters in 2024.

Elisabetta Ferrari is a lecturer in Italian studies in the School of Languages and Linguistics at the University of Melbourne. Her research focuses primarily on teaching innovation, experiential learning pedagogy and virtual reality to enhance the teaching of Italian and its cultures. She has additional expertise in Italian cinema and is currently leading a research project on the Italian cinemas of Melbourne from the 1950s to the late 1970s with a podcast series and related published research outcomes.

Mary-Anne Gale is a visiting research fellow at the University of Adelaide and a former trainer with Tauondi Aboriginal Community College and TAFE SA. Her involvement with Aboriginal languages began in 1978 when she was teaching in bilingual schools at Milingimbi and Willowra, and later Yirrkala in the Northern Territory. This was followed by MA and PhD studies in linguistics. Since 2003, Mary-Anne has worked intensively with the Ngarrindjeri community in South Australia in reviving their language and producing numerous language resources. She has also offered support to the Pitjantjatjara, Boandik, Narungga and Kaurna communities in South Australia by coordinating and teaching formal language training programs for adults.

John Hajek is professor of Italian studies and a linguist in the School of Languages and Linguistics at the University of Melbourne, where he also serves as head of school. He completed his university education in Australia, Italy and the UK. John is also the director of the Research Unit for Multilingualism and Cross-Cultural Communication. He has been active in the tertiary languages education in Australia for decades, and was founding president of the Languages and Cultures Network for Australian Universities (LCNAU).

Barbara E. Hanna is French major convenor and senior lecturer in French in the School of Languages and Cultures at the University of Queensland, where she also supervises doctoral research in second language teaching and learning. With longstanding research interests in learner identities and study abroad programs, she also works with undergraduate students in the Bachelor of International Studies who are participating in a study abroad experience, exploring the changes intercultural experiences bring to them and the differences they can make to the world.

Birgit Lang is a professor in German studies at the University of Melbourne. She has published widely on the German and Austrian history of sexuality, as well as in exile and translation studies (see also findanexpert.unimelb.edu.au/display/person139542). She initiated the 'Queering the Curriculum Project', including the first launch of the *Teaching with Respect for Gender and Sexuality* Padlet as part of her role as associate dean, diversity and inclusion, in 2019. Her current collaborative ARC Discovery Project, DP190101816, 'Visual Evidence: Sex Research in Germany (1890s–1930s)' (with Katie Sutton, The Australian National University), focuses on the visual turn in sex research in the early twentieth century. Recent publications include 'Censorship in Flux: Sex and Sexological Knowledge at the Great Police Exhibition of 1926 in Weimar Germany', *Journal of the History of Sexuality*, *33*(1), 2024, 102–129.

Claire Maree is a professor of Japanese at the Asia Institute, University of Melbourne. Claire's work brings queer, linguistic and cultural studies approaches to the study of language. Her third monograph *queerqueen: Linguistic Excess in Japanese Media* (2020, OUP), examines the mediatisation of queerqueen styles. Claire leads the Gender, Environment and Migration Research Cluster and facilitates the Gender, Sexuality and Language Studies Research Group at the Asia Institute, University of Melbourne. She is a member of the Queering the Curriculum Working Group, Faculty of Arts, University of Melbourne, and co-founder of the International Network of Gender, Sexuality and Japanese Language Education.

Anna Mikhaylova PhD is a lecturer in the School of Languages and Cultures at the University of Queensland. Her broad research interests include the cognitive, social and pedagogical implications of bilingualism. More specifically, she is interested in the similarities and differences between language development in second language learners and heritage speakers. Her emerging research interest is the effects of community engagement in language teaching and learning, both in formal and community-led educational contexts.

Robyn Ober is a Mamu/Djirribal woman from Innisfail who has had a 30-year association with Batchelor Institute. She is currently the coordinator of the Indigenous Research Practice team. A lead researcher at Batchelor Institute, she has published in the areas of Aboriginal English, identity and culture, and both-ways and Indigenous tertiary education. Robyn has extensive teaching experience and has been involved in award-winning Indigenous higher education and vocational education training. Her research has included Indigenous educational leadership and both-ways teaching and learning, and her research outcomes have been presented at national conferences and in research journals. She has been at the front line in the development of both-ways pedagogy, in working to combine Indigenous and non-Indigenous ways of knowing, being and learning in teaching practice and in research. In 2019, she completed her doctoral research, investigating identity and culture expressed in Aboriginal English.

Grace Yue Qi PhD FHEA is a senior lecturer and researcher in the School of Humanities, Media and Creative Communication, Massey University, Aotearoa New Zealand. Her research interests lie in the epistemological and ontological intersections of language, culture and technology, emphasising the humanistic orientation of language education. Her projects and publications include work on language policy and planning in

Australasia, plurilingual education, language teacher and learner agency and identity development, and language learner intercultural communicative competences in real and online multimodal environments.

Roberta Trapè is an honorary fellow of the School of Languages and Linguistics at the University of Melbourne. Her research shifts between theory—travel writing, notions of space and movement in contemporary society, postcolonial studies—and close communication with contemporary Australian writers who have travelled in Italy and written about it in the last three decades. She has worked extensively on the theme of Australian travel to Italy in contemporary Australian fiction, non-fiction and poetry. Her ongoing research explores transnational digital learning spaces (virtual exchange), intercultural citizenship (gender studies) and active citizenship, and postcolonial and world literature in English in additional languages education.

Yuping Wang is an adjunct associate professor in the School of Humanities, Languages and Social Science, Griffith University. Her research investigates the linguistic, intercultural and technological affordances of various asynchronous and synchronous online learning environments. She has published on online learning design, blended learning pedagogy (for example, flipped classrooms), implementation strategies, and online teacher training and professional development.

1

Disrupting, decentring and diversifying languages and cultures in Australian higher education

Adriana Díaz, Barbara E. Hanna, Samantha Disbray, Anna Mikhaylova and Grace Yue Qi

1. Introduction

Disruption has long been part of the human experience. Arguably, however, since the start of the global pandemic in 2020, the type, pace and intensity of disruptive forces impacting our lives have multiplied exponentially. As language and culture educators and scholars, one thing we can confidently say is that the past few years have clearly demonstrated our collective capacity to evolve through, and also enact, disruption. The enforced refashioning of our pedagogical practices in response to emergency online teaching, for instance, required us to reflect on many of our taken-for-granted pedagogical principles, as well as on the agentic, emotional and physical labour involved in responding to unforeseen educational challenges (Deng & Barros, 2023; Jin et al., 2021; Warner & Diao, 2022).

Held in November 2021, at the tail end of the global pandemic travel restrictions, the 6th Languages and Cultures Network for Australian Universities (LCNAU) Biennial Colloquium invited submissions that not only defined but also exemplified and illuminated the concepts of *disrupting, decentring,* and *diversifying* languages and cultures within the context of Australian higher education. We conceived of these three notions as harbingers of emerging pathways with the potential to challenge traditional paradigms, foster inclusive perspectives and pave the way for more pluralistic research and teaching practices in our fields. Contributors were asked to capture the complexities and possibilities underpinning these phenomena, surfacing concerns regarding endangered educational values and, at the same time, illuminating the potential for purposeful reconfigurations of our disciplines, research and teaching practices. Many of these contributions shone a light on exciting interstices, where decentring and diversifying theoretical lenses, research and pedagogical practices are making important trans- and interdisciplinary impacts.

This volume comprises a carefully curated selection of these contributions that harness evolving strategies to deal with and enact disruption, decentring and diversification, and, in so doing, pave the way for renewed engagement with languages and cultures in Australia. Indeed, each of the contributions to this volume exemplifies these three key concepts and theorises languages and cultures teaching in the contemporary tertiary sector in Australia. Before delving into these contributions, we turn our attention to five critical questions that will help frame readers' engagement with each of the chapters. These questions helped us to conceptualise the interplay between disrupting, diversifying and decentring:

1. What does it mean to disrupt/decentre/diversify languages and cultures research and pedagogy?
2. What does it take to disrupt/decentre/diversify languages and cultures research and pedagogy?
3. Who are the agents of disruption/decentring/diversifying?
4. How permeable, impenetrable or subject to disruption *extra muros* are university language programs?
5. What do the contributions (and our observations) reveal about the elasticity of university language programs and universities in general as sites for disruption?

In this introductory chapter, we sketch possible answers to these questions. While acknowledging that these concepts/actions represent unfolding processes that may also intersect with one another, we nevertheless delineate key features that are foregrounded in each of the contributing chapters. We then provide an overview of each chapter, the selection of which was guided by our concern to bear testimony to the resilience and creativity of our colleagues, and not to document short-term solutions to emergency scenarios, nor put forth claims for 'lasting changes' that would themselves fossilise into unquestioned assumptions. Instead, this volume presents instances of disruption, decentring and diversification that take traction from, and are responses to, a variety of factors that impacted researchers and educators in their context at the time. We conclude by critically reflecting on future waves of disruption, decentring and diversification in our field.

2. A tripartite thematic framework

2.1. Disruption

The word disruption conjures a wide range of meanings and (polarising) reactions. Disruption can be conceptualised as driven by external forces, changes that are beyond individuals' control, changes that we try to make sense of and catch up with. Against this backdrop, disruptions can be considered so seismic that they immediately cause confusion and, possibly, resistance (Samier, 2013). While disruptions are typically unplanned and may appear chaotic and externally determined at the onset, disruptions affect those who experience them in principled ways as a function of their nature, scope and severity as well as context, resources and level of preparedness, and agency available at the time of onset and through the aftermath. Against this backdrop, disruptions are not typically considered a change within a paradigm but, rather, a paradigmatic shift. Some might argue that we, as practitioners, do not necessarily have the power to 'disrupt' or trigger disruptions, but that our individual and collective actions can align with and contribute to advancing paradigmatic-level disruptions. Others might argue that all we can do is 'ride the waves' of disruption. These individual responses can then become collective ways of 'harnessing' and leveraging disruptions.

As such, disruptions can also be conceived of as internally driven, deliberate, possibly local-level innovations (solution-driven strategies). These disruptions can further be conceptualised within the specific context from which they emerge, whether it be institutional-level, discipline-level, classroom-level, etc. Sometimes grassroots-level, practice-driven innovation can have further disruptive effects. We may thus find disruptions driven 'from outside' versus those generated from 'within', responding to centrifugal or centripetal forces. Indeed, while disruptions are typically conceived of as unexpected, when they emerge from 'within' to challenge the existing status quo and normative oppressive systems, they may become purposeful.

What we know is that disruptions and innovations become normalised over time. Perhaps what has changed is the pace at which these disruptions emerge and are then described as the 'new normal'. In this sense, various waves of disruption have become synonymous with emerging technology-enabled/enhanced teaching and learning. In this context, there is greater agency given to individuals—learners and teachers—who may or may not choose to use the affordances of the technology to transform their teaching, and who might, in fact, welcome the shockwaves such disruptions trigger.

2.2. Decentring

Decentring, the second prong of the tripartite theme, urges us to consider the (im)possibilities of moving away from the 'centre'—used metaphorically to represent the historically privileged canon and norms around which our discipline, teaching and research practices have traditionally gravitated. Part of this work entails recognising the pervasive power dynamics underpinning the process of coming to terms with how we have (un)consciously benefitted from such norms and complicity supported their perpetuation.

Decentring efforts in our field include exploring the onto-epistemological ruptures that have put into question knowledge and ways of being (Bojsen et al., 2023). Other efforts have called for a deconstruction—and, in some cases, the dismantling—of the established hierarchies of linguistic and cultural capital, towards promoting a more egalitarian and democratic learning space. As collectives, language teacher associations have also been called to take on the role of agents of change to support and advance decentring efforts in our field (see Banegas et al., 2022, in the case of English language teaching). When thinking about classroom power dynamics, one may also think of de-emphasising conventional teacher-centric models, thereby foregrounding student experience and empowering students to take ownership of their learning journeys (Johnson, 2022).

Thus, decentring can serve as a catalyst for disruption, challenging entrenched hierarchies and norms, while disruption can prompt a re-evaluation and realignment of our focal points, thereby facilitating the process of decentring. Together, these dynamics have the potential to foster a cycle of reflection and action, driving us towards more equitable and inclusive practices. Closely associated with (and possibly a corollary of) moving away from the 'centre' is the notion of 'diversifying' content and perspectives.

2.3. Diversifying

The third prong of our thematic framework advocates for an educational landscape that not only respects but also celebrates the rich tapestry of backgrounds, perspectives and experiences students bring to the learning environment. By championing diversity in all its forms (cultural and linguistic backgrounds, race, giftedness, gender, learning needs etc.), 'diversifying' actions aim to foster inclusivity and representation, promote a more equitable and holistic educational experience, and ensure that every student's voice is heard and valued (Anya & Randolph, 2019). Through this lens, diversification of language education may also entail broadening the spectrum of named languages taught and learnt within tertiary institutions, encompassing Indigenous languages, sign languages and other less commonly taught languages. This diversification challenges the traditional primacy of imperial languages, contributing to a more inclusive representation of Australia's linguistic and cultural tapestry. Diversification can thus be a response to wider patterns of diversity, not only within the classroom but also outside it. This stands in stark contrast to disruption, in which the response is often forced, and teachers may or may not be the main catalyst agents of change.

In diversification, there is a conscious choice to respond to a set of conditions, and that response is of a particular kind: it expands the range of perspectives. While calls to diversify the curriculum have often been conflated with decolonising efforts (see Grue, 2021), we argue that these are clearly distinct processes. In choosing to focus on the concept of diversification, we recognise it as a concrete and actionable pathway that aligns with the overarching goals of decolonisation and lays the groundwork for profound systemic changes. In so doing, we acknowledge that decolonisation is a broader, more complex project that seeks to address and rectify deep-seated legacies of colonialism (De Fina et al., 2023). Ultimately, the decolonising project not only entails a radical revisioning of curricula, pedagogies and institutional frameworks, but also:

> [giving] land and resources back to the people from whom they were taken and, in an imperial context, [ensuring] that power and reparations are given to those in the metropole who are there as a direct result of colonisation.
>
> (Grue, 2021, p. 165)

All three concepts operate in concert within the larger ecosystem of language education, their interplay serving as the foundation for dismantling colonial legacies and promoting social justice, an imperative pursuit in our field (see, inter alia, Bouamer & Bourdeau, 2022; Criser & Malakaj, 2020; Herlihy-Mera, 2022; Hird, 2023; Ortaçtepe Hart, 2023; Padilla & Vana, 2024; Reagan & Osborn, 2020; Wassell & Glynn, 2022).

3. Three interlinked concepts at play

Figure 1.1 provides a visual representation that attempts to capture the nature of each of the concepts. The dynamic interplay among them is shown in Figure 1.2. Each concept is symbolised by a unique shape, distinguished by its distinct edges, which serve to metaphorically represent the nature of the actions/processes these concepts may trigger. The 'disrupting' piece features sharp, jagged edges that serve as a compelling visual metaphor, capturing the concept's profound and unforeseen impact, and symbolising the forceful shattering of the conventional as it cleaves through the familiar to forge paths towards entirely new paradigms. The abrupt angles and pointed lines vividly convey the idea of disruption as a catalyst for groundbreaking change, effectively breaking down existing barriers and paving the way for innovative approaches and perspectives.

The 'decentring' piece has edges that radiate outward like the rays of the sun, symbolising a pivotal shift from a singular, centralised focus to a landscape marked by numerous centres of interest and influence. This radiant design encapsulates the move away from Eurocentric, monocultural, or monolingual paradigms towards a more pluri/multipolar comprehension of knowledge. By employing sun-like rays as a metaphor, the diagram attempts to illustrate the dispersion of intellectual and cultural authority, shedding light on diverse perspectives and voices.

The 'diversifying' piece is characterised by outward-reaching arrows, each symbolising the expansion of perspectives and the embrace of a rich tapestry of voices and experiences. The arrows, pointing in multiple directions, encapsulate the essence of diversification as an active, ongoing process of reaching beyond traditional boundaries to foster an inclusive and vibrant educational landscape.

In Figure 1.2, these three visual representations interact, their edges overlapping and interweaving, portraying the dynamic and synergistic relationship between them. This visual interplay underscores their collective potential to re-imagine and reshape the languages and cultures teaching and research landscape. This design aims to highlight the notion that disrupting, decentring and diversifying are not isolated actions but are deeply interrelated forces that, together, hold the power to innovate and enhance the way we teach, learn and research languages and cultures.

The LCNAU 2021 Colloquium tripartite thematic framework emerged in response to the profound and ongoing reverberations of the COVID-19 pandemic. Acknowledging the aftermath of this external disruption, we see the complex and fluid interrelationships among the three dimensions emerging throughout the volume's chapters. As intimated earlier, disruption can be a driving force, and so some chapters situate their research in the COVID-19 emergency online teaching circumstances that required frontline teachers and researchers to reflect and quickly react and respond to the disruption. When it comes to decentring knowledge and integrating Indigenous languages and cultures into a community language learning context, the ways in which decentring is navigated and implemented expect collective and reciprocal efforts involving key stakeholders (for example, educators, students, community members, administrative support team, university leadership and policymakers). Diversifying the curriculum and pedagogy becomes a facilitative and powerful process for (continued) educational innovation. Educators' active responsiveness to consolidating multilayered and complex disruptions has ensured the potential of diversifying knowledge contributions to embrace and foster the cultural identities of students to support multilingualism and multiculturalism in Australian tertiary classroom practices. The impact of such practices will be longitudinal and beneficial to reshaping societal understandings of diversity, equity and justice—the core values of humanity.

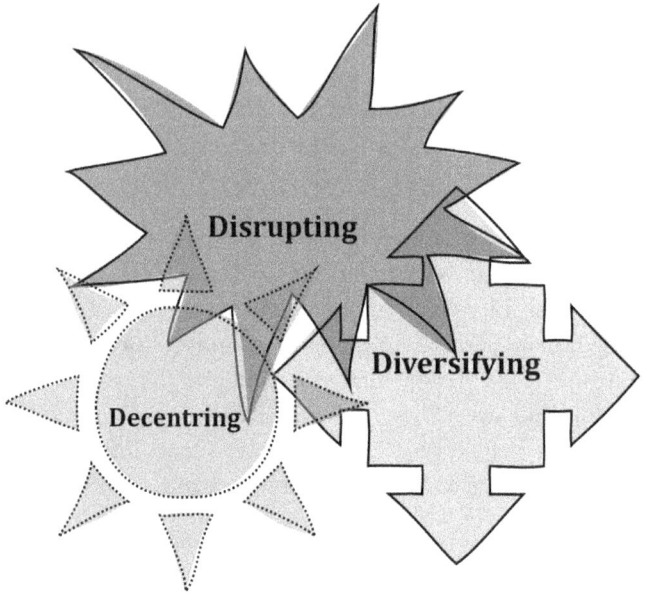

Figure 1.1. Visual representation of disrupting, decentring and diversifying forces
Source: Authors.

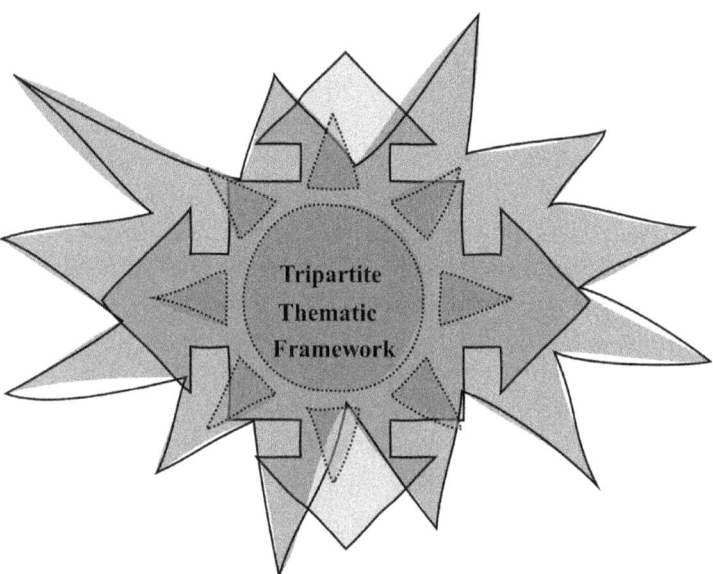

Figure 1.2. Visualising the interplay of disrupting, decentring and diversifying forces
Source: Authors.

It is also important to note that, since all three notions are dynamic processes, they need to be executed and managed, but not necessarily by the same people, creating opportunities for resistance and collaboration and requiring specific resources. For the pedagogical practices resulting from these processes to be successful and positively impact more stakeholders, they should be sustainable.

These three dimensions—disrupting, decentring and diversifying—have enabled us to exercise critical reflexivity of the research–teaching nexus and to reconsider and revamp our professional identities as language teachers, teacher educators, language researchers, and multilingual and multicultural advocates in our respective courses, programs, institutions and communities. Valuing and appreciating 'differences' to enrich diversity in languages, cultures and knowledge are just the beginning. The conceptualisation of diversifying, disrupting and decentring reflects the varied possibilities and potentials to convey and foster the ongoing exploration and development of languages and cultures in different learning contexts, different learning environments and for different learning needs. We encourage readers to keep the three dimensions in mind as they browse the contributions of this volume. We invite you to join us in reflecting on how each dimension or the combination of dimensions is positioned and interpreted in specific contexts of languages and cultures education and research.

4. Overview of the volume

The volume comprises 10 chapters. In Chapter 2, Robyn Ober, a First Nations educator and researcher, discusses the ways of being, doing and knowing among Indigenous Australian teacher education students as they navigate and make meaning of new professional and academic orientations during their tertiary studies. Using three research-informed metaphors— slipping and sliding, *kapati* ('cup of tea') and the guitar—Ober presents a strong sense of intersection between language, culture, identity and learning interpreted by Aboriginal English speakers who draw on their own social, cultural and linguistic repertoires to construct and make meaning of new knowledge from their own perspective. The pedagogical implications of this study make a significant contribution to the critical discourse on 'decentring' and 'diversifying' within the Australian tertiary education sector, particularly emphasising the necessity for Indigenous students to engage with curriculum content in ways that are both meaningful and accessible.

By advocating for equitable and just learning opportunities, this research underscores the imperative to recognise and value the unique abilities of Aboriginal students in approaching, comprehending and interacting with new knowledge through their Indigenous knowledge systems. Incorporating their distinct modes of thinking, acting and understanding not only enriches the academic knowledge-building process but also strengthens collective engagement in knowledge production within academic settings.

In Chapter 3, Mary-Anne Gale and Rob Amery report on substantial advances made in teaching Aboriginal languages in South Australia in the adult education sector over the last two decades or so, and comment on future plans and prospects. Their chapter discusses why Aboriginal languages continue to fall through the cracks of government bureaucracy and institutional policies and, in so doing, presents a series of proposals on how each of these cracks could possibly be closed (or at least reduced), thus ensuring a positive future for adult learners and teachers of Aboriginal languages in the state. This chapter tackles the decentring of power and control concerning the recognition and teaching of Aboriginal languages, a process that involves re-evaluating who has the authority to acknowledge Aboriginal languages officially and determining the extent of their inclusion within educational institutions.

Recognising a range of affordances brought by the disruptive power of digital communications technology, Levi Durbidge's chapter offers alternative forms of pedagogy to support the decentralisation of certain idealisations in language learning and communication. By probing into a selected dialogue from a Japanese elementary school textbook, Durbidge argues that textbook communicative practices typically draw on idealisation, which stands in contrast to current understandings of the heterogenous, dynamic, negotiated and complex nature of language, as well as the pedagogical purposes of language learning for socialisation (Steffensen & Kramsch, 2017). Leveraging the affordances of Instagram, Durbidge offers two examples emerging from his own disrupting attempts to engage students in the complex realities of contextually situated and structured semiotic practices of Japanese-speaking communities. These include having students observe hashtag use in Japanese language Instagram posts and create their own tags. His innovative approach, grounded in research on the practical application of digital technology and pedagogical strategies, demonstrates how learners benefit from engaging with the richness of language in real-world communications. This method provides learners with the opportunity to reflect on concepts of communication, comparing the idealised versions presented in textbooks with the more nuanced and sometimes challenging realities of language use encountered during interactions with Japanese-speaking communities.

In Chapter 5, Birgit Lang and Claire Maree delve into the concepts of diversifying and decentring by highlighting the critical need for a paradigmatic shift in tertiary language education that emphasises gender justice. They argue that this shift becomes evident through the active embrace and affirmation of a broad spectrum of sexual orientation, gender identity and expression, and sex characteristics, referred to as SOGIESC. Their chapter focuses on German and Japanese language education and critically examines and discusses the impact that language teaching institutional frameworks in Australia have on curriculum development. The authors focus on pronouns as a key aspect of gender justice that is often challenging to convey effectively in foreign language classrooms. They propose practical alternatives to demonstrate how this practice can be co-constructed by both students and teachers. By advocating for a shift away from cis-heteronormative biases in language teaching, they emphasise the importance of integrating linguistic, cultural and sociopolitical perspectives on gender expressions and diversity into curriculum development.

Matt Absalom and Roberta Trapè's chapter explores how travel restrictions in response to the COVID-19 pandemic led to the development of a virtual exchange program for Italian language learners. This initiative was designed to enhance global intercultural citizenship, diversifying students' learning experiences by providing them with broader cultural and linguistic exposure. They forged telecollaboration links to support language learners' connections with the world during the challenging period when it was not possible to experience in-country exchange. Their virtual exchange program included four iterative rounds. In 2021, they attempted to activate learners' curiosity about their international peers through the discussion of topics of interest that simulated their intercultural reflection. In 2022, active global citizenship was highlighted. Here students were asked to engage in pre-virtual activities in class before interacting with their overseas partners, allowing them to brainstorm activities centred around global citizenship with peers in face-to-face lessons as well as online via the university learning management system (LMS). Both models of virtual exchange provided students with a rich experience evidenced by students' positive comments on mediating their intercultural relationship through language use that extended along a continuum of formality. In addition to pedagogical diversification, the authors engage with the concept of decentring, positioning it as a shift of the shared collaborative space from physical to online that offers a lens on disruption at cognitive, attitudinal and behavioural levels within the individual, which may result from experiencing and reflecting upon this virtual exchange. The chapter highlights the potential of technology to support virtual exchanges that can be integrated into language subjects for all students, alleviating the financial burden of traditional in-country experiences.

In Chapter 7, Grace Qi, Yuping Wang and Nian-Shing Chen focus on the disruptive power of technology, exploring and implementing a design pattern to support frontline language practitioners in developing tailored curriculum and activities for adult learners. Their design pattern comprises four components: context, problem, solution and diversification. To present an overarching view of the design stages across the four components, they consider factors such as people, things, place, information, ubiquitous technologies, space and time. They suggest that language educators implement the design pattern in a specific context and learning activity. Their study demonstrates how language practitioners can collaborate with instructional designers and educational technologists to design innovative robot-assisted language learning that supports the desire of adult learners for personalised learning.

The Italian podcasting project presented by Riccardo Amorati, Elisabetta Ferrari and John Hajek in Chapter 8, through its decentring or recentring of the language classroom, challenges the traditional power structures in which language teaching is embedded. In so doing, it opens a space for students to perform orally that is more motivating and less stressful than in-class oral instruction. Working within the project-based paradigm, students are guided towards the production of a podcast in Italian on a topic of their choice—an outcome that has multiple meaningful afterlives. First, the project represents a personal achievement for learners who report that the artefact is meaningful to them. Second, the podcasts, as student-generated content, function as discussion starters for the final weeks of the semester. Third, they are broadcast on SBS Italian for a wider audience of Italian speakers. In this way, the project disrupts conventional ideas of L2 speakers as defined by marginality, 'authentifies' students as Italian speakers and is consistent with calls to diversify content to include more non-L2 speaker productions (see McGregor et al., 2021). The result for students is increased intrinsic motivation and an accompanying reduction in reported levels of anxiety associated with speaking.

Elisabetta Ferrari and Mitch Buzza's chapter reports on the pedagogical opportunities arising from virtual reality (VR) environment projects in two undergraduate Italian language courses at the University of Melbourne. While initially conceptualised as a response to the disruption of the COVID-19 pandemic and constraints of online teaching, the projects continue to serve multimodal content delivery as an experiential active learning opportunity. The non-immersive, interactive desktop VR in a 3D environment in the first project, aimed at post-beginner students, combines exports from Google Earth, Google Streetview and 5P interactive video with links to other authentic and educational resources and a voiceover. The second project, targeting more advanced students in the post-pandemic context, was inspired by the success of the first and resulted in two fully immersive VR 3D videos accessible either through Oculus Quest headsets or computers/tablets. In this project, VR learning not only promoted students' experiential learning but also supported the agency of language teachers as researchers in the techniques of VR learning, enabling learners to engage in innovative creation in line with the notion of 'disrupting' as developed in this volume. The experience gained from planning, developing and implementing the two projects, in conjunction with project-based group work, demonstrates teachers' agency in harnessing external disruption. Through the development of learner-centred activities, and with the help of VR technology (available at low cost and compatible with the university LMS), they were able to develop innovative learner-centred teaching resources—itself a form of disruption.

In Chapter 10, Ducasse critically engages with the theme of decentring to consider a radical revision of written assessment practices in the context of a tertiary Spanish language course. Rather than students being tested on recall of materials taught by their classroom teacher, a new protocol for a process of guided drafting encourages students to use online tools as potential sources of epistemological authority. Direct teacher correction is dropped in favour of encouragement of student agency, including individualised consultation of tools such as dictionaries, concordances, grammar checkers and machine translation. The design and implementation of the protocol over two semesters of a Spanish course are described and evaluated, leading to an argument in favour of a disruption to the previous exclusion of these tools from accepted writing practices.

Circling back to our initial questions, we can thus conclude that disruption can be unexpected, unwelcome and limiting when coming from an external agent, but can also be purposeful, empowering and creative when triggered or carried out by internal agents. Decentring and diversifying pedagogical practice can be both a response; a reclamation of agency in the context of external disruption; and, possibly/eventually, a trigger for further disruption of practices and power structures in tertiary languages education. It takes agents who are both focused on the ultimate goal of their research and teaching practice and open to innovation and paradigmatic shift, whether in their response to external disruption or in their pursuit of disruption from within.

On the one hand, university language programs (that is, complex dynamic multi-agent systems embedded into even more complex systems) can be quite rigid and slow to take up innovation and are often reactive to disruption. On the other hand, the changes within paradigms and paradigmatic shifts are led by the individual and collective agency of invested practitioners. Ultimately, the success of engaging with disrupting, decentring and diversifying practices is determined by how much they meet the changing needs of the stakeholders and how much agency is allowed by the environment in which they function.

5. What disruptive futures await?

At the time of writing, our discipline faces a new wave of disruptive forces, some of which have the potential to shake the very foundations of our practice. We embrace these looming waves of disruption driving the transformation of education across sectors with hope. Generative artificial intelligence (Gen AI), for example, is already reshaping the landscape of communication, enhancing our ability to comprehend and navigate the intricate nuances of human languages. Yet, as our contributors' research illuminates, our work transcends the capabilities of Gen AI. In envisioning our present and future amid the rise of Gen AI and the metaverse, it is crucial that human agency remains central in promoting multilingualism and multiculturalism alongside technological advancements. This principle is fundamental to understanding our humanity and the significance of our collective human experience.

It is also crucial to recognise that learning is not an automatic process devoid of human intervention. Agency, described by Ahearn (2001, p. 112) as 'the socioculturally mediated capacity to act', underscores the significance of individual learners' actions, decisions and their engagement with the opportunities presented by their learning environment (White, 2018).

As we delve deeper into the possibilities presented by AI-enabled learning environments and contexts for language and cultural studies in higher education, it is only a matter of time before we fully understand their potential. This exploration ought to emphasise the dynamic interplay between individual learners and their surroundings, as well as the impact of emerging digital technologies, thereby shedding light on how these interactions are likely to shape the educational experience.

Against this backdrop, we are also painfully aware of the importance of embracing disruptive technological innovations for our own disciplinary survival. Higher education institutions in the Anglosphere have been quick to exploit the advent of AI as a convenient pretext to slash language programs, citing budgetary constraints and a perceived lack of relevance against the powers of AI-powered, real-time, automatic translators (Harrison & McLelland, 2023; Miller & Neigert, 2024; Muradás-Taylor, 2023). Such narratives spread and become ever more pervasive, particularly among the parents of prospective (language) learners.

While part of the answer seems to involve synergistically leveraging these new technologies to enhance language learning, it is equally important to continue emphasising the human factor that underpins communication and cross-cultural understanding to foster empathy and critical perspective taking. Such critical perspectives can help engage with the range of social justice issues underlying these and other emerging technologies, among which voice-cloning and accent-altering technologies (Payne et al., 2024) perpetuate 'colonialingual' patterns in our field (Meighan, 2023).

As we reflect on the human factor, specifically, what makes us human, we cannot forget that this, too, has been weaponised, turning us against each other and dehumanising entire communities to justify unthinkable atrocities. Indeed, we cannot conclude the introduction to this volume without acknowledging the heart-wrenching events that are unfolding in real time. As languages and cultures scholars and educators committed to disrupting, decentring and diversifying our disciplines and profession, we cannot turn our gaze away from unspeakable violence and human suffering. In our pursuit of a more equitable and just educational paradigm, we recognise that our work is intrinsically linked to broader societal challenges.

We also understand that finding answers to all these matters lies beyond the present volume. We hope this volume demonstrates that language and culture teaching and its concerns are not primitive responses to linguistic diversity and, as such, cannot be superseded by the advent of technological tools. In this volume, we see evidence of the criticality of practice, of paradigm shifts. As we contemplate how these waves of disruption unfold, we find hope in the cyclical nature that characterises these processes. We thus look forward to learning about the new kinds of disruption that the 'normalisation' of previous waves might trigger. While reflection on these matters makes us painfully aware of the perennially vulnerable state of being in our discipline, it also reminds us of the resilience and constant innovation that lies in readying ourselves and our learners to deal with change and transformation.

Acknowledgements

We would like to acknowledge the collective efforts that have shaped this scholarly endeavour. We extend our heartfelt gratitude to the diverse community of scholars, activists and thinkers who have enriched our work. We also extend our deepest gratitude to all the contributors to this volume. Their dedication, expertise and innovative perspectives have been instrumental in shaping the richness and depth of this collection. We would also like to thank each of the peer reviewers who lent their time and expertise to supporting authors in enhancing their contributions: Katelyn Barney, Chantal Crozet, Melinda Dooly, Angela Giovanangeli, Tiare González Vidal, Scott Grant, Angela Harrison, Min Jung Jee, Kathleen Loysen, Daniel Martin, Troy McConachy, Paul Moore, Kerry Mullan, Hugues Peters, Celeste Rodríguez Louro, Kelly Shoecraft, Antonella Strambi, Priscilla Strasek-Barker and Sara Visocnik. We are also indebted to the LCNAU Executive Committee and to the LCNAU Studies Editorial Board, especially Professor Emerita Jean Fornasiero for her unwavering support and guidance throughout this process.

References

Ahearn, L. M. (2001). Language and agency. *Annual Review of Anthropology, 30*(1), 109–137. doi.org/10.1146/annurev.anthro.30.1.109.

Anya, U. & Randolph, L. (2019). Diversifying language educators and learners. *The Language Educator*, Oct/Nov. actfl.org/uploads/files/general/TLE_OctNov 19_Article.pdf.

Banegas, D. L., Bullock, D., Kiely, R., Kuchah, K., Padwad, A., Smith, R. & Wedell, M. (2022). Decentring ELT: Teacher associations as agents of change. *ELT Journal, 76*(1), 69–76. doi.org/10.1093/elt/ccab090.

Bojsen, H., Daryai-Hansen, P., Holmen, A. & Risager, K. (Eds.). (2023). *Translanguaging and epistemological decentring in higher education and research*. Channel View Publications.

Bouamer, S. & Bourdeau, L. (Eds.). (2022). *Diversity and decolonization in French studies*. Springer.

Criser, R. & Malakaj, E. (Eds.). (2020). *Diversity and decolonization in German studies*. Springer.

De Fina, A., Oostendorp, M. & Ortega, L. (2023). Sketches toward a decolonial applied linguistics. *Applied Linguistics, 44*(5), 819–832. doi.org/10.1093/applin/amad059.

Deng, M. & Barros, S. (2023). Learning to teach world language online during COVID-19 pandemic: A phenomenographic study. *Foreign Language Annals, 57*(2), 382–402. doi.org/10.1111/flan.12729.

Grue, M. (2021). Diversify or decolonise? What you can do right now and how to get started. In D. S. P. Thomas & J. Arday (Eds.), *Doing equity and diversity for success in higher education* (pp. 161–172). Springer. doi.org/10.1007/978-3-030-65668-3_13.

Harrison, K. & McLelland, N. (2023). Research in languages, cultures and societies: Voices of researchers in the UK. *Modern Languages Open, 1*(22), 1–36. doi.org/10.3828/mlo.v0i0.476.

Herlihy-Mera, J. (2022). *Decolonizing American Spanish: Eurocentrism and the limits of foreignness in the imperial ecosystem*. University of Pittsburgh Press.

Hird, D. (2023). *Critical pedagogies for modern languages education: Criticality, decolonization, and social justice*. Bloomsbury Publishing.

Jin, L., Deifell, E. & Angus, K. (2021). Emergency remote language teaching and learning in disruptive times. *Calico Journal, 39*(1), i–x. doi.org/10.1558/cj.20858.

Johnson, S. M. (2022). Who is at the center of our language teaching? *Second Language Research & Practice, 3*(1), 116–127. hdl.handle.net/10125/69871.

McGregor, J., Diao, W. & Trentman, E. (2021). An investigation of L2 learning peer interactions in short-term study abroad. In W. Diao & E. Trentman (Eds.), *Language learning in study abroad: The multilingual turn* (pp. 72–96). Multilingual Matters. doi.org/10.21832/9781800411340-006.

Meighan, P. J. (2023). *Colonialingualism*: Colonial legacies, imperial mindsets, and inequitable practices in English language education. *Diaspora, Indigenous, and Minority Education, 17*(2), 146–155. doi.org/10.1080/15595692.2022.2082406.

Miller, G. & Neigert, M. (2024, 15 March). Lost in translation: The geopolitical risks of declining foreign language learning in Australia and NZ. *The Conversation*. theconversation.com/lost-in-translation-the-geopolitical-risks-of-declining-foreign-language-learning-in-australia-and-nz-225787.

Muradás-Taylor, B. (2023). Undergraduate language programmes in England: A widening participation crisis. *Arts and Humanities in Higher Education, 22*(3), 322–342. doi.org/10.1177/14740222231156812.

Ortaçtepe Hart, D. (2023). *Social justice and the language classroom: Reflection, action, and transformation*. Edinburgh University Press.

Padilla, L. & Vana, R. (Eds.). (2024). *Representation, inclusion and social justice in world language teaching: Research and pedagogy for inclusive classrooms*. Taylor & Francis.

Payne, A. L., Austin, T. & Clemons, A. M. (2024). Beyond the front yard: The dehumanizing message of accent-altering technology. *Applied Linguistics, 45*(3), 1–8. doi.org/10.1093/applin/amae002.

Reagan, T. G. & Osborn, T. A. (2020). *World language education as critical pedagogy: The promise of social justice*. Routledge.

Samier, E. A. (2013). Where have the disruptions gone? Educational administration's theoretical capacity for analysing or fomenting disruption. *International Journal of Leadership in Education, 16*(2), 234–244. doi.org/10.1080/13603124.2012.762172.

Steffensen, S. V. & Kramsch, C. (2017). The ecology of second language acquisition and socialization. In P. A. Duff & S. May (Eds.), *Language socialization— Encyclopedia of language and education* (pp. 17–32). Springer. doi.org/10.1007/978-3-319-02327-4_2-1.

Warner, C. & Diao, W. (2022). Caring is pedagogy: Foreign language teachers' emotion labor in crisis. *Linguistics and Education, 71*, 101100. doi.org/10.1016/j.linged.2022.101100.

Wassell, B. & Glynn, C. (2022). *Transforming world language teaching and teacher education for equity and justice: Pushing boundaries in US contexts*. Channel View Publications.

White, C. J. (2018). Agency and emotion in narrative accounts of emergent conflict in an L2 classroom. *Applied Linguistics, 39*(4), 579–598. doi.org/10.1093/applin/amw026.

2

Slipping and sliding: Knowledge production, innovation and creativity from an Indigenous educational perspective

Robyn Ober

1. Introduction

Aboriginal and Torres Strait Islander people draw on their own ways of being, doing and knowing in all aspects of their lives, including learning in various educational sectors. Indigenous epistemologies (ways of knowing), ontologies (ways of being) and axiologies (ways of doing) are impossible to separate because they are integral and intrinsic to how people view and understand the worlds they engage in. This chapter explores the ways of being, doing and knowing among Indigenous Australian teacher education students as they process and make meaning of new professional and academic concepts and understandings in their tertiary studies. I present three metaphors and the data that motivated them that were central to recent research carried out with Indigenous tertiary educators and teacher education students (Ober, 2019). Three metaphors emerge from the research: slipping and sliding, *kapati* and the guitar. They weave strong threads of language, culture, identity and learning to demonstrate how

Aboriginal English speakers draw on their own social, cultural and linguistic repertoires to make meaning and construct new knowledge emerging from their own Indigenous standpoint.

1.1. Positioning myself

I position myself as a First Nations educator and researcher. I am a Mamu/Djirribal woman from North Queensland with social, cultural and linguistic connections with First Nations people in this region. I was a lecturer in teacher education at Batchelor Institute, the Northern Territory, from 1991 to 2006, before transferring to the Higher Education and Research division. I have long been interested in learning, communication and knowledge creation, and have been engaged in the development and implementation of both-ways pedagogy in teacher education, incorporating this approach into Indigenous research methodologies.

1.2. Batchelor Institute and both-ways learning

Batchelor Institute is an Indigenous tertiary education provider in the Top End of the Northern Territory, Australia. The main campus is located 100 kilometres south of Darwin in the township of Batchelor, with another campus, the Desert Knowledge Centre, in Alice Springs. Batchelor Institute has a long history of providing vocational and higher education to Aboriginal and Torres Strait Islander students, firstly in the Northern Territory and later throughout Australia. In 2024, Batchelor Institute celebrates 50 years of working with Aboriginal and Torres Strait Islander people in tertiary education through a both-ways educational approach:

> The Institute gives precedence to its philosophy of Both Ways: positioning First Nations peoples as knowledge holders in all educational transactions with Western knowledge systems as well as privileging First Nations ways of learning and teaching to underpin our engagement with mainstream education systems and society more broadly.
>
> (Batchelor Institute of Indigenous Tertiary Education, 2020, p. 3)

Both-ways acknowledges that there are at least two knowledge systems in play for Indigenous students: Aboriginal and Torres Strait Islander knowledge systems and the Western academic system. These two knowledge systems are recognised, celebrated and drawn on to create innovative knowledge, something that is new, fresh, vibrant and alive (Ober, 2009, p. 36).

Both-ways as a philosophy is a continual question that challenges Indigenous and non-Indigenous educators and researchers when engaging with Aboriginal and Torres Strait Islander adult students, community members and communities. The question of alternative ways of working and engaging presents a challenging but important opportunity to explore culturally inclusive and responsive processes, practices and philosophies relevant to the context (Morgan, 1988). Contested spaces often emerge when Indigenous and non-Indigenous researchers, educators and adult learners work towards mutual understanding and creating new knowledge. These sites of contestation stimulate feelings of discomfort and discontentment from various perspectives and standpoints, triggering new ways of thinking about teaching and learning. Such moments occur during a real but often turbulent and rigorous process revolving around curriculum content, pedagogy, assessment and delivery. The both-ways space makes room for contested sites where negotiation, disagreements and debates can take place, and where, finally, mutual understanding is reached on common ground. Both-ways has become a part of my practice and philosophy as an educator and researcher. It influences how I conduct research that is culturally responsive, appropriate and safe (Ober, 2019, pp. 8–9). When undertaking research with Aboriginal and Torres Strait Islander people, it is important to acknowledge that the methodologies utilised reflect our epistemologies, axiologies and ontologies. This means that Indigenous methodologies make visible what is meaningful and logical in our understanding of ourselves and the world and apply this to the research process (Porsanger, 2004, as cited in Moreton-Robinson & Walter, 2009, p. 2). Indigenous ways of being, doing and knowing are interrelated and continuously engaged, ensuring that we bring our true, authentic selves into the research and educational domain. It is about our knowledge systems, how we know what we know and what gives our knowledge validity and truth, because it is both truth and reality from our standpoint. Indigenous researchers in Australia and globally are beginning to push the boundaries of the traditional Western research space and are shifting the cultural dynamics to reflect an Indigenous standpoint. Indigenous researchers Moreton-Robinson and Walter (2009, p. 3) state that 'while European colonisation of certain countries and peoples disrupted Indigenous ways of life and ways of living, Indigenous knowledge systems remain intact and continue to develop as living, relational schemas'.

Both-ways philosophy recognises diverse knowledge systems, including language systems. Among the many Indigenous languages known and spoken across the nation, new linguistic varieties, such as Aboriginal English (AE), are used and shared by many Indigenous people, including the adult learners at Batchelor Institute.

2. Aboriginal English as a social, cultural and identity marker

The horrific historical atrocities deriving from racist policies since white contact have impacted massively on Aboriginal and Torres Strait Islander people. Young Indigenous children were forbidden to speak their traditional languages as part of the assimilation policy implemented by government officials and people in power, causing fear and humiliation. Over time, new ways of communication emerged with Aboriginal people speaking new varieties of English, referred to by linguists as AE, as well as English-based Kriols in some parts of the Northern Territory, Cape York Peninsula and Torres Strait (Mühlhäusler, 1986). AE is now recognised as the first language of many Aboriginal people in Australia, mainly in urban, rural and regional centres. Ober and Bell (2012, p. 60) describe this form of communication as a 'rich, highly structured and … complex form of the English language' that is 'widely appropriated in the social and cultural domains of Aboriginal Australia'. According to Eades (1993, p. 2), 'about 250 languages [were] spoken in this country before the British invasion, with at least 600 distinct dialects'. More recent estimates propose over 400 distinct languages (Bowern, 2023). Widespread massacres, introduced diseases, dispossession of land and enforced racist policies over several generations profoundly damaged many Indigenous Australian languages and speech communities, and some were totally wiped out. However, Bell (2002, p. 43) points out that, while many Aboriginal languages have not survived intact, some have survived in 'varying degrees of healthiness'. Reclamation and revitalisation efforts have been galvanised nationwide through language programs and projects (Hobson et al., 2010).

AE's varieties sit on a language continuum ranging from Standard Australian English (SAE) at one end to Australian Kriol at the other. It is important to remember that one variety is not superior to the other, and that all varieties are recognised 'depending on your social and cultural upbringing, including one's geographical location' (Ober & Bell, 2012). It is quite common for Aboriginal people to recognise the social and cultural group of individual speakers by intently listening to their talk:

> The accent, vocabulary and grammatical patterns of AE enable Aboriginal people from all over the country to recognise other Aboriginal people, even in contexts where visible markers of identity are not present.
>
> (Eades, 2013, p. 82)

AE is viewed as a 'non-standard English' variety by the dominant, mainstream society; unspoken stereotypical labels of unintelligence or inferiority are applied and equated with the inability to articulate abstract and complex concepts. According to Ober and Bell (2012, p. 63), in 'earlier decades, the emerging varieties of Aboriginal English were often unrecognised or misunderstood by outsiders and were generally considered to be "bad English"'. This kind of prejudice was noted by a non-Indigenous colleague:

> There is an assumption if someone can't articulate themselves in Standard Australian English, then this is in some way is a reflection of their intelligence. Whereas actually, someone can be highly, highly intelligent but not able to express that in SAE, so for me it's about creating the bridge between the two languages for them.
>
> (Individual Staff, Kapati 18–11–14)

Students enrolled at Batchelor Institute are of Aboriginal and/or Torres Strait Islander cultural heritage and therefore draw upon their own linguistic repertoire, which in the wider society may be frowned upon and judged against SAE. This brings to the fore the socially assigned status of language varieties. Indeed, the idea of 'standard' is not inherent or naturally occurring; it results from a process of status elevation, possibly alongside codification and uniformisation, that takes place over time, steered by power dynamics and dominant social norms. A single, uniform, standard language, deemed to be of 'high status', is often conceived of in contrast to a 'non-standard' variety, of lower status, as is the case with SAE and AE. However, in the growing literature of multiculturalism, it has emerged that the notion of a standard language 'may be best viewed as an ideology' (Walsh, 2021, p. 774), and, according to McLelland (2021), one that is monolinguistic.

An alternate positioning that stems from multilingualism scholarship posits that multilingual and bilingual speakers 'have *one linguistic repertoire* from which they select features *strategically* to communicate effectively' (García, 2012, p. 1, original emphasis). In a both-ways teaching and learning context, such a linguistic repertoire is recognised, acknowledged and celebrated as a language in its own right, corresponding to high levels of intellectual ability. Both-ways philosophy adopts a strengths-based approach, drawing on students' linguistic repertoire as a foundation for, and springboard to, new academic and professional knowledge. There is an understanding that:

> students bring with them their own conceptual framework that is rich and highly intellectual, but it becomes difficult and frustrating when students try to communicate that high-level knowledge in a language that is not their own.
>
> (Ober, 2019, p. 126)

Trying to communicate and engage in a language that is 'not their own' results in a watered-down understanding of professional concepts, bringing misunderstanding, misinterpretation and confusion. There is value in language and cultural inclusivity within the teaching and learning space, ensuring students are supported and encouraged to draw on their own social, cultural and linguistic repertoire through authentic and genuine means. Encouraging students to draw on their Indigenous literacies in conjunction with their heritage language provides a medium to relay important knowledge, concepts and understanding through a strength-based approach. Indigenous literacies may be in the form of 'traditional symbols, markings, designs on bark, or in contemporary forms such as batik, paper, clay, lino prints and other mediums' (Ober, 2001, p. 62).

Aboriginal students at all levels enter the educational academy with a rich social, cultural and linguistic repertoire. Over time they gradually learn to navigate the educational space, drawing on their strengths and communicative capabilities, which are evolving and developing from their life experiences, both positive and negative. The 'slips and slides' are the trials and errors, the risk-taking, the challenges and, ultimately, the rewards once they have completed the course of study, whether at the early childhood, primary, secondary or tertiary phases of education.

3. Exploring emerging metaphors

Metaphors are widely used by Indigenous people to communicate important and complex messages in creative yet clear ways. There is a long history of using metaphor to research and reflect on the development of the philosophy of Batchelor Institute's 'both-ways education'. For instance, in the 1990s, teacher education students used metaphors from their local natural environment. Berna Timaepatua spoke about the ebb and flow of the tide, representing both-ways as a Tiwi Islander, student and educator:

> As the tide comes in, it is known knowledge, as it goes out it takes new knowledge that is gained to be used and applied to real situations. She (Berna) spoke about the stone being dropped in the water, which signifies the beginning of the educational learning journey, creating ripple effects back in the community. Taking new knowledge home and applying it in a real-life context.
>
> (Stage 4 Teacher Education Students, 1998, p. 14)

Yolngu (Aboriginal people) in north-east Arnhem Land capture both-ways education using the metaphor of 'Ganma', which is an actual lagoon situated in the mangroves. The lagoon represents a mutually respected and balanced place where Yolngu and Balanda (non-Aboriginal) knowledge can meet. The fresh water represents Yolngu knowledge from the land and the salt water represents Balanda knowledge from the sea. The surface of the lagoon is quiet and still, while strong undercurrents move beneath the water to represent contested sites and knowledge production, as described by Marika:

> The swelling and retreating of the tides and the wet season floods can be seen in the two bodies of water. Water is often taken to represent knowledge in Yolngu philosophy. What we see happening in the school is a process of knowledge production where we have two different cultures, Balanda and Yolngu, working together. Both cultures need to be presented in a way where each one is preserved and respected.
>
> (Marika, 1999, pp. 112–113)

Metaphors are powerful tools for creating and communicating educational philosophies in deep and meaningful ways, drawing on Indigenous knowledge systems and using strength-based approaches to learning. The Ganma metaphor draws on Yolngu philosophy to show the two bodies of water, meeting and swirling together, not mixing as an ugly brew but rather intertwining with a marbling effect, indicating the balance, collaboration and enhancement of the two distinct knowledge systems. The metaphor holds rich and intrinsic cultural knowledge, which only Yolngu people can represent from their standpoint to explain and unpack the notion of both-ways education.

According to Indigenous scholars Karen Martin and Booran Mirraboopa:

> to represent our worlds is ultimately something we can only do for ourselves using our own processes to articulate our experiences, realities, and understanding. Anything else is an imposed view that excludes the existence of our ontology and the interrelationship between our ways of knowing, ways of being and ways of doing.
>
> (Martin & Mirraboopa, 2003, p. 211)

In the research detailed here, metaphors serve as powerful tools to communicate abstract ideas and concepts in meaningful and accessible ways. By exploring and being guided by these, I stay true to my identity as a both-ways practitioner in the research and tertiary educational space. This approach allows me not only to be true to my Indigenous ways of doing and making meaning, but also to push through and forge ahead into new, untouched knowledge bases, in particular, the use of AE in tertiary educational domains. Three powerful metaphors in this study are *kapati*, slipping and sliding, and the guitar. As *kapati* is very much a metaphorical methodology, I will start with it to detail the research method for this study.

4. Study methods: The *kapati* metaphor

Like yarning (Bessarab & Ng'andu, 2010; Kennedy et al., 2022), the *kapati* or 'cup of tea' methodology emerged to serve Indigenist research principles, which foreground lived experience, cultural protocols, cultural safety through participant agency and the collaborative construction of interaction, meaning and story. The *kapati* approach is based on narrative enquiry, which rests on the 'epistemological assumption that we as human beings make sense of random experience by the imposition of story structures' (Bell, 2002, p. 207).

For my family, *kapati* signalled making time to pause, reflect and exchange stories about life in general, through socialising and engaging in conversation around a 'cuppa'. It seems a simple event, but, in fact, *kapati* times were when important knowledge, stories, news and events were shared, including sorry news, celebrations and times of humour through acting, music, song and dance. The kettle or billycan would always be ready for deep conversation and yarns to occur in a comfortable and culturally safe family environment. This Indigenous social practice can be extended in the research domain as a way of bringing familiar ways of sharing information from the home environment into the academic research space.

My experience of using a Western-style guided interview technique with an older male family member highlighted the need for a different approach. Early in the interview, which was also early in my research journey, my family member challenged me on my identity, asking 'who are you and why are you speaking like a white fella?' This was a confrontational conversation, showing me that my research methodology was distant and different from my social and cultural identity, bringing an unauthentic and fake persona to my researcher's position and perspective. The following quotation presents my reflections on and analysis of the formal interview, and highlights the challenges and tensions during the interview:

> The interview began quite well, with a clear recount of a family situation, where miscommunication occurred between hospital staff and the extended family of the informant. Although the beginning stages of the interview were smooth with information flowing easily, it gradually became evident that the participant began to struggle when asked to respond to the next question in isolation to the previous one.
>
> The participant seemed to be uncomfortable with the short, sharp response expected from the researcher's questioning structure and technique. There seemed to be some resistance by the participant to make isolated comments against each question without referring to what was previously stated.
>
> As a result, the participant found it easier to just openly share the critical incident through storytelling and then give me the opportunity in collaboration with him to search for appropriate responses to the five set interview questions. Once the obstacle of responding to specific questions was removed, it was obvious the participant's verbal accounts of the critical incident flowed freely and richly with a touch of humour. The verbal and facial expressions as well as feelings and emotions replaced the uneasiness and awkwardness of the formal interview.
>
> (Ober, 2017, p. 10)

As the principal researcher in the current research, I knew it was important to draw on Indigenous ways of doing research, which were familiar, homely and authentic, resulting in real conversations drawing on students' social and linguistic repertoire. The conversations seemed to flow easily, 'sometimes with many voices in small groups, while at other times there were silences and long pauses as participants pondered and thought about questions'. At these times I was content to sit and wait until respondents were ready to share their perspectives.

Fortunately, the both-ways philosophical foundation at Batchelor Institute provided a rich space for the *kapati* method in the study. Data collection for the study occurred through observation and 11 recorded (audio/video) sessions, in staff gatherings, student *kapatis* and teacher education workshops. This approach allowed me to work collaboratively with participants to explore AE as an expression of cultural identity in a both-ways teaching and learning space. The strength, integrity and purpose of *kapati* from my standpoint was to share these stories in an inclusive, collaborative, authentic and genuine way, in which participants felt culturally safe and supported.

5. Participants and data

This research focused on speakers of AE who were enrolled in the Bachelor of Education (Primary Teaching) and Bachelor of Education Early Childhood Teaching through the Australian Centre of Indigenous Knowledge and Education, a partnership between Batchelor Institute and Charles Darwin University. Student participants were recruited through initial discussions with the senior lecturer from the teacher education course who then invited me to present the study, plain language statement and informed consent to the student group.

There were four groups of participants: teacher education students who spoke AE as their first or other language, postgraduate candidates, current and previous non-Aboriginal teacher education staff involved in teaching AE speakers and current Indigenous staff who spoke AE as their first language but were not directly involved in the teacher education course. The total number of student participants was 19, and the total number of staff members was 13.

Eleven transcripts were collected and analysed. These included student stories, individual and group yarns or *kapatis*, student engagement in workshops and individual interviews with staff and students. The data collection method of *kapati* was coined based on my family's way of sharing information in the home environment as described above. The data were analysed by identifying key themes, topics, patterns and emergent ideas to determine the relationship between language, culture, identity and learning within the Indigenous tertiary teaching and learning space. Ethical clearance for the study was granted by the Batchelor Institute Research Committee (11–07–12 Application Number: 201202).

6. Slipping and sliding

'Slipping and sliding' emerged in the *kapati* data as a key notion. It was coined by an Indigenous senior lecturer in her reflection on teaching students in the common units—Public Communications and Telling Histories—compulsory courses in the higher education programs.

6.1. Aboriginal staff *kapati*

The metaphor of slipping and sliding emerged as the lecturer reflected on the process that Aboriginal and Torres Strait Islander staff and students followed to communicate and make meaning of new academic concepts introduced in the common unit workshops. The extract below shows the lecturer explaining the learning and communication in the class, and her description of this as slipping and sliding. P1 indicates the Aboriginal staff participant and R1 is the researcher:

> P1: If you know the educational theories and you know the jargon, and you can actually argue for your right to speak, what you want. You've got the jargon; you can say this is a Piaget model of—y'know what I mean.
>
> R1: Yeah, yeah.
>
> P1: Y'know what I mean, you can sit at the table if you've got that toolbox with you.
>
> R1: Yeah, but I think what is really important, is that you understand the theories.
>
> P1: Yeah.
>
> R1: And I think that people y'know, yes you can go back in your own dialects and language, but you have to have that understanding first, so that you can communicate in your own way if you like.
>
> P1: And you can argue your right to do that then, when you got those theories under your belt.
>
> R1: Yeah, and I think you done it a bit when you were doing the common units.
>
> P1: Yeah we did it—it slipped and slided often.
>
> R1: I like that, slipped and slided. I'm gonna write that down. Explain that a bit more.

> P1: It was depending on the group and stuff. You would find it would happen naturally anyway, because there's so much standing and talking. You would find that you're trying to, y'know, create understanding, so um yeah so we slipped and slided from SAE to AE and—all the time and it was quite a fluid process.

Although there is mention of the two codes—SAE and AE—P1 is really explaining how adult students moved in and out of diverse social, cultural and linguistic spaces as they engaged in the academic discourse, by drawing on their own repertoires. This powerful yet simple, subtle, and organic phenomenon expresses how Aboriginal and Torres Strait Islander academics and students engage, move and interact within the social, cultural and linguistic spaces of educational contexts. Slipping and sliding is a good example of 'both-ways' in action, helping students to consolidate and validate new knowledge as they socially, culturally and linguistically engage with fellow students and Aboriginal and non-Aboriginal staff members.

The slipping and sliding metaphor captures the fluidity, flexibility, contestations, challenges and rewards of teaching and learning in an intercultural context using a both-ways educational approach to learning. The picture of children slipping and sliding in muddy terrain during playtime captures the fun, failures, messiness, fluidity, smoothness and ease of the slips and slides, but also the tensions and contestations at the dry points of the slide. This signifies moments of difficulty, hardship, confusion, misunderstanding and misinterpretation. The slips and slides vary between those of ease and those of unease.

6.2. Student *kapati*

The uneasiness of conversing in academic English emerged as a site of contestation for students who expressed their frustration at the inability of lecturers to understand their verbal interactions in discussions. The phrase 'they just don't get it' highlighted students' frustration with lecturers who unknowingly misunderstood and misinterpreted their ideas, opinions and perspectives. In the extract below, S1 and S2 are two such students:

> S2: That's why I was saying before … [lecturers] just don't get what we say. When they aims they aims too high for us and when we say, what you mean by that, and then they go too high again, and we say, 'Aww don't worry about it then, y'know, if you can't tell us the second time what you mean the first time then.'
> S1: We want you to break it down, not bring it up.

S1 wanted the content to be broken down—not diluted, weakened or watered-down, but clarified, making it deeper, more analytical and richer, thereby giving students access to conceptual understandings that are critical to the profession and practice of teacher education. The 'hit and miss' approach in multilingual educational contexts is common and unfortunately leaves students guessing; many give the impression that they understand the content when, in fact, they are struggling to grasp important concepts. Feelings of shame and humiliation stem from scenarios such as these, setting students up for academic failure. The teaching and learning environment can be constructed to provide opportunities for real analytical discussions and debates to take place, encouraging students to draw on their own linguistic repertoire to bring understanding in a meaningful way. There is potential to produce new professional knowledge through slipping and sliding between Aboriginal and Western academic mindsets and conceptual constructs through a both-ways educational approach.

Slipping and sliding is like the linguistic phenomenon of 'translanguaging' introduced by García and Li (2014), in which the focus is on the movement and fluidity of language relating to 'multiple discursive practices in which bilinguals engage in order to make sense of their bilingual worlds' (García, 2009, p. 45). Teacher education students who participated in the study all identified as being of Aboriginal and/or Torres Strait Islander heritage and the majority spoke SAE as an additional language, therefore engaging in the multiple discursive practices described by García (2009). Like translanguaging, slipping and sliding is more than code switching and code mixing, in that it goes beyond the edifice of spoken language, encompassing and embedding the ontologies, epistemologies and axiologies that are integral to, and evolving within, Indigenous knowledge systems. García and Li (2014, p. 22) support this notion, explaining that:

> translanguaging differs from the notion of code-switching in that it refers not simply to a shift or a shuttle between two languages, but to the speakers' construction and use of original and complex interrelated discursive practices that cannot be easily assigned to one or another traditional definition of a language, but that make up the speakers' complete language repertoire.

6.3. Workshop transcript

Slipping and sliding between AE and SAE is evident in the teaching and learning context. At a post-practicum workshop, a small group of senior teacher education students discussed cultural aspects and values of their school placements. The group consisted of three females and one male plus the lecturer (ST in the transcript below). I joined the workshop as an observer, recording the interaction between the students and the lecturer. It was obvious that the four students and the lecturer had established a good rapport and relationship over the course of study, and student 1 (S1) seemed quite comfortable in putting her query to the group:

> S1: Umm—I'm trying to say the motto, I'm not even quite sure if motto's the right, right word, but it's a—at … school, they got that safe respect for learners and how do I say that? Cos normally when I'm sitting on the chair I'm, and then A [child] did something wrong then I say 'A, are you doing the right thing? Are you being safe? Are you being respectful? Are you being a learner?', so that's three things that I threw back at him. Then he knew straight away what I was talking about, because that's our safe respect for learner, so what, what, what word am I looking for to put there—motto?
>
> ST1: School motto or school philosophy.
>
> S1: Philosophy.

In essence, S1 was trying to find a suitable word that captured the school's values, beliefs and expectations. She told a story of an actual incident so that others in the group could comprehend and picture the situation. She slipped into AE by using terminology that was familiar to Aboriginal people in the group, such as 'so that's three things that I threw back at him', meaning, 'I am reminding you these are the three things that are important to our school, and you're not doing it at the moment' (Ober, 2019, p. 131). 'Then he knows straight away what I was talking about', meaning, 'he knew immediately' the type of behaviour expected from him. The transcript displays an ease and confidence in sharing the story in AE among other AE speakers. There is no apology for the slipping and sliding; rather, there is a sense of cultural and linguistic pride in conversing in her first language of AE.

This way of communicating is a familiar form of interaction to the rest of the teacher education group—a quick and easy way to say something that AE speakers comprehend. If spoken in SAE, the story would lack richness and authenticity and would result in awkwardness and discomfort among the student group. There are invisible boundaries, protocols and processes that Aboriginal adults and children are aware of, and are continually checking against, within specific speech events:

> [such] cultural protocols, rules and invisible boundaries [are] set in place to guide us in our interactions with various members of our family and community. Community may include family, work, sporting clubs, church, student groups, or just social and cultural groups in general. We are taught these social rules, laws, and guidelines from birth and they are continually strengthened, reinforced and developed as we mature from childhood to adulthood.
>
> (Ober & Bat, 2007, p. 67)

6.4. Classroom observation

'The look' is an example of non-verbal communication through which young children are made aware that behavioural boundaries have been breached, with consequences forthcoming. The student teacher (S1) explains to a peer (S2) how using 'the look' is a way to remind, guide and lead the child to behave according to the school's values and philosophy:

> S1: Yeah I just put it back on the … and sometimes I didn't have to speak, I just gave them that look to let them know they were doing the wrong thing and I kinda stopped and looked and (pause).
>
> S2: Hesitated.
>
> S1: Hesitated for a little while, then I looked at them to—they knew straight away to come back.

The student teacher has brought her way of guiding children's behaviour from the home environment to the classroom environment. AE is the primary language for most children at this school, and it is appropriate to incorporate 'the look', which some people refer to as the 'black look', as a way to guide, remind and lead children to behave according to the school's values and philosophy. As I have written elsewhere:

> This is a good teaching strategy and one that I expect most experienced teachers would use. However, in this case, the student teacher would most certainly be related to and, therefore, connected socially, with the children. With that relationship would come certain obligations, such as respect, trust and authority.
>
> (Ober, 2019, p. 131)

Aboriginal children are familiar with 'the look' as a disciplining gesture, especially when relationships between the adult and child are established, as with many Aboriginal teachers and students. This is a good example of drawing on Indigenous ways of being, doing and knowing and bringing them into the teaching and learning context.

6.5. The guitar metaphor

The guitar metaphor was coined in dialogue with one of our senior postgraduate candidates, also a recognised Elder, at Batchelor Institute.

6.5.1. Postgraduate *kapati*

The conversation took place at the postgraduates' *kapati*, which involved Indigenous staff and postgraduate students. The discussion generally focused on the status, position and purpose of SAE in the teaching and learning context, including the home environment. Prior to responding to the question, there was a long pause from the senior Elder who thoughtfully considered the question before presenting the 'guitar' metaphor in an articulate, clever and culturally responsive way. In the two transcripts below, postgraduate 1 (PG1) described the importance of not prioritising one language over another through the metaphor of playing a guitar. He cleverly likened the guitar strings to the diverse language groups represented at Batchelor Institute, including the English varieties, creoles and dialects:

> PG 1: If you look at those strings as people coming from different backgrounds, different language backgrounds or cultures, see they come in from a knowledge base—whether the string is small string or it's a big string—it might be a big tribe or might be small tribe, but they all important, they got that value of importance. And to tune that guitar—right to that deadly tune you want to sing—the singer, the player must recognise that.
>
> Researcher (R1): Where do you see English in all of this, would you see this as one of the strings, one of the big strings or one of the strings or would you see that as something dominant coming from the teacher?
>
> PG1: Different people in respect to different Elders because they come from their high knowledge or their knowledge's or their high knowledge's view, they know that English is there, so it depends on—umm—how they see it—English is one of that strings.
>
> R1 and PG2 (in unison): And I guess it depends on who's playing the guitar.

PG 1 draws on his knowledge as a musician and singer, where the guitar is used as the main musical instrument in contemporary songs and dances. The guitar is used as a meaning-making and constructive metaphor to explain and describe the linguistic repertoire that is available for Indigenous students as they navigate between academic, cultural and knowledge production spaces. It helps to deepen our understanding of slipping and sliding. The guitar is made up of six strings, three thin and three thick; therefore, the explanation of big or thick strings represents critical and important languages for that context. The thin strings represent the lesser or 'not so important' languages for that context. No one string, or language, is more important than the other; rather, it is the contextual situation, including the topic, content, speakers and relevant language, that is the determining factor. The guitar metaphor also contributes to the notion of slipping and sliding by privileging many languages as well as recognising SAE. In the home environment, English, including SAE, is recognised as just another string that is pressed upon in collaboration with other strings to make meaning within intercultural spaces and to play that 'deadly tune'. That 'deadly tune' is about making meaning, through producing new and creative ways to communicate ideas and concepts in a culturally responsive and inclusive way.

6.6. Student *kapati*

As stated above, it is common for Batchelor Institute students to be fluent in multiple Indigenous Australian languages, including creoles and AEs. Therefore, there are multiple ways of thinking about and conceptualising professional educational constructs. This brings a sense of normalisation, where slipping and sliding happens organically and is expected to occur when Aboriginal and Torres Strait Islander people gather in social interactions. Outside the academic environment, students default to slipping and sliding, drawing on their own linguistic repertoire, so why does it seem abnormal for this practice to continue within the tertiary teaching and learning context? This is a strength-based and commonsense approach to learning, drawing on known and familiar knowledge and connecting with new and professional conceptual knowledge systems and structures. Student participants expressed the value of discussing, conversing and debating academic and technical issues in their small groups. For example, the introduction of 'Learnline', an online learning platform, at Charles Darwin University was quite confusing and challenging for most students. They found regular discussions among themselves, using their own ways of making meaning, to be an important tool for understanding and accessing the platform. The students (S2, S3) express their frustrations and resolutions to the researcher (R1) in the transcription below:

> S3: Bit of trial and error wasn't it?
>
> S2: It was more frustrating for us, cos we didn't know our way around it and we only had half an hour, 45 mins on it and that was it. The rest of it we had to find out, and just talking amongst ourselves. We kinda found out y'know a lot.
>
> R1: So you find that support in your group—that helps?
>
> S2: Without our group we wouldn't be here.

In a culturally safe and supportive environment, students felt at ease presenting challenges, questions and difficulties. The relationship and rapport between the students created an environment in which individual voices were listened to respectfully, no question seemed too silly, and students felt comfortable drawing on their own languages/dialects through slipping and sliding to ensure their ideas and thoughts were communicated clearly. In a both-ways educational environment, these collaborative and supportive ways of working were not only demonstrated but also expected, both by staff and students in the workshops.

7. Conclusion

Among teachers of Indigenous learners, there needs to be an awareness that young and adult students enter the classroom with a range of different language and linguistic capabilities. The fact that Indigenous students enter educational centres with a rich cultural heritage should be celebrated and acknowledged as a strength, not as a weakness.

AE is the first language for many Aboriginal people in Australia. As such, it needs to be recognised as a language of identity, thought processing and meaning-making. Having AE speakers in the classroom is critical to students' educational success and essential in settings where there are high enrolments of Indigenous students. It ensures that students are able to engage with the content of the curriculum in ways that are meaningful and accessible for them. This must be considered as one among other measures to ensure equity and access for Indigenous students in tertiary settings (Frawley et al., 2017). Both-ways educational philosophy has the potential to provide opportunities for Aboriginal students to confidently draw on their social, cultural and linguistic repertoires through a powerful, creative and innovative approach. Metaphors deriving from a student's home environment are instrumental in unlocking new knowledge and making it accessible and meaningful. They enable students to take ownership and show leadership in producing their own metaphors, thereby generating new knowledge. This chapter has provided evidence that Aboriginal students and educators are capable of drawing on their own knowledge systems through a strength-based approach, generating new knowledge and ways of teaching and learning in an academic context.

References

Batchelor Institute of Indigenous Tertiary Education. (2020). *Strategic Plan 2020–2022. Batchelor Institute of Indigenous Tertiary Education.* batchelor.edu.au/uploads/About/Stragetic-Plan-2020-2022_V1.3.pdf (page discontinued).

Bell, J. S. (2002). Narrative research in TESOL: Narrative enquiry: More than just telling stories. *TESOL Quarterly, 36*(2), 207–212. doi.org/10.2307/3588331.

Bessarab, D. & Ng'andu, B. (2010). Yarning about yarning as a legitimate method in Indigenous research. *International Journal of Critical Indigenous Studies, 3*(1), 37–50. doi.org/10.5204/ijcis.v3i1.57.

Bowern, C. (2023). How many languages are and were spoken in Australia? In C. Bowern (Ed.), *The Oxford guide to Australian languages* (pp. 56–64). Oxford University Press. doi.org/10.1093/oso/9780198824978.003.0007.

Eades, D. (1993). *Aboriginal English, PEN 93.* Primary English Teaching Association.

Eades, D. (2013). *Aboriginal Ways of Using English.* Aboriginal Studies Press.

Frawley, J., Ober, R., Olcay, M. & Smith, J. A. (2017). *Indigenous achievement in higher education and the role of self-efficacy: Rippling stories of success.* National Centre for Student Equity in Higher Education.

García, O. (2009). *Bilingual education in the 21st century: A global perspective.* Wiley-Blackwell.

García, O. (2012). Theorizing translanguaging for educators. In C. M. Celic & K. Seltzer, *Translanguaging: A CUNY-NYSIEB guide for educators* (pp. 1–6). CUNY-NYSIEB, The Graduate Center.

García, O. & Li W. (2014). *Translanguaging: Language, bilingualism, and education.* Palgrave Macmillan.

Hobson, J., Lowe, K., Poetsch, S. & Walsh, M. (Eds.). (2010). *Re-awakening languages: Theory and practice in the revitalisation of Australia's Indigenous languages*. Sydney University Press.

Kennedy, M., Maddox, R., Booth, K., Maidment, S., Chamberlain, C. & Bessarab, D. (2022). Decolonising qualitative research with respectful, reciprocal, and responsible research practice: A narrative review of the application of Yarning method in qualitative Aboriginal and Torres Strait Islander health research. *International Journal for Equity in Health, 21*(1), 134. doi.org/10.1186/s12939-022-01738-w.

Marika, R. (1999). Milthun latju wana romgu Yolnu: Valuing Yolnu knowledge in the education system. *Ngoonjook: Journal of Australian Indigenous Issues, 16*, 107–120. search.informit.org/doi/10.3316/informit.964748961603912.

Martin, K. & Mirraboopa, B. (2003). Ways of knowing, being and doing: A theoretical framework and methods for Indigenous and indigenist research. *Journal of Australian Studies, 27*(76), 203–214. doi.org/10.1080/14443050309387838.

McLelland, N. (2021). Language standards, standardisation and standard ideologies in multilingual contexts. *Journal of Multilingual and Multicultural Development, 42*(2), 109–124. doi.org/10.1080/01434632.2019.1708918.

Moreton-Robinson, A. & Walter, M. (2009). Indigenous methodologies in social research. In Walter, M. (Ed.) *Social research methods: An Australian perspective* (2nd ed., pp. 1–18). Oxford University Press.

Morgan, D. (1988). The role of Batchelor College in Aboriginal teacher training in the Northern Territory. An historical perspective 1953–1988. *Ngoonjook: Journal of Australian Indigenous Issues*, 1, 5–12. search.informit.org/doi/10.3316/informit.151469979372784.

Mühlhäusler, P. (1986). *Pidgin and creole linguistics*. Basil Blackwell.

Ober, R. (2001). The use of Indigenous literacy in tertiary education. *Ngoonjook: Journal of Australian Indigenous Issues, 19*, 60–64. search.informit.org/doi/epdf/10.3316/informit.995927608709015.

Ober, R. (2009). Both-ways: Learning from yesterday, celebrating today, strengthening tomorrow. *The Australian Journal of Indigenous Education, 38* (S1), 34–39.

Ober, R. (2017). Kapati time: Storytelling as a data collection method in Indigenous research. *International Journal of Learning in Social Contexts, 22*, 8–15. doi.org/10.18793/LCJ2017.22.02.

Ober, R. (2019). *Aboriginal English as a social, cultural and identity marker in Indigenous tertiary educational contexts*. [Unpublished doctoral dissertation]. Batchelor Institute.

Ober, R. & Bat, M. (2007). Paper 1: Both-ways: The philosophy. *Ngoonjook: Journal of Australian Indigenous Issues, 31*, 64–86.

Ober, R. & Bell, J. (2012). English language as juggernaut—Aboriginal English and Indigenous languages in Australia. In V. Rapatahana & P. Bunce (Eds.), *English Language as hydra: Its impact on non-English language cultures* (pp. 60–75). Multilingual Matters.

Porsanger, J. (2004). An essay about Indigenous methodology. *Nordlit, 15*(July), 105–120. doi.org/10.7557/13.1910.

Stage 4 Teacher Education Students. (1998). *Developing Aboriginal pedagogy. A collection of writings by Batchelor College Stage 4 Teacher Education Students*. Batchelor College.

Walsh, O. (2021). Introduction: In the shadow of the standard. Standard language ideology and attitudes towards 'non-standard' varieties and usages. *Journal of Multilingual and Multicultural Development, 42*(9), 773–782. doi.org/10.1080/01434632.2020.1813146.

3

Falling between the cracks: Learning and teaching Aboriginal languages in the adult education sector in South Australia

Mary-Anne Gale and Rob Amery

1. Introduction

> Fall between the cracks: To be overlooked, neglected or ignored, especially due to mismanagement or disarray in the midst of a large or complex situation.
>
> (The Free Dictionary, 2024)

Colonisation *disrupted* any normal means of learning and teaching Aboriginal languages intergenerationally or intragenerationally, particularly across southern Australia. The inevitable language and cultural breakdown in the post-colonisation era resulted in the *decentring* of power and control over whether Aboriginal languages were recognised by the government and taught in educational institutions. Fortunately, in recent years, the range of languages being taught in adult educational institutions and some universities has *diversified*. This chapter examines what is being taught formally in the state of South Australia (SA) and the outcomes of this effort.

Over the last few decades, an exciting resurgence of interest in reclaiming one's own language and culture has slowly emerged, both nationwide and globally, among Indigenous communities (Gale, 2023; Grenoble & Whaley, 2006; Hinton et al., 2018). Within SA, in response to some strong demands, particularly from Aboriginal people living in the more urbanised regions, newly accredited language courses were developed for adults and offered from 2011. The first full course taught by Technical and Further Education (TAFE) institutions was at the Certificate III level, 'Learning an Endangered Aboriginal Language'. By 2021, there were 85 Aboriginal TAFE graduates in SA who had studied one of the seven languages offered: Kaurna, Ngarrindjeri, Wirangu, Narungga, Adnyamathanha, Boandik and Pitjantjatjara. The last is the only language in SA that is still being acquired by children as a first language.

This chapter focuses on the formal teaching and learning of Aboriginal languages by adult Aboriginal students. When we refer to 'our graduates', we are talking about Aboriginal people in SA who have completed formal courses in an effort to learn their own language or languages as a means of redressing the disruption of the past, and as a means of empowering themselves to work in the field of Aboriginal languages in the future. In fact, 19 of our Aboriginal language graduates went on to complete a Certificate IV in 'Training and Assessment', which qualifies them as adult trainers of other adults wanting to study their own languages. In 2022, several new adult cohorts embarked on studying the newly written and accredited Certificate II course, 'Learning an Australian First Nation's Language', developed by Tauondi Aboriginal Community College, with either a Kaurna or Ngarrindjeri focus. This new course is being taught by our Certificate III and Certificate IV Training and Assessment (TAE) graduates. In fact, the new course outline stipulates that the language course must be taught by Aboriginal trainers.

Apart from celebrating these humble successes, the primary purpose of this chapter is to examine the 'cracks' within state government departments, adult training institutions and the school system that our Aboriginal graduates, and all Aboriginal people in SA, are perpetually falling through. This occurs despite the financial support offered and provided for languages by the federal government and the indisputable resurgence in Indigenous languages worldwide.

One of the main contributing causes is a mismatch between the federal and state governments. The federal government provides money and support for Aboriginal language activities, projects, resources and training programs, but it is the state government that controls and funds the schools and adult education sector. The SA government pays lip service to recognising Aboriginal languages, but, unfortunately, that is where it tends to end. Following the changes in state and federal governments in 2022, there were signs of dialogue on Aboriginal language education, prompting faint glimmers of hope for better cooperation and support in the future.

This chapter also briefly discusses the limited Aboriginal language offerings in the university sector (Amery, 2020; Gale et al., 2020). However, this is not the primary focus, which is to highlight the lack of formal institutional recognition and career paths for our language graduates. As hourly paid language instructors in schools, they get no job security, no superannuation and no holiday pay. They are incentivised solely by their passion for their languages. So, our purpose here is to highlight the problems and offer some solutions that will hopefully trigger the government and the institutions they fund to help close the ever-widening cracks in the system.

2. A brief history of Aboriginal language training in South Australia

SA has offered formal training in Aboriginal languages to adults, in one form or another, since the 1960s when Pitjantjatjara was first offered at the University of Adelaide (see Gale et al., 2020). But it was not until the 1990s that training was offered to Aboriginal people themselves wanting to revive their own languages.

Formal education opportunities for adults wanting to learn their own Aboriginal language began at Tauondi Aboriginal Community College as part of other certificate courses on offer in the 1990s. The trainer, Mike Gray, wrote a single (accredited) unit in 1995 that introduced adult learners to basic greetings and phrases in an Aboriginal language. The course was offered by Nelson Varcoe and Cherie Watkins within the popular cultural tourism course taught by the Narungga man and cultural trainer Kevin (Dookie) O'Loughlin at Tauondi College. Rob Amery introduced a short-lived Kaurna TAFE course, Kaurna Warra Patpangga (Kaurna Language in the South), exclusively for Kaurna people and run at Warriparinga in 1996 (Amery, 2016, pp. 180–181, 197).

The single introductory unit on Aboriginal languages developed at Tauondi College in 1995 was resurrected in 2007 when adult Ngarrindjeri students at Murray Bridge demanded formal training beyond the informal language classes that had been offered since 2004 by the linguist Mary-Anne Gale, alongside Elders. In 2007, the unit was offered within the Introduction to Vocational Education Certificate (IVEC), a Certificate I course, to 17 adult Ngarrindjeri students, with federal government funding via the University of Adelaide. The IVEC course was accredited by TAFE SA. The course was taught by Gale and her University of Adelaide colleague Peter Mickan, with the support of two Ngarrindjeri Elders, the late Eileen McHughes and Julia Yandell. (For a review of this course, see Gale & Mickan, 2007.)

As soon as those keen adult students graduated with their IVEC Certificate I, they said, 'We want more'. But there was no more. So Gale set about applying for a grant through the Commonwealth Department of Communications, Information Technology and the Arts to write higher-level certificate courses for adults wanting to learn their own Aboriginal language. The application was successful, and Gale was employed by the SA Department of Further Education, Employment, Science and Technology to write new Certificate III and Certificate IV courses in 'Learning an Endangered Aboriginal Language' and 'Teaching an Endangered Aboriginal Language', respectively. The new courses gained accreditation on 1 January 2011. Backed by Commonwealth funding, Gale immediately began offering formal classes in Ngarrindjeri at Murray Bridge, eagerly supported by the two Elders, McHughes and Yandell. With the same bucket of funding, the linguist Paul Monaghan offered the Certificate III for Wirangu to adult students at Ceduna, with the support of the late Elder Gladys Miller. On 1 January 2016, the two courses were re-accredited under the auspices of TAFE SA.[1]

In 2021, 10 years after the first courses were accredited, SA could proudly boast that it had 85 graduates of the Certificate III in seven different languages, plus 12 graduates of the Certificate IV (from five languages). These two certificate courses expired on 31 December 2020. Because TAFE SA chose not to re-accredit them, Tauondi College has since developed three new language certificate courses, which were approved by the Australian Skills Quality Authority (ASQA) in October 2020. They are the Certificate II and III in 'Learning an Australian First Nation's Language',

---

1   Adult vocational training courses have a five-year life span. They must undergo a re-accreditation process every five years under ASQA guidelines.

and Certificate IV in 'Teaching an Australian First Nation's Language'. In early 2022, after a year spent preparing and writing the teaching and assessment materials, as demanded by ASQA, three student cohorts began studying the new Certificate II for the Kaurna language, and two cohorts for the Ngarrindjeri language.

It must be said that these apparent successes in SA with language graduate numbers have been reached *despite* the South Australian education sector, not because of it. Without the financial support of the federal government over the years, none of this training would/could have occurred. (Note Tauondi College lost *all* its core funding from the SA Liberal government in 2020.) The SA Department for Education offers partnerships with a few Aboriginal community corporations (of up to $33,000 per year), but the support is just financial, and any training and/or support for languages is (unreasonably) left entirely up to individual language communities. The successes in SA, therefore, are due to the determination of Aboriginal people themselves who have demanded training and found willing non-Aboriginal linguists and experienced language teachers to support them in making it happen.

When informal adult classes started at Murray Bridge in 2004, it was the late Elder Eileen McHughes who said she wanted to learn to give welcome speeches in full Ngarrindjeri without any English words, just like the neighbouring Kaurna people could. These Kaurna cousins had started giving welcome speeches in full Kaurna in the early 1990s, so gradually some Ngarrindjeri women began to feel their code-mixed speech of English, peppered with remembered Ngarrindjeri words, was not enough. Aunty Eileen wanted more than just words; she wanted whole sentences in full Ngarrindjeri. To do that, she needed to learn some grammar. A little grammar was offered in the 2007 IVEC course but, again, it was Aunty Eileen who demanded more formal training and more grammar in a higher-level certificate course. Gale et al. (2012) reviews those early days of language revival by Aunty Eileen and other women pioneers.

When grammar became a bigger part of formal training—it had a unit of its own—in the new Certificate III course accredited in 2011, some within the TAFE sector, who had little understanding of how to revive a language, voiced concerns (see Gale, 2012). But Gale persisted, finding many exceptional Aboriginal adult learners (usually younger members) who enjoyed the grammar lessons and asked for the complexities to be explained in more detail. For them, learning grammar was empowering. They are the current and future teachers/trainers of adults.

Formal training began in the Kaurna language as early as 1990, when Amery offered a course developed by the Centre for Australian Languages and Linguistics at Batchelor College (later Batchelor Institute) in the Northern Territory (NT) to adult students at Kaurna Plains School, Adelaide.[2] This was followed by several informal workshops. In 1994, Amery worked with Kaurna language pioneers Nelson Varcoe and Cherie Watkins to develop a senior secondary level Kaurna language course through the Australian Indigenous Languages Framework (AILF). Varcoe taught it to Aboriginal (and non-Aboriginal) adults at Elizabeth West Adult Campus (renamed Para West Adult Campus), while Watkins taught it to adolescents at Elizabeth City High School. This course taught adults to give acknowledgement or welcome to country speeches, and to speak basic phrases in Kaurna. Soon after, around 1995, a Kaurna course for adults taught by Varcoe and Watkins was included in the cultural tourism course developed by Mike Gray at Tauondi College. Teachers at Kaurna Plains School attended the newly established Kaurna course at the University of Adelaide, which was taught in the late afternoon (after school) in 1997 and 1998. In subsequent years, a handful of teachers were supported by the Department for Education's Mother Tongue Retraining program to also attend the university course. This course was open to members of the public to audit upon payment of a small fee. This fee was initially paid by the Adelaide City Council to enable members of the Kaurna community to attend. However, the audit scheme was withdrawn some years later, thus making it more difficult for members of the Kaurna community to access the course.

In 2004, Amery wrote a Kaurna Stage 1 (that is, Year 11) course on offer through the School of Languages and taught this course himself, first at Adelaide High School and then, in 2005, at the Living Kaurna Cultural Centre at Warriparinga. Although it was a Year 11 course, all the students were, in fact, adults, some of them active teachers in schools, or university students and lecturers. An important minority of the student cohort were Kaurna adults. It was through these classes that Jack Kanya Buckskin, the most fluent current speaker of Kaurna, was recruited (see Amery & Buckskin, 2012). Buckskin took over teaching this course from Amery, and

---

2   Kaurna Plains School is an urban Aboriginal school established in the north of Adelaide in 1987.

also taught Kaurna language at various schools, including Kaurna Plains School, Adelaide High School, Salisbury High School and Le Fevre High School, and later at Tauondi College.

In 2012, Amery and Gale offered the new TAFE Certificate III to Kaurna adults; however, by this stage, the giving of welcome speeches in Kaurna was well entrenched. Indeed, it was this growing fluency in Kaurna that made Aunty Eileen envious. A little bit of 'tribal jealously' has proven to be a great motivator to kick things along among the different language groups in SA. Similarly, Gale kickstarted workshops on the Boandik language of Mount Gambier in 2009, with the support of linguist Barry Blake. Subsequently, Boandik man David Moon offered the Certificate III for Boandik people, due to increasing community demand, with 10 graduates in 2020.

In 2021, there were 27 graduates with a Certificate III in Learning an Endangered Aboriginal Language in Kaurna, with the latest cohort of 12 graduating at Tauondi College on 31 May that year. For Ngarrindjeri, the Certificate III was offered to various cohorts beginning at Murray Bridge in 2011; since 2013, it has been offered regularly to adults at Victor Harbor and/or nearby Goolwa; and, from 2018, in Adelaide at Tauondi Aboriginal College. By the end of 2020, 31 students had graduated with a Certificate III in Learning an Endangered Aboriginal Language in Ngarrindjeri, with a further 17 with a skill set of five units.[3]

The Certificate IV in Teaching an Endangered Aboriginal Language is designed to train language teachers. It was undertaken by selected Certificate III graduates in 2013. Two Ngarrindjeri, two Kaurna, one Adnyamathanha and one Narungga speaking student have completed the course. As mentioned, nine Ngarrindjeri adults went on to complete a Certificate IV TAE in May 2021, along with six adults from the Kaurna language classes.[4] The TAE course is a general one for all adult trainers; it does not teach specific skills for Aboriginal languages. Since 2022, some TAE graduates have been formally teaching the Certificate II course for Ngarrindjeri and Kaurna at various training sites.[5]

---

3   This skill set was part of the Certificate III, which they would have finished but for COVID-19 interruptions.
4   See news story celebrating this achievement: Marchant (2021).
5   Two younger TAE graduates and trainers of Kaurna at Tauondi, Jack Buckskin and Kira Bain, were in high demand for teaching Kaurna and cultural awareness to non-Aboriginal people. They are no longer offering formal training in Kaurna to Aboriginal students, hence the need for more TAE graduates. They are now freelance, and offering informal Kaurna and cultural awareness classes to non-Aboriginal people.

Training has also been offered to Pitjantjatjara tutors/teachers from the remote north-west of the state who speak their language fluently. With the support of Paul Eckert, Gale offered the Certificate III to 11 Pitjantjatjara adults in 2013. Six Pitjantjatjara adults completed a Certificate IV with on-the-job training between 2014 and 2015 while teaching the intensive Pitjantjatjara summer school course offered annually by the University of South Australia. This was an excellent training model and convincingly improved the teaching skills of the participating Pitjantjatjara tutors. The certificate training gave them a much deeper understanding of their own language, which they could then explain to their non-Aboriginal adult students (see Gale et al., 2020, for a discussion of the summer school program).

Table 3.1 summarises the number of graduates of language training courses in SA since 2011 in various languages.

Table 3.1. Graduates of South Australian language training courses since 2011

SA language	Certificate III Learning an Endangered Aboriginal Language	Skill set (5 units) Certificate III Learning an Endangered Aboriginal Language	Certificate IV Teaching an Endangered Aboriginal Language	TAE Certificate IV Training and Assessment (graduates holding Cert III in an Aboriginal language)
Ngarrindjeri	31	17	2	10
Kaurna	27	–	2	9
Wirangu	4	–	–	–
Adnyamathanha	1	–	1	–
Narungga	1	–	1	–
Boandik	10	–	–	–
Pitjantjatjara	11	–	6	–
TOTAL	**85**	**17**	**12**	**19**

Source: Authors.

3. The Senior Secondary Assessment Board of South Australia and Aboriginal languages

The Senior Secondary Assessment Board of South Australia (SSABSA), later renamed the South Australian Certificate of Education Board, was the independent education statutory authority that oversaw the senior secondary curriculum and examinations in SA and the NT (Year 12 only). In 1994, the SSABSA developed the AILF for the introduction of accredited Year 11 and 12 subjects in Aboriginal languages throughout Australia (see Mercurio & Amery, 1996). Amery was the first project officer. The manager, Tony Mercurio, and Amery realised that the biggest challenge would be finding teachers to teach the subject. They successfully applied for federal government funding to offer a series of professional development workshops for teachers of Aboriginal languages. Subsequently, run across the nation—at Worawa College at Healesville, Victoria, and at Port Augusta, Adelaide and Alice Springs—the groundbreaking project met with much enthusiasm. This professional development opportunity was highly valued by participants from SA and interstate, but it was non-accredited and was funded by a one-off grant with no continuity beyond the life of the grant. The SA Department of Education also held professional development workshops throughout the 1990s, often at the Balyana Conference Centre at Belair, Adelaide. Sometimes successful language teachers of other languages, such as German, were brought in to share their teaching strategies and methods with the group. But, again, these professional development opportunities were eventually discontinued, and there have been no such workshops on Aboriginal languages, run or organised by the (now) SA Department for Education, for more than a decade.

Lacking a sufficient number of trained Aboriginal teachers with the knowledge and skills to teach Aboriginal languages, the AILF project promoted the formation of teams consisting of Aboriginal language and culture specialists and teachers, with additional support from linguists. This was the model operating in the early to mid-1990s when Kaurna programs were introduced at Elizabeth City High School and Elizabeth West Adult Campus. This led to official recognition of the skills of Kaurna language and culture specialist Cherie Warrara Watkins, who was issued 'provisional registration' by the SA Teachers Registration Board. Some years later, Jack Kanya Buckskin was also issued provisional registration. These were short-term arrangements awarded on a case-by-case basis. The significance of this is that while some non-trained Aboriginal teachers, with well-developed skills in the Kaurna language, were given recognition for their skills in the form of 'provisional registration' to teach the Kaurna language, such recognition has not been repeated in SA in the last decade or so.

4. The current policy situation in South Australia

Truscott and Malcolm (2010, p. 6) contend that in some states and territories within Australia:

> a de facto or invisible form of language policy exists that is not explicitly written but is implicitly created: it privileges monolingualism over multilingualism and impedes full revitalisation and maintenance of Indigenous languages … [This] goes against certain human rights and has significant implications in the field of health, education, law and social justice.

This section provides an overview of the current language teaching situation and difficulties in SA from a policy perspective. The SA Department for Education released its *Aboriginal Education Strategy 2019 to 2029* in 2019. It has five 'principles' that 'guide the implementation' of the strategy. The third principle, on 'Culture and identity', states:

> We will acknowledge, value and respect Aboriginal knowledge, wisdom and expertise, including our existing Aboriginal staff and students and we will adopt local approaches to teaching Aboriginal histories, cultures and languages.

In the glossy, colourful and surprisingly brief (23-page) booklet outlining the strategy, there is minimal reference to Aboriginal languages. However, under the subheading 'Languages', it mentions some aspirations:

> Strengthen and reinvigorate the learning of Aboriginal languages in children's centres, preschools and schools, including language revival and maintaining strong active languages. Recognise the linguistic rights of Aboriginal children and students, building on home languages through family and community engagement. Move toward a bilingual education model that ensures proficiency for Anangu [*sic*] children in Pitjantjatjara or Yankunytjatjara and Standard Australian English as an additional language.
>
> (SA Department for Education, 2019, p. 19)

However, as this chapter argues, it is in the implementation of such strategies that the SA department fails, with its good intent 'falling through the cracks'. The 'Implementation' section of the strategy states:

> We will engage with teachers, leaders and support services to drive action locally. Implementation plans will set out key actions and milestones that can be monitored and supported through our accountability mechanisms, using feedback, evaluation and evidence to adjust our approach and continually improve.
>
> (SA Department for Education, 2019, p. 21)

One could argue that this statement lacks practical detail; indeed, it reads like a motherhood statement (that is, vague, general and uncontroversial). By contrast, the strategy lists various measures, including NAPLAN (five mentions), PAT M and PAT R tests,[6] and phonics screening that relate to English; however, none of these apply to Aboriginal languages.

SA was once a leader in the development of curriculum in the field of Aboriginal studies. However, with the subsequent development, from 2010, of a national curriculum covering core subject areas, most funding and support in the field ceased.

5. National framework for Aboriginal languages

From 2014, all Australian schools were expected to follow the national curriculum in the core subject areas of English, mathematics, science, humanities and social sciences, health and physical education, technologies, the arts and languages.[7] The national curriculum includes a 'Framework for Aboriginal and Torres Strait Islander Languages' that outlines what communication skills and understandings are to be taught in all Aboriginal languages.[8] Unlike the national curricula for other languages (such as Japanese, Spanish, Italian, etc.), the framework is not specific to any particular Aboriginal language. Therefore, it is up to individual language teachers to provide the content and detail.

---

6   NAPLAN stands for National Assessment Program—Literacy and Numeracy; PAT M and PAT R tests are Progressive Achievement Tests in Mathematics and Reading Comprehension, respectively.
7   See Australian Government, Department of Education (2024).
8   See Australian Curriculum (2018).

In recent years, the Curriculum Branch of the SA Department for Education has offered some support. The most active language revival groups in SA schools (Ngarrindjeri, Kaurna, Adnyamathanha and Narungga) have been offered monetary support to 'populate' the framework with examples of words and phrases from their own languages. The department has signed formal partnerships with a few selected language communities in SA, offering grants of $15,000–$33,000 annually to incorporated Aboriginal organisations. The expectation is that the money will be used to incorporate their languages into the national Aboriginal Languages Framework. Yet community members do not necessarily have the expertise to fulfil these specialist tasks, especially on such a limited budget.

In 2020, the SA department funded two trained teachers for a six-month trial to develop examples for the Kaurna language within the National Framework with a 'Scope and Sequence' curriculum document. The aim was to outline the elements of the language to teach and when to teach them, from Reception to Year 6. In 2022, similar work commenced with selected employees representing the Ngarrindjeri and Narungga communities. Ironically, in 2023, the Framework for Aboriginal and Torres Strait Islander Languages was reviewed and revised, due to feedback from teachers that it was 'cluttered', 'repetitive' and 'overwhelming'.[9] The revised document (Version 9) was released in December 2023, rendering much of the work done on the old version possibly redundant.

It is disappointing that the SA Department for Education's support for the implementation of Aboriginal language education ends here. There is no official departmental strategy or planned means of implementing the curriculum. Implementation is being left up to schools, yet current teachers do not have the knowledge or skills to teach these languages.[10] Should schools (quite rightly) wish to draw on Aboriginal community members to assist in the teaching of Aboriginal languages in their schools, there is no provision for professional development for these Aboriginal people, as there was in the 1990s. Any such training has been left entirely up to others, hence the development of the independent Aboriginal language

---

9   These were terms used by the reviewers from the Australian Curriculum, Assessment and Reporting Authority in a First Languages Australia information session offered through Teams on 18 October 2023 regarding the framework revisions.
10 See SA Department for Education (2024), which outlines the schools (minimally) funded to teach one of seven Aboriginal languages in SA. There are no departmental checks on whether this teaching is actually happening, which is concerning given there is a huge shortage of skilled teachers with the necessary language capabilities.

training courses discussed in this paper. Aboriginal language graduates of the certificate courses worry that the department will eventually employ trained (non-Aboriginal) teachers to teach their languages, using Scope and Sequence curriculum documents, and that their own substantial skills and training will go unrecognised. They feel that their knowledge and training will continue to be dismissed and that they will remain without the jobs and the language careers they hoped and trained for. As a result, some graduates are reluctant to cooperate with any Scope and Sequence writing process or to share their language knowledge with the department.[11]

The support, training and recognition offered to Aboriginal language specialists by the Western Australia (WA) Department of Education can only be envied in SA. In WA:

> for the past 20 years, [they have] been running a professional development traineeship for people who want to teach their languages in schools. The course, known as the 'Aboriginal Languages Teacher Training Traineeship', is a three-year program, completion of which allows the graduates' schools to apply for Limited Registration to teach.
>
> (First Languages Australia, 2022, p. 66)

Ironically, this three-year traineeship, which is recognised by the WA Department of Education and offers a career path for its graduates, is not an accredited course. By contrast, SA has an accredited course, yet its graduates are not recognised by the department. (For further details on the support offered to Aboriginal language teachers in other states, see First Languages Australia [2022].)

6. The cracks

This section outlines the many specific cracks that our adult language graduates are falling through in their efforts to teach their own languages. We argue that the idiom 'falling through the cracks' describes not only

---

11   Again, it should be acknowledged that the SA Department for Education was once a leader in the field of Aboriginal studies and there was once a large, well-staffed curriculum and resource unit that supported such work. Similarly, professional development on Aboriginal languages is also sadly missed by Aboriginal people working in SA schools today. Missed, too, is the support offered by the Aboriginal Languages Standing Committee that once oversaw issues relating to Aboriginal language being taught in schools in SA. This committee was disbanded 15 years ago.

the situation of teaching Aboriginal languages in the adult education and Vocational Education and Training (VET) sector in SA, but also the struggle for schools to teach Aboriginal languages in the state.

Crack 1

- Universities do not offer degree courses for Aboriginal people to learn to speak and write in their own languages, nor do they offer training to teach their own languages in schools or elsewhere. The only three[12] university subjects offered in SA Aboriginal languages are:
    - 'Reclaiming Languages: A Kaurna Case Study' at the University of Adelaide taught as a summer school. This course focuses on the linguistic strategies and methods used to reclaim a 'sleeping' language.
    - 'Australian Indigenous Languages (Kaurna Focus)' introduced at the University of Adelaide in 2022 as a semester-length course directed at language students with more emphasis on Kaurna language learning and less emphasis on the source material.
    - 'Pitjantjatjara Language and Culture' at the University of SA (UniSA), taught as an intensive summer school course.
- All three courses are taught by non-Indigenous academics in collaboration with members of the respective communities. In the case of Pitjantjatjara at UniSA, Anangu tutors teach conversational Pitjantjatjara to their respective student groups. The vast majority of students in all three courses are non-Indigenous, though, significantly, the number of Indigenous students is slowly increasing, albeit from a very low base.

Crack 2

- The SA Department for Education is primarily concerned with curriculum, especially 'populating' the national Aboriginal Languages Framework, and the writing of Scope and Sequence documents based on the Australian curriculum.
- Implementation of the curriculum is not currently on the SA department's agenda, and there is no in-house training or professional development for Aboriginal language teachers within the department.

---

12   An additional Australian Indigenous Languages summer school is also offered at the University of Adelaide, being a general introduction from both linguistic and sociolinguistic perspectives to the Indigenous languages of Australia.

Crack 3

- The accredited Aboriginal language certificate courses offered in the VET sector in SA are not recognised by the authorising bodies associated with schools. The SA Department for Education does not (as yet) recognise and reward Certificate III and IV qualifications for graduates wanting to teach Aboriginal languages in schools.
- The SA Teachers Registration Board will only offer temporary provisional registration to (unregistered) Aboriginal language teachers, and only if no other degree-qualified teacher applies for the same job. There have been no provisional registration offers for Aboriginal language teachers in SA for over a decade.

Crack 4

- Most funding in SA for learning, teaching, resource production and other projects involving Aboriginal languages comes from the federal government through the Indigenous Languages and the Arts program.
- The policies and implementation of services relating to Aboriginal languages in SA (especially in the education arena) are all determined at the whim of the state government and not in legislation.

Crack 5

- There is no SA state government legislation that acknowledges and guarantees support for the state's Aboriginal languages, as there is in New South Wales (NSW). Unlike in WA and NSW, there is minimal state government funding for Aboriginal languages, and the amount is dependent on the government of the day.

Crack 6

- The SA government's *Aboriginal Education Strategy 2019 to 2029*, in particular, its reference to Aboriginal languages, lacks substance and any commitment or process for the implementation of teaching Aboriginal languages in schools (unlike Victoria and NSW).

Crack 7

- There is no legal obligation for schools to abide by the protocol statements that appear at the beginning of the Aboriginal Languages Framework as set out by the SA Department for Education.
- Schools are autonomous with regard to curriculum implementation and the teaching of Aboriginal language programs can happen without local language community approval and involvement, even if advised otherwise.

Crack 8

- There is a clear lack of coordination between the various agents that could ensure the successful delivery of quality Aboriginal language programs in schools in SA. Departmental curriculum officers and curriculum writers are primarily concerned with curriculum and do not address implementation or training issues.
- Training institutions are concerned with the viability of their own courses. Addressing the needs of schools is a secondary concern.
- The Teachers Registration Board is concerned with maintaining standards to the detriment of 'new' areas like Aboriginal languages that teachers actually have the knowledge and skills to teach.
- School principals, who have much autonomy in SA, are concerned with the day-to-day running of schools and other pressures such as NAPLAN results, often at the expense of Aboriginal languages and community concerns about their teaching.

7. Proposals for closing the cracks

There are a number of situations that work against Aboriginal languages being recognised and given more support by various institutions in SA. If these could be changed or remedied, the cracks that Aboriginal languages are falling through could possibly be reduced or even closed. The following are just a few of the remedies that could help rectify the current situation, resulting in a better outcome for Aboriginal languages and our graduates:

- The introduction of an Aboriginal Languages Act through state parliament (similar to that in NSW) that enshrines official status for SA's Aboriginal languages and guarantees ongoing financial support for their research, development, learning and teaching.
- The immediate recognition of the need for teaching teams in schools, including Aboriginal language and culture specialists supported by classroom teachers and linguists. This will require funding beyond the usual staffing formula. Existing Aboriginal Language Program Initiative funding could and should be used towards this end, but much additional funding will be needed.
- Adopting targeted strategies for the recruitment and training of Aboriginal language and culture specialists to teach Aboriginal languages in schools. All current Aboriginal employees working in schools should be offered an introductory workshop in the local Aboriginal language (for example, Kaurna on the Adelaide Plains). Such a workshop would be of benefit, in the first instance, to Aboriginal community education officers and Aboriginal secondary education transition officers, but would also benefit others with an interest in and passion for the teaching of Aboriginal languages in the future.
- The funding and provision of accredited training for Aboriginal language and culture specialists and teachers of Aboriginal languages. Such training opportunities are lacking within the university sector but are partially addressed through the certificate-level courses offered at Tauondi College (see Gale, 2020). However, the previous state government cut $2 million of core funding annually from Tauondi Aboriginal Community College in 2020. Tauondi is the primary training institution for Aboriginal people in the VET sector in SA, so its funding needs to be reinstated in full.
- The provision of ongoing professional development for teachers of Aboriginal languages, including Aboriginal language and culture specialists. There is a lack of government support and coordinated professional development for Aboriginal language teachers (unlike WA, NSW and Victoria, see First Languages Australia, [2021]). Some fully trained teachers have attended and are attending the certificate-level training at Tauondi College, for want of professional development opportunities within the department.

- Recognition of the current Certificate II, III and IV accredited Aboriginal language training courses, and any other relevant professional development opportunities, by the SA Department for Education, Teachers Registration Board and Australian Education Union.
- Offers of on-the-job training, as in WA, so that trainees are employed and have an income as they train and undertake their accredited certificate courses, along with mentoring from experienced teachers and language specialists.
- The development of clear career paths for specialist Aboriginal language teachers. These should be based on an award structure that incrementally remunerates training, professional development and years of experience.
- Aboriginal community aspirations and Aboriginal teachers of Aboriginal languages should be front and centre as expressed in Australia's *Action Plan for the International Decade of Indigenous Languages 2022–2032* (see First Languages Australia, 2023, p. 34). If this is taken as the starting point, then other points (the need for training, career paths and so on) should follow.
- The establishment of a task force that works with the many stakeholders and considers all aspects of Aboriginal language programs and their implementation. Such a task force needs to put Aboriginal community aspirations at the centre regarding the teaching of Aboriginal languages in schools.

8. Conclusion

In this chapter we have summarised the situation regarding the learning and teaching of Aboriginal languages in the adult vocational training sector in SA. We have also reflected on the major cracks that Aboriginal languages are falling through, often because of inadequate government policy and inaction on the part of the bureaucracy. The biggest barrier to furthering the training of Aboriginal language teachers in SA is, arguably, the complete lack of recognition given to our language graduates by the SA Department for Education, the Teachers Registration Board and the Education Union. Despite continuous lobbying—by trainers and graduates—for well over a decade, the demand for recognition seems to have fallen on deaf ears.

We titled this chapter 'Falling between the cracks', giving the SA Department for Education the benefit of the doubt, and seeing the current situation as one of benign neglect. But one cannot help but wonder whether the department does not wish to place the teaching of Aboriginal languages in the hands of Aboriginal community language and culture specialists. This was not the case in the early 1990s, when the department was willing to embrace the notion of 'teaching teams' promoted under the AILF project. We can only hope that the department does not intend to place the teaching of Aboriginal languages in the hands of trained and registered teachers, irrespective of their knowledge of the languages, thereby sidelining those to whom the languages belong.

Despite the many cracks in the system, and this lack of recognition for our Aboriginal language graduates, we have intentionally highlighted the positive things happening in this state by presenting an overview of the substantial advances made in the teaching of Aboriginal languages in the adult sector over the last decade. We trust that this work will help inspire those who can help to rectify the current situation to work alongside our wonderful and passionate Aboriginal language graduates and specialists. The theme for National Reconciliation Week in 2022 was 'Be Brave, Make Change'. Ma! Let's do it!

Acknowledgements

We thank two anonymous reviewers for their helpful comments and feedback. This chapter has been written with the support of an ARC Discovery grant DP190102413.

References

Amery, R. (2016). *Warraparna Kaurna! Reclaiming an Australian language.* University of Adelaide Press. library.oapen.org/handle/20.500.12657/32836.

Amery, R. (2020). Teaching Aboriginal languages at university: To what end? In J. Fornasiero, S. Reed, R. Amery, E. Bouvet, K. Enomoto & H. L. Xu (Eds.), *Intersections in language planning and policy: Establishing connections in language and cultures* (pp. 455–471). Springer Nature. doi.org/10.1007/978-3-030-50925-5_29.

Amery, R. & Buckskin, V. K. (2012). Handing on the teaching of Kaurna language to Kaurna youth. *Australian Aboriginal Studies, 2*, 31–41.

Australian Curriculum. (2018). Framework for Aboriginal languages and Torres Strait Islander languages. www.australiancurriculum.edu.au/curriculum-information/understand-this-learning-area/languages#framework-for-aboriginal-languages-and-torres-strait-islander-languages.

Australian Government, Department of Education. (2024). The Australian curriculum. education.gov.au/australian-curriculum.

First Languages Australia. (2021). *Yakilla: Training tracks: Professional learning opportunities in the first languages field.* firstlanguages.org.au/yakilla.

First Languages Australia. (2022). *Report on professional learning to support the teaching of Aboriginal and Torres Strait Islander Languages.*

First Languages Australia. (2023). *Voices of Country: Australia's action plan for the international decade of Indigenous languages 2022–2032.* First Languages Australia and Commonwealth of Australia.

Gale, M. (2012). Grammar rules, ok? What works when teaching a highly endangered Aboriginal language versus a stronger language. In M. Ponsonnet, L. Dao & M. Bowler (Eds.), *Proceedings of the 42nd Australian Linguistics Society Conference 2011* (pp. 75–96). Australian Linguistic Society.

Gale, M. (2020). Square peg in a round hole: Reflections on teaching Aboriginal languages through the TAFE sector in South Australia. In J. Fornasiero, S. Reed, R. Amery; E. Bouvet, K. Enomoto & H. L. Xu (Eds.), *Intersections in language planning and policy: Establishing connections in language and cultures* (pp. 455–471). Springer Nature. doi.org/10.1007/978-3-030-50925-5_28.

Gale, M. (2023). Language revival. In C. Bowern (Ed.) *Oxford guide to Australian languages* (pp. 738–753). Oxford University Press. doi.org/10.1093/oso/9780198824978.003.0064.

Gale, M., Bleby, D., Kulyuru, N. & Osborne, S. (2020). The Pitjantjatjara Yankunytjatjara summer school: *Kulila! Nyawa! Arkala!* Framing Aboriginal language learning pedagogy within a University Language Intensive Model. In J. Fornasiero, S. Reed, R. Amery, E. Bouvet, K. Enomoto & H. L. Xu (Eds.), *Intersections in language planning and policy: Establishing connections in languages and cultures* (pp. 491–505). Springer Nature. doi.org/10.1007/978-3-030-50925-5_30.

Gale, M. A., McHughes, E., Williams, P. & Koolmatrie, V. (2012). Lakun Ngarrindjeri thunggari: Weaving the Ngarrindjeri language back to health. *Australian Aboriginal Studies, 2,* 42–53. search.informit.org/doi/10.3316/informit.020722420053994.

Gale, M. & Mickan, P. (2007). Nripun your ko:pi: we want more than body parts, but how? In R. Amery & J. Nash, (Eds.), *Warra wiltaniappendi: Strengthening languages: Proceedings of the inaugural Indigenous languages conference (ILC) 2007* (pp. 81–88). University of Adelaide.

Grenoble, L. A. & Whaley, L. J. (2006). *Saving languages: An introduction to language revitalization.* Cambridge University Press. doi.org/10.1017/CBO9780511615931.

Hinton, L., Huss, L. & Roche, G. (2018). *Routledge handbook of language revitalization.* Routledge. doi.org/10.4324/9781315561271.

Marchant. G. (2021, 11 July). Aboriginal languages making comeback through new training program and dictionaries. *ABC News.* abc.net.au/news/2021-07-11/aboriginal-languages-boosted-by-new-dictionaries-and-education/100275646.

Mercurio, A. & Amery, R. (1996). Can teaching languages at senior secondary level help to maintain and strengthen Australia's Indigenous languages? In J. D. Bobaljik, R. Pensalfini & L. Storto (Eds.), *MIT Working papers in linguistics, Vol. 28 Papers on Language endangerment and the maintenance of linguistic diversity* (pp. 25–57). MIT Press.

SA Department for Education. (2019). *Aboriginal education strategy: 2019 to 2029.* education.sa.gov.au/docs/curriculum/aboriginal-education/dept-ed-aboriginal-education-strategy-2019-2029.pdf.

SA Department for Education. (2024). Aboriginal language—schools offering a program. www.education.sa.gov.au/parents-and-families/curriculum-and-learning/primary-and-secondary/languages/languages-offered-government-schools.

The Free Dictionary. (2024). Fall between the cracks. Farlex. idioms.thefreedictionary.com/fall+between+the+cracks.

Truscott, A. & Malcolm, I. (2010). Closing the policy–practice gap: Making Indigenous language policy more than empty rhetoric. In J. Hobson, K. Lowe, S. Poetsch & M. Walsh (Eds.), *Re-awakening languages: Theory and practice in the revitalisation of Australia's Indigenous languages* (pp. 6–21). Sydney University Press.

4

Disrupting idealisations of communication in language learning pedagogy: Digital possibilities

Levi Durbidge

1. Introduction

The advent of digital communications technology has thrust human society into the midst of vast and rapid change. Even as we continue to grapple with the affordances and impacts that hyperconnectivity produces, it is redefining our relationship to technology, ourselves and even language itself (Barton & Lee, 2013). The effects of these changes are visible in language learning classrooms, both in the proliferation of digital artefacts in physical teaching spaces and in technology-enabled teaching and delivery methods. As language learning and teaching grapple with the impact of technology, including an increased ability for students to pursue language learning away from the traditional bounds of the classroom, it is vital that we examine the materials and practices used in language education with an eye to rethinking what can be achieved through institutionalised education.

Against this backdrop, and perhaps in spite of it, textbooks have continued to remain central to the enterprise of institutionalised language teaching (Gray, 2016). A body of work has developed that uses critical perspectives to investigate and demonstrate how language learning textbooks reproduce ideological representations of communication within a given language community, the nature and composition of that community, and its cultural and political realities. Authors have pointed out, for example, how language learning textbooks construct ideological notions of gender and sexuality (Goldstein, 2015; Lee, 2014; Mustapha, 2015; Yoshida, 2023), race and ethnicity (Grose, 2012; Yamada, 2010), cultural and linguistic homogeneity (Heinrich, 2005; Su, 2016), as well as perpetuating and valorising neoliberalist ideology (Bori, 2018; Gray, 2010).

These analyses have been vital in demonstrating how specific perspectives are presented to textbook users in ways that, following the work of critical discourse theorists such as van Dijk (2008), can be seen as natural and self-evident. This chapter argues that what is presented in language textbooks inevitably reproduces particular ideological perspectives due to the nature of pedagogical processes (Bernstein, 2000).

In this chapter I employ the notion of the 'communicative event' developed by Hymes (1974) as a means to understand how ideology is instantiated in contexts of language teaching, with particular reference to language textbooks, while also offering the means to disrupt those same ideologies. In doing this, I draw on the concept of idealisation found in the philosophy of science (Nowak, 1980) and on Bernstein's (2000) 'pedagogic device' to conceptualise the way that certain ideological notions are instantiated through example interactions presented in language learning textbooks. Although identifying the ideological underpinnings of language learning materials is crucial to the critical applied linguistic project (e.g. Pennycook, 2021; Risager, 2018), I seek in this chapter to show how these materials can be responded to by teachers through methods that circumvent some of their problematic aspects. My aim is not to suggest how materials development should be changed or improved; rather, it is to suggest ways that identified deficiencies or biases in the language learning materials can be subverted through alternative forms of pedagogy.

Digital communications technology offers a range of affordances that facilitate observation and participation in the communicative practices of a speech community without the need for proximity. It therefore provides opportunities to rethink the boundedness of the language classroom and its connection to speech communities (Kessler, 2018; Warschauer & Kern, 2000). With this in mind, I offer two examples that show how digital communications technology can be used to decentre *idealisations of communication* in students' language learning practice and disrupt ideologies of language and communication that are often implicitly absorbed by learning through said idealisations. Thus, I conceive of this chapter as contributing both to a conceptual and critical understanding of language learning materials and offering ideas for creating pedagogical disruptions in and beyond the language learning classroom. To this end, I draw examples from Japanese language teaching and learning practice in an Australian higher education institution; however, the general conceptual thrust of the chapter can be understood as applying more broadly.

2. From communicative reality to idealisation

Hymes's (1964) notion of the communicative event, which he understood as central to developing a sophisticated and holistic understanding of language use, consists of particular patterns of interaction that the speech community itself recognises as governed by particular norms, such as a conversation, lecture or sermon. This notion informed the development of the now widespread practice of communicative language teaching, based on the idea that participation in communicative events is a productive means to enable linguistic development (Savignon, 1987; Thornbury, 2016).

For many individuals learning a new language, the opportunity to engage in real-life scenarios where these communicative events organically occur can be quite restricted (Widdowson, 1990). Without direct access to these interactions, the potential for developing understanding of socially and politically appropriate ways of participating in a given communicative event is constrained by the materials available, instructors' directions and students' own experiences. Examinations of language textbooks have frequently pointed to how portrayals of communication through dialogues can significantly influence students' comprehension of how specific communicative events take place, including what is and is not considered normal and expected (e.g. Inawati, 2016; Jakupčević & Ćavar Portolan, 2021; McConachy, 2009). Having said that, the demands of institutionalised learning require that the complex, contextually situated and structured semiotic practices deployed in any given communicative event are transformed to fit pedagogical objectives.

The tensions that necessarily arise from these transformations, particularly the way that textbook-based dialogues fail to reflect communication as it occurs, have been frequently noted and examined (Jones & Ono, 2005; Matsumoto & Okamoto, 2003; McConachy & Hata, 2013; Wong, 2002), including debates about the role of 'authentic' materials (Breen, 1985;

Widdowson, 1990) and corpora-based findings (Carter, 1998) in language learning. Given this ongoing issue in language education, I suggest that better conceptualising the inevitable inability of language presented for pedagogic purposes to reflect organic communication would allow its constructiveness and the rationales it serves to be made more visible.

In this, I believe that the notion of 'idealisation' as it appears in the philosophy of science offers significant conceptual value when repurposed to describe communicative events as they are represented in language learning materials. Famously identified by Nowak (1980), idealisations are created in response to the complexity and dynamism of phenomena as they naturally appear. This complexity makes it notoriously difficult to generate models that can accurately and completely account for particular phenomena and make accurate predictions about how they will function. In order to overcome this, deliberate omissions or false assumptions about the way phenomena occur are made in order to generate models that are more easily understood and solved. Looking at the field of second language learning, for example, Ellis (2015) has pointed out how theories of order-of-acquisition are idealisations, ignoring the variations found across different individuals' developmental trajectories. He argues that while these theories are disputed and not universally applicable, they hold value that can serve in teacher education and enable theory testing across domains. Importantly for this chapter, idealisations exist conceptually as deliberately incomplete and sometimes false representations of actual phenomena that, through the removal of complexity, are instrumental in developing generalisable findings. Turning to the way communicative events are represented in textbooks, we can observe that they fulfil a similar function—presenting a deliberately incomplete or false representation of a complex reality for the purpose of generating understandings that can be generalised by those doing the learning.

Note, I am not suggesting that processes of language learning are directly comparable to the building of scientific theories, but, rather, that these similarities make the concept of idealisation useful. By labelling the types of communicative events found in language learning textbooks as *idealisations of communication*, their purpose as pedagogical resources and their inability to comprehensively represent actual interactive realities is made more apparent. That is to say that communicative events, as they are represented in textbook examples, are largely emptied of their situated complexity through their transformation for pedagogical purposes. Indeed, a primary aim of language learning pedagogy is to take a language as it is used within a given speech community and recontextualise it to allow those learning to appropriate its forms and usages in structured ways (Widdowson, 2000). This requires a degree of simplification since the complexity and breadth of actual language use cannot be immediately apprehended by those unfamiliar with it. These idealisations, as they are presented in textbooks, serve to develop users' linguistic repertoires, mediating their learning through structured introduction and practice of specific communicative practices, serving as important resources for language learning.

Although *idealisations of communication* serve a pedagogical purpose, they also present a number of issues. As the critical work referred to earlier has shown, language learning textbooks serve to reproduce particular ideological discourses and the idealised communicative events they contain reflect this. With scientific theories or models, the process of idealisation should be a well-understood aspect of their use by practitioners. This cannot be said of learning materials that, following Luke et al. (1983), derive authority not only from their textual forms, but also from the institutional contexts that position them as optimal targets for learning. While it is certainly true that students and, indeed, teachers can respond to what is presented critically, this ability is predicated on an understanding of contextually dependent communicative norms, as Widdowson (1990, p. 45) has pointed out:

> the development of the authenticating ability calls for an effective internalization of form and capability of analysis which will allow for their use across a wide and unpredictable range of different contexts. In other words, the very learning process implies a focus on form as a necessary condition for the subsequent focus on meaning.

That is to say, attention to the patterning of language is a necessary precursor to developing an awareness of when, where and with whom particular patterns are deemed appropriate. Unless directed otherwise, students encountering *idealisations of communication* in learning materials have only these examples and their own previous experiences with language to draw upon when making judgements about appropriateness.

The processes taking place, and the links between the creation of *idealisations of communication* and ideology, can be understood as the workings of the pedagogic device as described by Bernstein (2000). According to Bernstein, knowledge comes from something he terms the field of production, which includes traditional practices of academic research and thought. This knowledge is then recontextualised for pedagogic practice in the field of recontextualisation, with this transformation being subject to a number of rules. The first of these are distributive rules, which regulate how knowledge is ordered and distributed and determine who has the power to transmit and receive that knowledge. The second are recontextualising rules, which determine what, specifically, will be appropriated and focused upon, and how various elements will relate to each other and other discourses. The third are evaluative rules, which determine how acquisition will be recognised. Finally, these pedagogised discourses are transmitted in the field of reproduction, wherein students are introduced to them and required to replicate them to demonstrate understanding.

Looking at how communicative events are presented in language learning materials, we can note the ways in which the development of *idealisations of communication* is subjected to various ideological considerations. As explicated above, understandings of phenomena typically emerge from academic and scientific practice, and it is from here that selections of what will be taught in institutional settings are made. However, the development of language learning materials, including textbooks, draws its understanding of the way in which communicative events take place, not from empirical observations of those events, but directly from the intuitions of those producing the materials themselves (Biber et al., 1994; Boxer & Pickering, 1995). Even when corpora are used to avoid the pitfalls inherent in professional assumptions, processes of decontextualisation, underrepresentation and pedagogisation are still at work (G. Cook, 1998; Flowerdew, 2009).

When it comes to *idealisations of communication* in language learning textbooks, the field of production is therefore merged with the field of recontextualisation. The elements of communication and the relationships between them that will be emphasised in a textbook are based on the judgements of those producing the materials. Leung (2005, p. 127), for example, has observed that, in conceptions of communicative competence in language education, 'the social now resides in the pedagogic projections of the expert knower, the expert teacher', which generates disjunctions with the directly observable communicative practices of language users themselves.

The field of recontextualisation is, therefore, the principal site for knowledge about both what constitutes communication in a given speech community and what elements of that knowledge will be included in any idealisations that are produced for pedagogic purposes. The process of pedagogisation, which is already 'a space in which ideology can play' (Bernstein, 2000, p. 32), is made more problematic by the fact that the role of expert knower has traditionally been conflated with that of the native speaker and its deep-seated connections to race and ethnicity (Hashimoto, 2018; Tupas, 2022). While critical work over the past several decades has gone some way to picking apart this relationship at an academic level (Canagarajah, 2013; Rampton, 1990), these categories remain synonymous for many who work in, or engage with, language education. Harsanti and Manara (2021), for example, point out that while English teachers in Indonesia recognise the plurality of World Englishes, they continue to display a preference for textbooks that come from 'native speaking' authors in dominant Anglophone countries, primarily the United States. *Idealisations of communication* as they appear in learning materials are therefore also likely to privilege and reflect the ideological preferences of specific groups of expert knowers.

3. Idealisation in language learning materials

To illustrate how specific communicative events in language teaching textbooks represent *idealisations of communication*, I will analyse an example of dialogue from one of the most popular introductory Japanese language teaching textbooks and illustrate how the linguistic choices made by the authors reflect certain ideological and pedagogical positions that lead it to deviate from observations in the empirical literature.

In analysing this example, I draw on Halliday's (2013) insight that the notion of choice is an organising principle of communication. That is to say, when participating in communicative events, users of language must opt for a particular means of realising meaning from among various possible alternatives where they exist. The probability of any given choice being made by a user in a given communicative event is governed by a number of factors, of which Hymes's (1974) SPEAKING/PARLANT model represents a highly productive taxonomy (see McConachy [2009], for an example of how this can be applied to textbook dialogues). Importantly, though, Halliday (2013) observed that choices that deviated from those considered the default or norm in a given situation would be seen by other users as 'marked'.

For the purposes of this chapter, this insight is productive since we can observe that language learning materials, specifically representations of particular communicative events, are produced through a series of semiotic choices. Other scholars have previously demonstrated that research that draws from an observable communicative reality, including discourse studies (Jones & Ono, 2005) and corpus linguistics (Holmes, 1988), can highlight divergences between that communicative reality and textbook dialogues. By applying these types of comparisons, we can identify where choices have been made (explicitly or implicitly) about what language (and whose voice) has been included and how it has been presented. That is to say, the constructed nature of the particular idealisation of communication and the ideological processes at work become more readily apprehensible.

The example used in this analysis is taken from the second edition of Banno et al.'s (2011) *Genki: An Integrated Course in Elementary Japanese*, which is used widely in Japanese language classes throughout Australian universities. I have selected Dialogue II in Lesson 3 of the textbook (reproduced below). Its location in the textbook means it would be encountered by a majority of students using the text early in their learning and, therefore, it would be influential in shaping their understanding of Japanese communicative practices. The example presents a communicative event involving an American study abroad student and her host mother, on which there is already a body of applied and sociolinguistic work that can inform the analysis. Drawing on this academic scholarship, I demonstrate how semiotic choices made in the constitution of the dialogue represent idealised notions of communication and serve to produce a particular view of how this communicative event would take place. Additionally, I have provided a reproduction of the English translation included in the textbook. Although I recognise its important relationship to the text being analysed, I will not address it in the analysis below for reasons of space and complexity.

To contextualise the extract, Mary, introduced in previous chapters in the textbook as a Japanese major from the University of Arizona, has arrived in Japan to study at a local university. In the immediately preceding dialogue, a local university student, Takeshi, invites Mary to see a movie with him, which exhibits the same linguistic characteristics as the example below:

On Sunday morning, at Mary's host family's.

メアリー：おはようございます。
お母さん：おはよう。早いですね。
メアリー：ええ。今日は京都に行きます。京都で映画を見ます。
お母さん：いいですね。何時ごろ帰りますか。

メアリー：九時<ruby>く<rt>く</rt></ruby>ごろです。
お母さん：晩ご飯は？
メアリー：食べません。
お母さん：そうですか。じゃあ、いってらっしゃい。
メアリー：いってきます。

Mary: Good morning.

Host mother: Good morning. You are early, aren't you?

Mary: Yes, I'm going to Kyoto today. I will see a movie in Kyoto.

Host mother: Good. Around what time will you come back?

Mary: Around nine.

Host mother: How about dinner?

Mary: I will not eat.

Host mother: I see. Well, have a nice day.

Mary: Good-bye.

(Banno et al., 2011, pp. 84–85)

Following Hymes (1974), the participants and the setting shape the nature of the communicative events, influencing the linguistic choices made in its realisation. Although it can be inferred from the dialogue above and the accompanying image in the textbook itself (not reproduced here) that the interaction is taking place in a domestic setting, it is also important to observe the approximate geographical setting that can be deduced from the dialogue itself. In line 3, Mary states 京都で映画を見ます (*kyōto de eiga wo mimasu* / I will see a movie in Kyōto), which locates the dialogue as taking place somewhere in the Kansai region of Japan where Kyōto is located. This is an important detail since, as is widely recognised among Japanese speech communities and extensively discussed in the sociolinguistic and anthropological literature (e.g. Doerr, 2015; Keum, 2005; Sreetharan, 2004), varieties of Japanese widely used in this area are distinctly different from the Tōkyō-originating varieties construed as *hyōjyungo* or 'standard' Japanese.

Throughout the interaction, however, both Mary and the host mother use only forms that appear as part of Tōkyō-originating *hyōjyungo*. Examples of alternative linguistic choices that would highlight the existence of dialectical variations in the Kansai region include おはようさん (*ohayōsan*) instead of おはよう (*ohayō*), ええですね (*ee desu ne*) or ええやん (*ee yan*) instead of いいですね (*ii desu ne*) and 食べへん (*tabehen*) instead of 食べません (*tabemasen*). The selections made by the authors are not particularly surprising, though, as they follow longstanding norms in Japanese foreign language education of presenting *hyōjyungo* as the only variety used (Matsumoto & Okamoto, 2003). The decision to present the dialogue in this way represents both a semiotic and pedagogic choice—a choice that is not visible to a student who is encountering this type of communicative event through the text, unaware that dialectical differences exist.

As the academic literature has pointed out, knowledge of these dialects among those studying abroad in Kansai is widespread (Takamura & Naito, 2016), and they are often encountered within homestay settings (Iino, 2006). Further, Iino (2006) points out that while there may be a tendency among families to switch to *hyōjyungo* when addressing students they host, the interactive reality is decidedly heterogenous. While it is certainly conceivable that a sojourner staying in the Kansai region of Japan would encounter nothing but *hyōjyungo* within the host family, the fact that other prominent linguistic possibilities for this setting do not appear, and are not even acknowledged, effectively erases them. Instead, linguistic choices have been made to present specific forms of Japanese as universal and standardised.

Further, language learning abroad research has shown how interactions are often negotiated around the linguistic repertoire of interactants, with translanguaging practices often an important feature of sojourners' interactions (Diao & Trentman, 2021), including in homestay settings (Durbidge, 2024). Although the reasons for presenting interactions wholly in the target language require little pedagogical justification, the communicative reality in homestay situations is that interactants may often move between and across linguistic varieties according to their needs, abilities and desires. The homogenised dialogues found throughout language learning textbooks, including the example above, in this way, represent an idealisation of actual communication.

The second main issue I wish to examine is the fact that both Mary and the host mother predominantly use formalistic suffixes, namely ます (*masu*) and です (*desu*), throughout this communicative event, with at least one instance appearing in each conversational turn. In a comprehensive sociolinguistic analysis of the use of *masu* forms among Japanese speakers and their occurrence in interactions with those learning Japanese, H. M. Cook (2008) demonstrates the conditions under which they are used within family interactions. Analysing the dinnertime interactions of nine Japanese families hosting American and British students, Cook shows that the use of *masu* within Japanese-speaking families is generally limited to specific utterances and communicative events: for example, set phrases, teaching about things they have authority on (for example, Japanese culture), indicating they are in charge of a particular activity, reporting speech or categorising playfulness. Significantly for our analysis, Cook finds that hosts positioned the exchange students as members of the host family and, therefore, adopted conventions of using more informal or intimate forms outside of the instances listed above. As for the exchange students themselves, while deviation from these norms was more prevalent among those with less experience with the language, it was nearly absent among advanced users.

However, for one family in Cook's study, marked use of *masu* forms occurred more frequently. Cook demonstrates that these instances co-occurred with other marked features, such as the use of first- and second-person pronouns where they would not be expected. Moreover, Cook shows that these instances of marked usage often occurred as rephrasings of utterances initially presented in plain form. The exchange student Alice is noted to be a novice user of Japanese, and Cook identifies the use of marked *masu* forms as an accommodation strategy adopted by the host family in response to issues of comprehension. These findings cohere with other studies of interactions between host families and international students in Japan that show that the marked use of *masu* and *desu* forms is adopted as a form of accommodation and is often used to rephrase expressions initially expressed in plain form (Iino, 1996; McMeekin, 2006).

Other studies demonstrate that international students in Japan quickly adopt plain forms in most interactions soon after their arrival (Okunishi, 2019; Taguchi, 2015). Viewed alongside these studies, we can observe that, overwhelmingly, the use of plain forms would be the default choice in the particular communicative event presented in Figure 4.1. However, in what is presented, there are only two instances in which less formalistic forms have been selected: the host mother's use of おはよう (*ohayō* / good morning) in line 2 and the truncated question 晩ご飯は？ (*ban gohan wa*? / how about dinner?) in line 6. Clearly, through the processes of pedagogisation, choices have been made to use formalistic language to represent a communicative event where its use would normally be highly restricted. The convention of presenting formalistic structures in Japanese textbooks before introducing plain forms has been noted by Matsumoto and Okamoto (2003). Locating its genesis in ideologies that essentialise notions of group-orientedness and hierarchy as aspects of Japanese interactional styles, they prioritise the acquisition of registers that adhere to interactional strategies that emphasise these notions. What we see, therefore, is formalistic interaction styles presented as the default mode of communication, even in the intimate confines of a homestay where they may be considered contextually inappropriate.

Finally, the idealised nature of this example is made more apparent by the way it, like almost all constructed dialogues, is free from the disfluencies and overlaps that characterise normal conversational interaction; nor does it exhibit the hesitations, negotiations, repairs and repetitions that would usually occur (Jones & Ono, 2005). This is a particularly important point, as those in the early stages of learning a language variety would arguably benefit the most from these types of conversational strategies. This presentation, therefore, carries an implication that these types of communicative events may occur between speakers free from disfluency and negotiation and serve as models for the reproduction of similarly pristine interactions.

My point here is not simply to re-emphasise that textbook dialogues diverge from naturally occurring interactions. Rather, the point I wish to make is that the presentation of these idealised communicative events in language learning textbooks serves underlying pedagogical and ideological rationales. Any communicative event necessarily involves actions of linguistic choice, and those presented in learning materials will always be an idealisation, given that the complexity of interaction is removed in service of pedagogical objectives. As Luke (2015, pp. 8–9) has pointed out, any attempt to structure the learning of language and communication must necessarily involve purposive and normative inclusions of specific texts and discourses, skills and competences, knowledges and ideologies from a virtually infinite archive of possible selections.

The issue, though, is that the rationales that have driven these selections may not be immediately apparent to students, or, for that matter, teachers who use these idealisations in the classroom. They may, therefore, come to stand as models of appropriate interaction in the absence of additional or alternative examples that can reveal the choices that have been made. The ideas they convey about the communicative practices of a particular speech community—their homogeneity, formality, rigidity—stand in contrast to current understandings that emphasise their heterogenous, dynamic and negotiated nature. The complexity of language, its relationship to other semiotic practices, and its entanglement with the social, cultural and political dimensions of communities are well documented (Block, 2014; Douglas Fir Group, 2016; Kramsch, 2020; Norton & Toohey, 2011). Language learning is a process of socialised linguistic appropriation that is entwined with social, cultural and political socialisation and renegotiation (Steffensen & Kramsch, 2017). In this sense, I believe that the appropriate response to these idealisations, which do in themselves serve important pedagogical purposes, is to reveal to students their idealised nature through direct observation and engagement with the communicative practices of speech communities in all their complexity and messiness. Indeed, this has traditionally been the remit of many study abroad programs, yet the logistics and economic imposition of these programs can limit their accessibility and practicality.

As discussed earlier, the advent and rapid development of digital communications technology have induced widespread changes in the ways we interact and relate to each other. However, the disruption that these changes have introduced to the learning and teaching of language also offers affordances that can bring students into immediate contact with speech communities without the need for proximity, particularly through interactive technologies such as social media, videoconferencing and messaging services. These platforms provide opportunities for students to directly engage with the communicative practices of a given speech community as they appear beyond the recontextualisation processes that produce the idealisations found in textbooks.

4. Towards a praxis of decentring and disrupting idealisations in language learning pedagogy: Examples of practice

The idealised communicative events found in textbooks serve useful practical and pedagogical purposes; however, it is vital that students are also provided with encounters that can disrupt the ideological notions of language and community that become embedded within them. To this effect, I offer examples that have come from my own attempts to directly engage students with the communicative events in Japanese speech communities by leveraging the affordances of digital communications technology. This includes having students perform observations of hashtag use in Japanese language Instagram posts, noting their linguistic diversity and appropriate common practices for the creation of their own social media posts. It also includes an 'online language exchange' program in which participation in interactions allows students to observe the co-constructed and heteroglossic nature of interaction, de-emphasising the importance of maintaining perfect grammatical accuracy in achieving meaning. These examples are not comprehensive prescriptions but simply examples from my own praxis of disruption.

4.1. Disrupting idealisations through exposure to digital discourse

The first example draws on the language learning possibilities available through digital discourse as it emerges in the online interactions of a given speech community (for further discussion, see Durbidge & McClelland, 2023). Social media provides rich ground for students to observe communicative practices directly, both in the monologic practices of posting and in the interactions that emerge through commenting. While the language varieties used online can be idiosyncratic, digital communication has also made a range of vernacular practices more public and easily accessible (Barton & Lee, 2013; Spilioti, 2019). Moreover, online interaction is often multimodal, incorporating digital and visual literacies that students may already possess competence in, allowing them to readily engage with more advanced members of a given speech community (e.g. Jin, 2018).

Working from the premise that social media posts are a type of communicative event, students in an introductory Japanese language class were required to produce a post containing an image that described a past activity they had engaged in. In preparing for this activity, students needed to perform a limited investigation of Instagram posts produced in Japanese on the activity they wished to write on, specifically observing and documenting the hashtags used. These observations were then used to prompt instructor-led critical reflections on the linguistic composition and affordances of hashtags and how they function in Japanese language posts on Instagram. These observations and reflections included commentary on the way Japanese orthography does not use spaces within sentences, facilitating the inclusion of more complex utterances as hashtags; the use of other language varieties, particularly English, in posts that are primarily written for a Japanese-using audience; and the use of both formalistic and informal language. Given their limited syntactical complexity and students' familiarity with them from their own use of social media, hashtags are generally easy for those with limited understanding of Japanese communication to grasp and appropriate for their own use.

While the language that students observe and deploy through this activity may be restricted to specific online contexts, the objective of these activities is to develop a critical awareness of the heterogeneity of actual linguistic practice. Moreover, the language they encounter emerges more organically, with students investigating usage as it relates to their own needs and interests. The examples are then contrasted with the idealised pedagogic recontextualisations they encounter elsewhere in their learning to generate further insights about linguistic choices. Importantly, student engagement with these instantiations of organically occurring language happens through teacher-directed observations and reflections that highlight the divergences.

4.2. Disrupting idealisations through online interactions

The second example makes use of now widespread videoconferencing software to foster interactions between students of different speech communities. While the approaches and varieties of online language exchanges are highly varied (Colpaert, 2020), they share the idea of allowing users of different languages to engage in interaction with the objective of promoting language development in all participants. Referred to in the literature as 'telecollaboration' or 'virtual exchange', this approach to learning was embraced by tertiary institutions around the world that were pursuing alternatives to in-person international exchange during the COVID-19 pandemic (O'Dowd, 2021). Research has focused on the immediate linguistic and cultural learning outcomes of these exchanges (Colpaert, 2020); however, they are also highly valuable for the affordances they offer for participants to interact directly with speech community members. The spontaneity and practical demands of the interactions that occur bring them into direct contrast with *idealisations of communication* as ordered, homogeneous and requiring near-perfect adherence to grammatical norms.

In a project conducted on a voluntary online language exchange program between students learning Japanese at an Australian tertiary institution in Queensland and English at a Japanese tertiary institution in Osaka, participant responses indicated how engaging in interaction with each other led to realisations that disrupted their understandings of communication. The program, running since 2020, involves pairs of students from each institution meeting weekly online to interact and support each other's language learning in Japanese and English for at least 30 minutes a week for a minimum of four weeks. After completing the minimum four weeks, participants were asked to answer a survey on their experiences. From over 100 participants in the program between 2021 and 2023, a total of 41 responded to the survey.

The survey captured a range of data, including frequency and duration of meetings, the main activities focused on in sessions, motivations for participating and responses to a variety of statements regarding outcomes. While the research project did not specifically seek to investigate the effects of the language exchange on participants' ideas of communication, a number of responses to the optional question 'Did you gain anything else (that was not in your original aims) from the teletandem?' indicated that interactions led participants from both Japan and Australia to re-evaluate their assumptions about communicating in their target language. For example, one Australian participant stated:

> I gained some confidence in speaking Japanese and a courage to try without fear of getting the sentence completely wrong.
>
> (Participant 3)

Students from Japan also provided responses that indicated renewed perspectives on communicating in English:

> 私が話そうと思えば、つたない会話でも相手と話すことができることを学びました。
>
> I learned that if I think I can talk [with my partner], then even if what I say is clumsy, I'm still able to converse with them.
>
> (Participant 7)

> 分からなくても頑張って英語を話して、伝えることができれば会話を楽しめることがわかり、英語での会話が楽しいと思えるようになったこと。
>
> I realized that even if I don't understand something, if I try hard to speak English and can communicate, I can enjoy having conversations. I've started to think that having conversations in English is fun.
>
> (Participant 8)

These reflections suggest that participants developed an understanding of interaction that was more collaborative than they imagined before beginning the program. Indeed, Blake and Zyzik (2003) noted in their study of a telecollaborative program involving Spanish that partner exchanges were highly negotiated and featured a range of interactional strategies as pairs continually worked together to achieve meaning. Consequently, it appears that through interactions with a language partner online, students become aware that communication can be achieved, not through perfect comprehension of syntactically normative utterances, but through deviations from these norms.

Australian participants also indicated that participation in the program had raised their understanding of the heterogeneity of the Japanese language:

> I learnt more about socially appropriate language.
>
> (Participant 10)

> I learned lots about how language works and also learned little bits and pieces of language that are more 'locally' known in Japan.
>
> (Participant 28)

By using the expression 'socially appropriate language', Participant 10 indicates that their online interactions have contributed to a greater awareness of how linguistic variation functions across different social settings in Japanese (as discussed in the previous analysis). Participant 28 indicates that their participation in the program taught them forms that they associate with localised communicative practices. As both of these participants indicate, interaction with members of the speech community brought them to a greater awareness of different varieties of Japanese and how they function within that community. Further, as one participant from Japan indicated, interacting with someone learning the language gave them cause to reflect on how Japanese actually functioned:

> パートナーに自分の言語について話す中で、日本語についても改めて考え直す機会ができた
>
> While talking to my partner about my language, I had the opportunity to rethink my Japanese as well.
>
> (Participant 40)

Taken together, these responses suggest direct interactions with members of a given speech community can contribute to an increased awareness of the nature of language and work to disrupt idealisations of communication encountered in language learning textbooks.

5. Discussion and conclusion

While each of the practical examples above draws on different genres, modalities and functions of digital communications technology, they both leverage its affordances to bring students into direct contact with the living communicative practices of speech community members. These examples serve to illustrate how technology and the ensuing development of attendant social media platforms present opportunities to decentre more traditional language learning materials and pedagogy in the classroom. The ability to observe, analyse and participate in instances of communication among members of a speech community without the need for immediate temporal or spatial proximity opens up new possibilities for critical language education. Communicative events lie at the heart of a speech community's linguistic practice, and allowing students to directly engage with and reflect on them as they emerge organically offers possibilities for disrupting the notions of communication instantiated in idealisations found elsewhere.

Although the identification of ideologies as they are transmitted through learning materials is an important aspect of the critical applied linguistic project, the reality is that any pedagogised notion of communicative practice necessarily involves simplification and transformation of the complex realities of contextually situated and structured semiotic practices of a speech community. Intentional or otherwise, the *idealisations of communication* that are used to teach language through learning materials such as textbooks will necessarily carry traces of the ideological processes that inform their creation (Bernstein, 2000). The production of learning materials will always involve processes of pedagogisation. However, as Kubota and Miller (2017, p. 147) have noted, the challenge for critical applied linguistic work is to move beyond a 'concept/theory fetish' and close the gap between theory and practice. It is therefore imperative that we follow the problematising of naturalised assumptions in learning materials with a praxis that seeks to disrupt these assumptions.

One response, as demonstrated above, is to ensure that students also encounter and engage with communicative events as they appear organically. It is through these examples that their co-constructed nature, their performativeness and their contextual situatedness can be more fully realised. As Blommaert (2018, p. 4) notes, 'language is context, it is the architecture of social behaviour itself', and allowing students to encounter language as it is deployed in the service of actual lived interaction means it is encountered in its complex fullness. That is not to say that *idealisations of communication* have no place in structured learning. Their role as simplified, fragmentary models of communication allows specific concepts to be illustrated, comprehended and scaffolded, particularly among those with more limited understandings of the communicative norms of the language practices being studied. As practitioners, though, we need to consider the degree to which these idealisations are centred in our teaching practice, the effect this has on students and the methods we can adopt to disrupt their problematic aspects.

Building on the examples provided above, students can be introduced to the tools of ethnography and critical applied linguistics, even in limited forms, that can foster their ability to critically reflect, evaluate and understand the language they encounter through structured learning sources and actual communicative practice. The availability of online communication platforms provides opportunities to train students in critical and ethnographic methods of observation and language learning that can then disrupt the reproduction of linguistic ideologies. Although this analysis has focused on idealisations as they appear in language learning textbooks, the proliferation of technologies that are promoted as enabling language learning, including language learning apps and language learning video channels on platforms such as YouTube, also requires critical engagement.

Critical appraisals of structured learning materials readily available online can serve to highlight and inform students of their ideological underpinnings, particularly when combined with actual experience and the communicative practices of a given community. Although the expert knower or teacher is required both for the structuring of learning materials and the contextualisation of those materials, there is a space within learning to present opportunities for learners to observe, analyse and participate in communicative events that contain members of the target speech community. Enabling students to encounter live instances of communication and interaction generates opportunities to reflect on notions of communication transmitted through *idealisations of communication* and reconcile them with the complex reality of actual use.

References

Banno, E., Ikeda, Y., Ohno, Y., Shinagawa, C. & Takashiki, K. (2011). *GENKI I: An Integrated Course in Elementary Japanese* (2nd edition). Japan Times.

Barton, D. & Lee, C. (2013). *Language online: Investigating digital texts and practices.* Routledge.

Bernstein, B. (2000). *Pedagogy, symbolic control, and identity: Theory, research, critique.* Rowman & Littlefield.

Biber, D., Conrad, S. & Reppen, R. (1994). Corpus-based approaches to issues in Applied Linguistics. *Applied Linguistics, 15*(2), 169–189. doi.org/10.1093/applin/15.2.169.

Blake, R. J. & Zyzik, E. C. (2003). Who's helping whom? Learner/heritage-speakers' networked discussions in Spanish. *Applied Linguistics, 24*(4), 519–544. doi.org/10.1093/applin/24.4.519.

Block, D. (2014). *Social class in applied linguistics.* Routledge.

Blommaert, J. (2018). *Dialogues with ethnography: Notes on classics, and how I read them.* Multilingual Matters.

Bori, P. (2018). *Language textbooks in the era of neoliberalism.* Routledge. doi.org/10.4324/9781315405544.

Boxer, D. & Pickering, L. (1995). Problems in the presentation of speech acts in ELT materials: The case of complaints. *ELT Journal, 49*(1), 44–58. doi.org/10.1093/elt/49.1.44.

Breen, M. P. (1985). Authenticity in the language classroom. *Applied Linguistics, 6*(1), 60–70. doi.org/10.1093/applin/6.1.60.

Canagarajah, A. S. (2013). Interrogating the 'native speaker fallacy': Non-linguistic roots, non-pedagogical results. In G. Braine (Ed.), *Non-native educators in English language teaching* (pp. 77–92). Routledge.

Carter, R. (1998). Orders of reality: CANCODE, communication, and culture. *ELT Journal, 52*(1), 43–56. doi.org/10.1093/elt/52.1.43.

Colpaert, J. (2020). Editorial position paper: How virtual is your research? *Computer Assisted Language Learning, 33*(7), 653–664. doi.org/10.1080/09588221.2020.1824059.

Cook, G. (1998). The uses of reality: A reply to Ronald Carter. *ELT Journal, 52*(1), 57–63. doi.org/10.1093/elt/52.1.57.

Cook, H. M. (2008). *Socializing identities through speech style: Learners of Japanese as a foreign language*. Multilingual Matters. doi.org/10.21832/9781847691026.

Diao, W. & Trentman, E. (2021). *Language learning in study abroad: The multilingual turn*. Multilingual Matters.

Doerr, N. M. (2015). Standardization and paradoxical highlighting of linguistic diversity in Japan. *Japanese Language and Literature, 49*(2), 389–403. jstor.org/stable/24615144.

Douglas Fir Group. (2016). A transdisciplinary framework for SLA in a multilingual world. *The Modern Language Journal, 100*(S1), 19–47. doi.org/10.1111/modl.12301.

Durbidge, L. (2024). *Language learning, digital communications and study abroad: Identity and belonging in translocal contexts*. Multilingual Matters. doi.org/10.21832/9781800415065.

Durbidge, L. & McClelland, G. (2023). Japanese language learning and teaching during COVID-19: Challenges and opportunities. *Japanese Studies, 43*(3), 237–250. doi.org/10.1080/10371397.2022.2072821.

Ellis, R. (2015). Researching acquisition sequences: Idealization and de-idealization in SLA. *Language Learning, 65*(1), 181–209. doi.org/10.1111/lang.12089.

Flowerdew, L. (2009). Applying corpus linguistics to pedagogy: A critical evaluation. *International Journal of Corpus Linguistics, 14*(3), 393–417. doi.org/10.1075/ijcl.14.3.05flo.

Goldstein, B. (2015). LGBT invisibility in language learning materials. *Language Issues: The ESOL Journal, 26*(2), 35–40.

Gray, J. (2010). The branding of English and the culture of the new capitalism: Representations of the world of work in English language textbooks. *Applied Linguistics, 31*(5), 714–733. doi.org/10.1093/applin/amq034.

Gray, J. (2016). ELT materials: Claims, critiques and controversies. In G. Hall (Ed.), *The Routledge handbook of English language teaching* (pp. 95–108). Routledge.

Grose, T. (2012). Uyghur language textbooks: Competing images of a multi-ethnic China. *Asian Studies Review, 36*(3), 369–389. doi.org/10.1080/10357823.2012.711809.

Halliday, M. A. K. (2013). Meaning as choice. In L. Fontaine, T. Bartlett & G. O'Grady (Eds.), *Systemic functional linguistics exploring choice* (1st ed., pp. 15–36). Cambridge University Press. doi.org/10.1017/CBO9781139583077.003.

Harsanti, H. G. R. & Manara, C. (2021). 'I have to teach the "English" English': Nativespeakerism ideology among the English teachers. *Indonesian Journal of Applied Linguistics, 11*(2), 330–340. doi.org/10.17509/ijal.v11i2.26379.

Hashimoto, K. (2018). 'Mother tongue speakers' or 'native speakers'? Assumptions surrounding the teaching of Japanese as a foreign language in Japan. In S. A. Houghton & K. Hashimoto, *Towards Post-Native-Speakerism* (pp. 61–77). Springer. doi.org/10.1007/978-981-10-7162-1_4.

Heinrich, P. (2005). Language ideology in JFL textbooks. *International Journal of the Sociology of Language, 2005*(175–176), 213–232. doi.org/10.1515/ijsl.2005.2005.175-176.213.

Holmes, J. (1988). Doubt and certainty in ESL textbooks. *Applied Linguistics, 9*(1), 21–44. doi.org/10.1093/applin/9.1.21.

Hymes, D. (1964). Introduction: Toward ethnographies of communication. In J. J. Gumperz & D. Hymes (Eds.), *The ethnography of communication* (pp. 1–34). Wiley Online Library.

Hymes, D. (1974). *Foundations in sociolinguistics: An ethnographic approach*. University of Pennsylvania Press.

Iino, M. (1996). *'Excellent foreigner!' Gaijinization of Japanese language and culture in contact situations. An ethnographic study of dinner table conversations between Japanese host families and American students* [Unpublished PhD thesis]. University of Pennsylvania.

Iino, M. (2006). Norms of interaction in a Japanese homestay setting: Toward a two-way flow of linguistic and cultural resources. In M. A. DuFon & E. Churchill (Eds.), *Language learners in study abroad contexts* (pp. 151–176). Multilingual Matters.

Inawati, I. (2016). The pragmatics of greetings reflected in the textbooks for teaching English as a foreign language in Indonesia. *Ahmad Dahlan Journal of English Studies, 3*(2), 1–10. doi.org/10.26555/adjes.v3i2.4984.

Jakupčević, E. & Ćavar Portolan, M. (2024). An analysis of pragmatic content in EFL textbooks for young learners in Croatia. *Language Teaching Research, 28*(1), 114–137. doi.org/10.1177/1362168820986936.

Jin, L. (2018). Digital affordances on WeChat: Learning Chinese as a second language. *Computer Assisted Language Learning, 31*(1–2), 27–52. doi.org/10.1080/09588221.2017.1376687.

Jones, K. & Ono, T. (2005). Discourse-centered approaches to Japanese language pedagogy. *Japanese Language and Literature, 39*(2), 237. doi.org/10.2307/30038901.

Kessler, G. (2018). Technology and the future of language teaching. *Foreign Language Annals, 51*(1), 205–218. doi.org/10.1111/flan.12318.

Keum, J. (2005). Nihongo hōgen ni okeru danwa hyōshiki no shutsugen keikō: Tōkyō hōgen, Ōsaka hōgen, Sendai hōgen no hikaku [Trends in the occurrence of discourse signs in Japanese dialects: A comparison of Tokyo, Osaka and Sendai dialects]. *Nihongo no kenkyū, 1*(2), 1–18.

Kramsch, C. (2020). *Language as symbolic power.* Cambridge University Press. doi.org/10.1017/9781108869386.

Kubota, R. & Miller, E. R. (2017). Re-examining and re-envisioning criticality in language studies: Theories and praxis. *Critical Inquiry in Language Studies, 14*(2–3), 129–157. doi.org/10.1080/15427587.2017.1290500.

Lee, J. F. K. (2014). A hidden curriculum in Japanese EFL textbooks: Gender representation. *Linguistics and Education, 27,* 39–53. doi.org/10.1016/j.linged.2014.07.002.

Leung, C. (2005). Convivial communication: Recontextualizing communicative competence. *International Journal of Applied Linguistics, 15*(2), 119–144. doi.org/10.1111/j.1473-4192.2005.00084.x.

Luke, A. (2015). Cultural content matters: A critical sociology of language and literacy curriculum. In X. L. Curdt-Christiansen & C. Weninger (Eds.), *Language, ideology and education: The politics of textbooks in language education* (pp. 207–220). Routledge. doi.org/10.4324/9781315814223.

Luke, C., de Castell, S. & Luke, A. (1983). Beyond criticism: The authority of the school text. *Curriculum Inquiry, 13*(2), 111–127. doi.org/10.2307/1179632.

Matsumoto, Y. & Okamoto, S. (2003). The construction of the Japanese language and culture in teaching Japanese as a foreign language. *Japanese Language and Literature, 37*(1), 27–48. doi.org/10.2307/3594874.

McConachy, T. (2009). Raising sociocultural awareness through contextual analysis: Some tools for teachers. *ELT Journal, 63*(2), 116–125. doi.org/10.1093/elt/ccn018.

McConachy, T. & Hata, K. (2013). Addressing textbook representations of pragmatics and culture. *ELT Journal, 67*(3), 294–301. doi.org/10.1093/elt/cct017.

McMeekin, A. (2006). Negotiation in a Japanese study abroad setting. In E. Churchill & M. A. DuFon (Eds.), *Language learners in study abroad contexts* (pp. 177–202). Multilingual Matters. doi.org/10.21832/9781853598531-011.

Mustapha, A. S. (2015). Gender positioning through visual images in English-language textbooks in Nigeria. In A. S. Mustapha & S. Mills (Eds.), *Gender representation in learning materials* (pp. 150–163). Routledge. doi.org/10.4324/9781315764092.

Norton, B. & Toohey, K. (2011). Identity, language learning, and social change. *Language Teaching, 44*(4), 412–446. doi.org/10.1017/S0261444811000309.

Nowak, L. (1980). *The structure of idealization: Towards a systematic interpretation of the Marxian idea of science.* Springer Dordrecht. doi.org/10.1007/978-94-015-7651-2.

O'Dowd, R. (2021). Virtual exchange: Moving forward into the next decade. *Computer Assisted Language Learning, 34*(3), 209–224. doi.org/10/gk49gk.

Okunishi, M. (2019). Dōkyūsei no nihongo bogowasha to no kaiwa ni mirareru ryūgakusei no futsūtai shiyō [International students' use of the plain form in conversations with native Japanese speaking peers]. *Journal of Japanese Language Teaching, 172,* 134–148. doi.org/10.20721/nihongokyoiku.172.0_134.

Pennycook, A. (2021). *Critical applied linguistics: A critical re-introduction* (2nd ed.). Routledge.

Rampton, M. B. H. (1990). Displacing the 'native speaker': Expertise, affiliation, and inheritance. *ELT Journal, 44*(2), 97–101. doi.org/10.1093/eltj/44.2.97.

Risager, K. (2018). *Representations of the world in language textbooks.* Multilingual Matters.

Savignon, S. J. (1987). Communicative language teaching. *Theory Into Practice, 26*(4), 235–242. doi.org/10/fj365s.

Spilioti, T. (2019). From transliteration to trans-scripting: Creativity and multilingual writing on the internet. *Discourse, Context & Media, 29,* 100294. doi.org/10.1016/j.dcm.2019.03.001.

Sreetharan, C. S. (2004). Japanese men's linguistic stereotypes and realities. In S. Okamoto & J. S. Shibamoto-Smith (Eds.), *Japanese Language, Gender, and Ideology: Cultural Models and Real People* (pp. 275–289). Oxford University Press.

Steffensen, S. V. & Kramsch, C. (2017). The ecology of second language acquisition and socialization. In P. Duff & S. May, S. (Eds). *Language Socialization* (pp. 17–32). Springer. doi.org/10.1007/978-3-319-02255-0_2.

Su, Y.-C. (2016). The international status of English for intercultural understanding in Taiwan's high school EFL textbooks. *Asia Pacific Journal of Education, 36*(3), 390–408. doi.org/10.1080/02188791.2014.959469.

Taguchi, N. (2015). *Developing interactional competence in a Japanese study abroad context*. Multilingual Matters.

Takamura, M. & Naito, M. (2016). Kansai zaijū tankiryūgakusei no hōgen ishiki to shūtoku iyoku [Dialectical awareness and motivation to learn among short-term international students in the Kansai region]. *Kansai Gakuin Daigaku Nihongo Kyōikusentā Kiyō, 5,* 23–30.

Thornbury, S. (2016). Communicative language teaching in theory and practice. In G. Hall (Ed.), *The Routledge handbook of English language teaching* (pp. 224–237). Routledge.

Tupas, R. (2022). The coloniality of native speakerism. *Asian Englishes, 24*(2), 147–159. doi.org/10.1080/13488678.2022.2056797.

van Dijk, T. A. (2008). *Discourse and power*. Palgrave Macmillan.

Warschauer, M. & Kern, R. (2000). *Network-based language teaching: Concepts and practice*. Cambridge University Press.

Widdowson, H. G. (1990). *Aspects of language teaching*. Oxford University Press.

Widdowson, H. G. (2000). On the limitations of linguistics applied. *Applied Linguistics, 21*(1), 3–25. doi.org/10.1093/applin/21.1.3.

Wong, J. (2002). Applying conversation analysis in applied linguistics: Evaluating dialogue in English as a second language textbooks. *International Review of Applied Linguistics in Language Teaching, 40*(1), 37–60. doi.org/10.1515/iral.2002.003.

Yamada, M. (2010). English as a multicultural language: Implications from a study of Japan's junior high schools' English language textbooks. *Journal of Multilingual and Multicultural Development, 31*(5), 491–506. doi.org/10.1080/01434632.2010.502967.

Yoshida, M. (2023). Representations of gender and sexual orientation over three editions of a Japanese language learning textbook series. *Gender and Language, 17*(2), 198–221. doi.org/10.1558/genl.23358.

5

In step: SOGIESC and language teaching, and learning and the linguistic diversification of gender justice

Birgit Lang and Claire Maree

1. Introduction

In many ways, the twentieth and twenty-first centuries have been an era of hard-fought LGBTQIA+ success. In Australia, as in many Western countries, radical legislative and societal shifts mean that, for example, a university teacher in their 50s who grew up in Tasmania might vividly remember the years before the decriminalisation of homosexuality in 1997. Likewise, today's tertiary undergraduate students would have witnessed the legal recognition of marriage equality during their high school years. While this rapid change has created considerable political backlash, nationally and internationally, it has put LGBTQIA+ history and issues on the agenda of young people. The Mission Australia Youth Survey Report 2021 (Tiller et al., 2021) identifies equity and discrimination, particularly along the lines of gender, sexuality and race, as central to the concerns of young people—after COVID-19 and climate change. Against this background, decentring and diversifying theoretical lenses to create more inclusive pedagogical practices in the language classroom seems of crucial relevance.

The 'queering' of language education is observed predominantly in the area of English language teaching (ELT) and identifies the importance of queer and trans-affirming pedagogies (Gray, 2016; Nelson, 2009; Paiz, 2019). The need to remain 'in step' with knowledge formulated in different languages seems of particular importance in the Australian tertiary sector where English remains the dominant language and concepts relating to sex and gender are often perceived from a monolingual perspective, which, in turn, does not necessarily correlate with linguistic developments in languages taught on campuses in Australia or with the everyday experiences of the diversity of students who come together in our learning spaces. Multilingual approaches to developing a critical pedagogy need to consider the complex interplay between gender justice and linguistic outcomes (Knisely, 2022, 2023), an area of research that is gaining currency at the moment.

In this chapter, we underline the importance of queering the foreign language classroom and affirming a plurality of sexual orientations, gender identities, expressions and sex characteristics (SOGIESC). First, we contextualise the ways in which gender justice can be envisaged against a multilingual background, taking German and Japanese as examples, to consider how the institutional framework of language teaching in the Australian tertiary sector affects curriculum development. We then focus on the ways in which we can provide safer classrooms for LGBTQIA+ learners and develop a relevant curriculum. In this context, we discuss how a narrow focus on pronouns as the main practice of gender justice is not easily transferred into the foreign language classroom and provide some alternative approaches/examples. In the last section, we highlight the benefit for universities in providing multilingual resources to challenge structural monolingualism in LGBTQIA+ contexts.

2. Gender-just how? Contexts of queering foreign languages

The foreign language classroom is a locus for the translingual negotiation of SOGIESC. In the Australian tertiary context, this includes a range of languages of different linguistic typological families with widely differing gender systems. In this chapter, we have chosen a European and an Asian language to investigate and showcase the differences in engaging with this topic. De Vincenti et al.'s (2007) exploration of integrating queer theory into world languages classrooms (Italian, French and Japanese) at tertiary level in Australia demonstrates the importance of taking an across-language perspective. The comparison of an Indo-European and a Japanoic language holds the further advantage of broadening out the scholarship on SOGIESC and language, which is currently dominated by the analysis of Indo-European languages (Paiz & Coda, 2021), in particular French (see Knisely, 2020, 2022, 2024) and, to a lesser extent, German (see below), and only occasionally extends beyond this realm. To examine how to queer the foreign language classroom (German and Japanese style), we must first map out the language ideologies around language, gender and sexuality, which are specific to the respective language, and which have left an imprint on the teaching and learning of that language.

2.1. Japanese

The standardised Japanese language is often touted as one of the most gendered due to the long-held belief in separate and discrete 'women's' and 'men's' languages. Within the ideology of Japanese women's language (JWL) and Japanese men's language (JML), linguistic resources such as self-referencing (for example, pronouns), vocabulary, verb endings and interactive particles (or sentence-final particles) are posited as being used differently by men and women to align with normative sociopragmatic regimes of politeness. Research has shown that JWL and JML are ideological conceptualisations and that the belief that all Japanese speakers use one or the other consistently across their language practice is a myth (see Inoue, 2006, 2020; Maree, 2007; Nakamura, 2007; Okamoto & Shibamoto-Smith, 2004).

The majority of mainstream textbooks aimed at novice and intermediate learners of Japanese, as well as grammar dictionaries, however, uphold heteronormative and cisnormative representations of language through reinforcing gendered usage of interactive particles and assigning pronoun usage to a gender binary. For instance, the informal first-person pronoun *boku* is regulated to be used by men, and JWL and JML styles are described as immutably fixed to a heteronormative cisgendered binary (Arimori, 2020; de Vincenti et al., 2007; Nagata & Sullivan, 2005; Siegal & Okamoto, 1996). Indeed, Yoshida's (2023) critical examination of three volumes of an internationally popular textbook demonstrates that, while most derogatory depictions of LGBTQIA+ people have been removed and there is some indication of gender and sexual diversity, heteronormative representations dominate the series.

2.2. German

German, too, has been conceptualised as a male language (Pusch, 1984). All nouns are grammatically classed into masculine, feminine and neuter (grammatical gender), and this gendered nature of German directly impacts the use of articles as well as personal and possessive pronouns. Examples relating to the gendered nature of German include the fact that, for instance, the female forms of nouns that denote human beings are based on the male form: *die Studentin* (female student) is formed through the suffix *-in* (singular), which is added to the relevant masculine noun, here *der Student*. Other examples include generic indefinite pronouns that are based on the masculine form alone. Further, the male form was traditionally seen to have a universalising meaning, by implicitly but not grammatically representing men and women and thus replicating power structures represented in society.

There exists a long history of gender bias in German textbooks aimed at learners of German as a second or foreign language (Moghaddam, 2010). Although some progress has been made in relation to representing men and women linguistically, when it comes to professions, some stereotypes are still perpetuated in textbook exercises (Elsen, 2020). Often textbooks use grammatical gender as a term uncritically, in that they present German nouns and pronouns as gendered (masculine, feminine and neuter), while not explaining the difference between grammatical gender and the workings of gender in society (a notable exception is Grenzenlos Deutsch [n.d.]). Teachers make the argument for the introduction of gender-just language based on providing students with a linguistic understanding of everyday life, rather than naming the communication of values as a prime motivator (Stark, 2021). The teaching of neopronouns to represent non-binary identities is not common, likely because a standardised form across the German-speaking world has yet to be established (Djavadghazaryans, 2020).

2.3. Challenging gender regimes

In German, the challenge to gender regimes was first expressed in the 1970s by feminist scholars such as Luise F. Pusch, who, for the first time, critiqued the inherent structure and use of German language as a mirror of patriarchal society (Pusch, 1984). The thrust for more equality was widely identified as a process of naming both male and female forms and, in doing so, making gender difference visible. By the 1990s, this attempt to address both female and male members of a given audience led to the development of the *Binnen-I* (internal I), which features a capitalised I in the female form, as a widely accepted way to address in writing both men and women in a more 'economical' form, for example, *Liebe KollegInnen* (Dear Colleagues) instead of *Liebe Kolleginnen und Kollegen*. This development is opposite to English, where the shift went from differentiation to simplification: for example, whereas in English the use of *actress* is often avoided, in German, it signals inclusion and representation of women. Based on this tradition of the *Binnen-I*, recent developments in German use an underscore or an asterisk to represent all genders and sexualities. While these measures work well for written discourse, they are harder to replicate in spoken language, although a pause in pronunciation—for example, *kolleg || innen*—is possible and has become common practice, particularly in public radio (less so in public television), as is the random use of masculine or feminine form for all human beings or the sole use of the feminine form to include all genders. There has also been a push for the use of neopronouns or for pronouns to be avoided, at least in addresses.

Today, gender diverse language is supported by EU guidelines (e.g. European Parliament, 2018) and is used by (local) government institutions across the German speaking world (e.g. City of Vienna, 2022; City of Zurich, 2022), by some universities (Goncalves, 2020; Hofbauer, 2022) and in the mass media (Stark, 2021). In 2020, the *Duden*, the standard reference work for German grammar, included new terms such as *genderneutral* (gender-neutral), *Genderstern* (gender asterisk) and *inklusiv*, and generally adopted a moderate position of support for making gender and sexual diversity grammatically visible. In 2023, *Duden* published a new work by Johanna Usinger titled *Gendern* in its guidebook series Einfach können (Usinger, 2023). The volume is based on the author's website *Geschickt Gendern*, literally 'gender cleverly', which she launched in 2015 and which she describes as a private undertaking.[1] A comparable website *Genderleicht*, literally 'gender easy', by the feminist journalists' association, Journalistinnenbund, is financially supported by the German Federal Ministry for Family Affairs, Senior Citizens, Women and Youth.[2] In this way, linguistic change is progressed by a combination of governmental and institutional drivers as well as relevant interest groups and individuals.

---

1   See geschicktgendern.de/.
2   See genderleicht.de/quellen/.

Critiques of these linguistic developments have been identified as, first, defending the linguistic status quo (39.4 per cent); second, sexism and cisgenderism (27.4 per cent); third, diminishing the issue and its proponents (26.9 per cent); and, last, a distractor in communication (6.3 per cent) (Vergoossen et al., 2020). Such motivation seems the case in the German example of the Verein Deutsche Sprache (German Language Association) that drives a nationalist linguistic agenda with a focus on maintaining German as a language of 'culture'. Scholarship has critiqued the underlying nationalist language regimes of such groups (see Lobin, 2021; Pfalzgraf, 2008; Wirth, 2010). When it comes to questions of comprehension and readability of gender-just texts, comprehension does not seem to be impacted by the use of internal I or the gender asterisk (Pöschko & Prieler, 2018), even though readability can be slowed. In particular, a study engaging with a focus on nouns in the singular rather than the plural identifies this issue, since in the singular not only the nouns themselves but also preceding articles need to be gendered—for example, der*die Student*in (Friedrich et al., 2021). However, in practice, this matter can be relatively easily circumvented through finding alternative formulations.

Early women's studies and feminist approaches to sexist language use also challenged the androcentric force within Japanese language conventions (Endō, 1987; 1992). Asymmetry in occupational titles, such as 医者 (*isha* doctor) and 女医 (*joi* woman/lady doctor), 作家 (*sakka* author) and 女流作家 (*joryū sakka* woman/lady author) were identified as sexist, as were courtesy titles such as 婦人 (*fujin* lady). Address forms used by married couples, were also critiqued for perpetuating asymmetrical power relations—for example, おい (*oi* hey) used by husband to wife as opposed to あなた (*anata* you) used by wife to husband. In 1975 a television commercial for noodles that contained the copy '*watashi tsukuru hito, boku taberu hito* (I am the person who cooks, I am the person who eats)' became the centre of controversy around gendered language usage. In the advertisement, the semi-formal, first-person pronoun *watashi* is used by the wife who cooks, and the informal, first-person pronoun *boku* is used by the husband who eats. The feminist group kōdō suru onnatachi no kai (Women's Action Group)[3] immediately took issue with the gendered division of tasks represented in the commercial, and successfully lobbied to have it taken off the air (Kōdō suru Kai Kiroku Henshū Iinkai, 1999).

---

3   This group was formed by activists working on feminist issues in the International Year of the Woman (1975).

The group also targeted national broadcaster NHK to include women as more than assistants to male newscasters, and to avoid sexist language that reflects asymmetrical social positions such as:

a. address terms for one's own husband
b. honorific titles for another's husband
c. phrases to express legal marriage
d. terms for parents and guardians.

(Kōdō suru Kai Kiroku Henshū Iinkai, 1999, p. 25)

Work that focused on linguistic sexism emerged not only from grassroots women's liberation groups, but also from within language studies (e.g. Jugaku, 1979). Kotoba to onna o kangaeru kai (Group Examining Women and Language) (1985) embarked on a comprehensive examination of national language dictionaries, identifying significant gender stereotyping in definitions and noting that examples listed for entry words more often featured men in the subject position than women. Similar gender bias was found in a critical analysis of Japanese–English dictionaries used by learners of Japanese (Maree, 1997, 2000).

Inroads have been made in public discourse, for example, through the use of non-gendered occupational titles. The suffix 師 (*shi*), which denotes expertise is now used in place of 婦 (*fu*), which denotes women. For example, 看護師 (*kangoshi* nurse) replaces 看護婦 (*kangofu* nurse). Rather than referring to an interlocutor's husband using the honorific term ご主人 (literally, honourable master), people increasingly use terms such as 連れ合い (*tsure ai* literally, companion) or パートナー (*pātonā* partner [from the loan word *partner*]). However, as Knisely (2020, p. 176) notes in relation to French, it is important to distinguish between movements for linguistic inclusivity that centre binary women and those that 'specifically … represent non-binary subject positions'. In relation to Japanese, the concerns identified by gender-just scholarship and trans and gender nonconforming linguistic inequity remain areas that are largely still in the realm of grassroots activism.

Recent awareness-raising around cisgendered language is noted on materials produced to encourage allyship within companies, local government service providers and in schools. Advocacy and community groups such as the Japan Alliance for LGBT Legislation (2022) and Pride House Tokyo, in association with GLAAD and Athlete Ally (2021), have released media guidelines to counteract media discrimination. The focus of materials aimed at LGBTQIA+ allies at the local government level seems to be on avoiding gendered references to intimate relationships and using terms such as 親 (*oya* parent) rather than 父母 (*fubo* father and mother) to be more inclusive of a diversity of family types (see Chiyoda City Ward, 2019).

3. Curriculum development within an institutional framework: Why and to what end

Institutions function 'both as a facilitator and natural constraint to building out TGNC [transgender nonconforming]-aware pedagogies and practices, even when institutions often embrace engaging with more pedestrian notions of diversity and inclusion of sexual minorities', Knisely and Paiz (2021, p. 38) remind us pointedly. This statement also holds true for the implementation of gender-just pedagogies in the Australian tertiary sector. Universities provide often bold strategic statements in their visioning for future planning, which are crucial for driving change. At the University of Melbourne, the *Advancing Melbourne* strategy paper identifies strengthening 'diversity and inclusion in the University community' as a key aim to be reached by 2030 (University of Melbourne, 2020, p. 9). Yet, the ways in which such vision is, and can be, put into practice are a result of complex factors. On the ground, the realities of the language classroom in the Australian tertiary sectors are defined largely by language programs, their disciplinary confines, as well as the preferences of individual subject coordinators. Depending on the relevant individual and program preferences, decisions are made to use textbooks and/or to teach language through culture, that is, authentic texts that are didactically prepared. For example, the teaching of German language and culture classes at the University of Melbourne is largely based on the use of authentic texts. Textbooks are only used for beginner levels (German 1 and 2, A1 in the Common European Framework of Reference for Languages/CEFR), while courses at proficiency levels from A2 to C1 are designed by the relevant subject coordinator. Both approaches hold advantages and disadvantages. As discussed above, German language textbooks have been criticised in secondary literature for perpetuating traditional gender roles and depictions of family units. At the same time, subject coordinators also teach from their own generational and SOGIESC positionality and might be more or less aware of developments such as linguistic shifts regarding gender diversity, even though localised discussions exist in the second and tertiary education sector (Kretzenbacher, 2022; Taeubner, 2023).

If most teaching is undertaken through authentic texts, as in the case of German, the research expertise of the educator is implicitly assumed to carry most of the pedagogical load. This leaves staff who do not specialise in gender studies or related fields, and who are in teaching positions, in need of professional development. Adequate textbooks could play a powerful role and lift some of this burden. Anecdotal evidence reported for German beginner students using Grenzenlos Deutsch at another Australian tertiary institution points out that teaching students about neopronouns and letting them choose their pronouns in German can have an emancipatory effect. Another approach is for institutions to provide pedagogical support in the form of teaching tools or seminars that enable the alignment of diversity frameworks with relevant pedagogical content, as well as professional development opportunities (Djavadghazaryans, 2020).

As with German, textbooks are widely used in the novice to intermediate streams of tertiary-level Japanese in Australia. For example, *Genki: An Integrated Course in Elementary Japanese* (Banno et al., 2020), now in its third edition, is used by 15 universities in New Zealand and Australia. The series is purported to have sold over 3 million copies worldwide. In response to feedback from educators globally and changing trends in Japanese language, society and culture, a greater 'emphasis on diversity and consideration of expressions (*tayōsei no jūshi to hyōgen e no hairyo*)' is highlighted as a feature of the revised third edition. The introductory notes mention that efforts have been made to 'avoid stereotypical representations of gender and sexuality (*jendā ya sekushuritī ni kanshitemo sutereotaipu na byōsha ya hyōgen ni naranai yō hairyo shimashita*)' (*Genki* online). As Yoshida (2023) notes, the textbook has gradually altered over its three editions. However, as with most Japanese language textbooks globally, there is little to no representation of queer, trans and/or gender nonconforming individuals in the textbook. The textbook series depicts a heterosexual romance and centralises the normative nuclear family. The gender binary is still introduced to explain gendered language styles, which, as we have noted above, have been thoroughly debunked in sociolinguistics and linguistic anthropology studies.

As Thomson Kinoshita and Otsuji (2009) note, textbooks are 'living things' and individual teachers can use the same textbook in markedly different ways. Arimori (2020) offers one approach whereby what Gray (2013) refers to as the erasure of LGBTQIA+ lives can be mitigated through the introduction of alternative images and phrases to refer to intimate partners and family members. Although this shifts the onus of recuperating materials onto the individual instructor, it is a crucial step when actioned across a department, placing the textbook in step with the teaching environment of a university that is committed to queer and trans inclusion.

The 'adopt early and often' approach (Knisely & Paiz, 2021) in which trans, non-binary and queer language and linguistic issues are incorporated into the everyday classroom, and not relegated to a special session, is often met with consternation for the supposed negative effects on learning this may have. Knisely's empirical exploration of the effect of introducing gender-neutral forms to an intermediate French language class demonstrates, however, that gender-just teaching can contribute 'to overall student linguistic competence development' (Knisely, 2022). Knisely and Paiz (2021, p. 30) advocate for trans affirming, queer, inquiry-based pedagogies that are not merely inclusive of trans, gender nonconforming or queer language learners, but aim to weave LGBTQIA+ into the curriculum, create welcoming spaces and challenge normativity (see also Paiz, 2020). How, then, can we facilitate classrooms in which misgendering is not excused, and fluidity and creativity are encouraged? We posit that this requires attention to both the creation and cultivation of 'safe(r) spaces' in which 'brave' choices can be enacted.

4. Brave teachers and safer classrooms

The notion of 'safe space' is part of the lexicon of diversity and social justice initiatives (Fast, 2018). It is widely thought that educators have 'an ethical obligation' (Barrett, 2010; Frusciante, 2008; García & Van Soest, 1997; Kaufman, 2008) to cultivate 'safe space'. However, the safe space classroom has been critiqued for disallowing critical thinking and dialogue (Boostrom, 1998; hooks, 1994). Further, it has been posited that the notion of 'safety' within a classroom reinforces power dynamics (Holley & Steiner, 2005; Hunter, 2008). Alternatives such as 'brave spaces' (Arao & Clemens, 2013), 'communities of disagreement' (Iversen, 2018) or classroom 'civility' rather than 'safety' (Barrett, 2010; Callan, 2016) have been proposed to destabilise any notion of 'safe space' that centres privileged positionalities.[4]

---

4 Many thanks to Safe(r) Space project collaborators Ryan Gustafsson, Benjamin Hegarty and Qiuping Pan for informing much of C. Maree's thinking in relation to scholarship in this field.

Brave space emerges from social justice pedagogies in the USA (see, in particular, Arao & Clemens, 2013) and is offered as an alternative that seeks to better engage both minoritised and privileged students alike. In the curation of brave spaces, Arao and Clemens posit that ground rules such as 'agree to disagree', 'don't take things personally', 'challenge by choice', 'respect' and 'no attacks' may lean heavily towards cultivating safety in such a way that participants are not 'brave in exploring content that pushes them to the edges of their comfort zones to maximise learning' (Arao & Clemens, 2013, p. 143). Ground rules such as these may be familiar to those in the tertiary language and culture sector as methods by which we engage students in thoughtful and respectful discussions, yet acknowledging the limits (Britzman, 1995) of such strategies may also enable bravery to tackle the complex and ongoing task of negotiating one's own personal identity in the target language. However, if the notion of 'brave space' is predicated on minoritised students doing much of the heavy lifting, then it is at risk of coming at considerable cost—with the potential to reinscribe stereotypes and institutionalised cisgenderism, rather than pursuing a gender-just pedagogy.

As educators in the Australian tertiary sector, how can we facilitate learning environments that are emboldened by gender-just approaches without centring the cisgender? Here we turn to Fast (2018, p. 2) who argues for the centring of the *cultivation* of safe space: 'Cultivating safe space requires the foregrounding of social differences and binaries (safe-unsafe, inclusive-exclusive) as well as recognizing the penetrability of such binaries'. To better encapsulate the understanding that space cannot ever be completely 'safe', we adopt the phrase 'safe(r) space'. Following Fast's lead, we posit that pursuing the cultivation of 'safe(r) spaces' can lead to the remaking of space through 'active interventions' (Fast, 2018, p. 14). For, if the impetus is on encouraging active risk-taking in conjunction with affirmation, (Cook-Sather, 2016, p. 1), then the notion of 'brave' may be part of our ongoing attempts to cultivate affirming spaces for queer, trans and gender nonconforming participants in the language classroom. The onus for active intervention, however, must not fall predominantly on the marginalised and minoritised within the gender-just framework.

4.1. From pronouns to questioning gender ideologies

When it comes to questions of gender and sexuality, safe(r) classrooms in English are often negotiated through the inclusive and considerate use of personal pronouns, and the sensitive use of pronouns in the classroom without creating a situation in which students feel forced to identify their pronouns. This can, for example, happen through the teacher introducing their pronouns, enabling students to do the same but not forcing the issue. The question of changes in first names can be easily addressed by handing out an attendance list without student first names for them to fill in. From anecdotal evidence, students appreciate such signalling, even if they do not identify as gender diverse; this observation ties in with the results of the Mission Australia Youth Survey Report 2021, which show that young people of all creeds have a heightened sensitivity to discrimination. But how can gender diversity be negotiated in languages where cisgenderism manifests in markedly different ways?

4.2. German pronouns and beyond

In German, as in English, personal and possessive pronouns are gendered in the third person. While in English the pronoun 'they/their/them' has historically been used as a way to avoid gendering a person, German does not allow a comparable construction. Earlier challenges to gender regimes, such as Pusch (1984), made gender difference more visible, and thus did little to address gender ambiguity (even though the gender asterisk builds on these forms). In the language classroom, with its communicative nature, it is not common to talk about a person who is present in the third person, and, therefore, this situation can usually be resolved by using the person's name. The way personal pronouns are used in German (that is, identifying someone else's sex/gender) means that mistakes can create confusing communicative situations and potentially cause some embarrassment. In an in-country situation, this would usually be attributed to the fact that the speaker is a learner and would not index them as LGBTQIA+. This might be different if students used neopronouns such as 'xier', which are not (yet) commonly used in German language and unfamiliar to large parts of the population.

The use of personal pronouns is first taught at beginner and consolidated at intermediate level. The following example outlines the teaching of gender-just grammar for a higher proficiency level (for a detailed analysis see Lang, 2025). In German 9, which focuses on the themes of self, language and identity and is targeted at C1-level, students read an excerpt of the recently published *Blutbuch* by Swiss author Kim de l'Horizon (2022). The autofictional novel has been celebrated as the first non-binary novel in German literature and has received the prestigious German Book Prize. Throughout the novel, the author uses gender-just language, often challenging the use of indefinite generalising pronouns. In the course, students have already been familiarised with the relevant grammar topic for constructions such as '*man*' (one) or '*jemand*' (somebody) and the fact that such structures are grammatically masculine (with a nod to feminist strategies to challenge this particular structure through the use of alternatives such as '*frau*' [woman] and '*jefrau*'). Reading the text allows students to build on previous learnings, since they are confronted with de l'Horizon's strategy to adapt the German language through the use of '*mensch*' (human being) and '*jemensch*' to signal inclusiveness. The text hence offers the opportunity to make gender norms visible and question them (Völkel, 2022). Students are tasked to write a review of the novel for a German newspaper of their choice in which they are asked to consistently apply one language form (normative, feminist, non-binary) and argue for their linguistic choice in particular reference to their choice of media. This example highlights the productive use of literature in the language classroom (Altun, 2023) and provides student self-determination by leaving choice, and thus agency, to students (Knisely & Paiz, 2021).

4.3. Questioning Japanese gender regimes

The topic of preferred pronouns in Japanese is not a self-evidently simple one, as self-reference and other-reference terms in Japanese index not only gender, but also formality, hierarchical relations, social distance and politeness. Indeed, pronouns (as they are understood in European languages) may not be grammatically required in many instances. Although the use of the equivalents of 'he/she' is found in contemporary Japanese (彼 *kare* / 彼女 *kanojo*), these emerged from the translation of European literature at the turn of the twentieth century. This historical period coincided with the adaptation of a standardised writing system that enabled the rendering of spoken Japanese into text, rather than the use of *kanbun* (or Literary Sinitic style) in public written discourse. The dialect of the Tōkyō Yamanote region was adopted as the basis for contemporary standardised Japanese that is taught in most textbooks today.

Both 彼 (*kare* him) and 彼女 (*kanojo* her) derive from the demonstratives 'this and that', which are part of the *ko-so-a-do* system in Japanese that is based on the relative distance (both spatial and social) of the interlocutors. In contemporary Japanese, the plural 彼ら (*karera* they) and 彼女ら (*kanojora* they) are formed by adding a plural suffix *-ra*. Thus, these terms index gender and may also suggest that social distancing, as referring to a third person, using either the singular or plural forms, can be interpreted as impersonal and even rude. Referring to others by demonstratives such as あの人 (*ano hito* that person) or the more polite あの方 (*ano kata*), which index distance, or by personal names, nicknames, kinship or occupational titles and using addressee suffixes with personal names, is also more common in everyday contexts. Addressee suffixes index gender and relative seniority, as well as formality of the interactive context. While it was once common for adults to refer to boys as name+くん (*kun*) and girls as name+ちゃん (*chan*) in educational settings, more schools and workplaces are adopting name+さん (*san*) as the gender-neutral alternative.

As sociolinguistic research on language, gender and sexuality has identified, Japanese has a complex system of multiple first-person and second-person pronouns that index not only gender but also relative seniority, social distance and formality (see Tables 1 and 2 in SturtzSreetharan, 2009, pp. 256–257, for an overview of the prescriptive account of mapping first- and second-person pronouns to context and gender). And, although interpersonal referencing in Japanese encompasses more than personal pronouns, the dominant heteronormative cis patriarchal language ideologies normatively expect gendered pronouns to be used in informal workplace settings and between friends and intimates. Here, asymmetrical usage of second-person pronouns あなた (*anata* you) by women to men and お前 (*omae* you) by men to women indexes both gender, relative social status and intimacy. Moral panics around the use of so-called masculine and/or boyish self-reference first-person pronouns 僕,俺 (*boku, ore*) by young women have recurred over time. Similarly, usage of hyper-feminine first-person pronouns あたし (*atashi*) by young men often leads to consternation.

Alongside the complex personal pronoun and addressee system, interactive particles have traditionally been categorised as components of JWL and JML. In prescriptive accounts, women are positioned as using, or being expected to use, less-assertive forms, and men as using more assertive forms. Although the prescriptive regulation of interactional particles vis-a-vis binary gender has been debunked in linguistic research (see Inoue, 2020, for an overview), it is still common to find notes reinforcing the necessity of caution for novice speakers. It is in this context that the usage of interactive particles categorised as feminine and part of JWL by cisgender men may invoke laughter (Yoshida, 2018) in the language classroom, thereby cultivating a decidedly unsafe space. Being brave in Japanese in the Japanese classroom, therefore, requires understanding the ideologies of gender and sexuality that shape representations of gendered language styles and deviance from prescriptive norms in both mainstream media and educational materials.

As is widely advocated by scholars and activists working in the gender-just area, in regard to pronouns, offering rather than expecting or requesting pronouns is a best practice approach (Knisely & Pais, 2021). In the context of Japanese, self-reference terms index not only gender, but also formality, hierarchical relations and politeness. Japanese users regularly use creative self-reference strategies, such as non-normative pronoun usage, self-referring with their personal name or nickname and/or avoiding personal pronoun usage to negotiate these cis-heteronormative gender ideologies (Abe, 2004, 2010, 2020; Lunsing & Maree, 2004; Maree, 2007). Rather than turning to the moral panics generated through supposed 'incorrect usage of boyish personal pronouns by girls', educators can turn to the ways in which Japanese speakers navigate and negotiate this area. To move away from textbook representations of binary gender as being one axis on which the pronoun system pivots, one has to look no further than popular media to find examples of a diversity of gendered language. Accounts of linguistic dexterity in navigating gendered styles can also be found in biographies and magazine articles. Self-referencing and other identity work forms a large part of novice language learning; therefore, raising awareness of the creative ways in which users self-refer is foundational to a gender-just and LGBTQIA+ inclusive approach (Siegal & Okamoto, 2003).

This approach inevitably brings concerns for educators who are focused on the experiences of students who travel abroad. Indeed, the axes of discrimination alter subtly within communities and social networks, and there is not often a lot of support available for LGBTQIA+ students embarking on study abroad programs. This brings us to the question of enabling brave decisions in the context of teaching for going abroad: do we protect students or let them make brave decisions? Here, again, the mantra of striving to cultivate safe(r) classrooms in the first instance should be a key motivator, equipping students with the skills to navigate and negotiate a range of linguistic situations rather than policing language as language teachers. Forward-planning for resistance from within the teaching and learning space, and within the interactive space is also strongly advocated for by gender-just and LGBTQIA+ inclusive language teaching, researchers and practitioners (e.g. Knisely & Paiz, 2021). This can be done by developing allies within and across language programs, referring to best practices identified in policies and governance documents, and pointing to examples that emerge from within the target language and culture.

4.4. Integrating language and content

As with German, at the advanced level of Japanese study, all materials are sourced for the subject content. At this stage it is not only language but also content—for example, literature, sociolinguistic variation, media and translation—that is the focus of learning. While queer pedagogical approaches to language learning and teaching clearly demonstrate that LGBTQIA+ issues should not be relegated to just one lesson, LGBTQIA+ issues are, by and large, still absent from Japanese studies classes. One approach from an advanced level content class that aims to foster media literacy is to integrate queer and trans-affirming pedagogy—through offering but not requesting pronouns, thereby affirming and not contesting alternative self-referencing strategies—with LGBTQIA+ content into the curriculum.

Claire Maree has combined a 'do early and do often' approach by integrating best practices for students' self-determination in self-reference usage with a curriculum in which queer and gender diverse examples are referred to regularly. The overarching focus of the subject is to develop critical media literacy around the mediatisation and problematisation of 'social issues' in Japan. Here, the aim is to critically reflect on what is considered newsworthy, and why, and to look to the social, economic, cultural and ideological concerns that motivate public discourse and the ways in which these are represented in a diversity of print, audiovisual and digital media. This facilitates a deeper understanding of the ways in which contemporary social and cultural issues are problematised as 'social issues in need of remedying' and the role that mainstream and alternative media play in the discursive construction of such 'issues'.

As societal, economic and cultural flows are constantly in motion, the subject first considers 'trends' and 'buzzwords' from the previous year that have been commodified and commercialised. The penultimate module focuses on developing analytical skills for the students' autonomous research project. In this module, global discourse around 'marriage equality' is juxtaposed with social media produced by individuals and groups from the LGBTQIA+ community in Japan. The aim is not to debate the merits of marriage equality, but to focus on representations, social media activism and the mainstreaming of queer issues through anime and manga. It functions as an exemplar of how critical analysis of contemporary print and digital media exposes the ways in which ideologies around issues are discursively constructed through multimodal media.

For both the German and Japanese examples discussed above, if conducted as a stand-alone, one-off, queer topic, these modules would risk contravening current applied linguistic emphasis on creating safe(r), brave spaces into which SOGIESC is woven into the very fabric of learning. However, if conducted within a gender-just framework in which reflexivity is central and the questioning of normative representations takes place, the modules reinforce that SOGIESC is relevant not only to queer, trans and/or gender nonconforming students but to all who participate in the learning environment.

5. LGBTQIA+ multilingual resources in English speaking contexts

As well as developing brave language learning spaces through co-creation and negotiation of target language norms, we also argue for providing multilingual resources that raise awareness of the diversity of linguistic approaches within the tertiary setting. Understanding what tools and resources are available from the LGBTQIA+ communities in the languages and cultures that we teach and learn on campus is integral to resource sharing and facilitating understanding. This is because, within the Australian tertiary language teaching context, there is a complex diversity of language backgrounds and lived experiences within the language learning cohort, and national surveys have indicated that safety remains an issue for many sex and gender diverse students.

The issue of safety, which we have mentioned above, became particularly prominent following the 2017 survey of student experiences across Australian universities. It was found that 'women were almost twice as likely to report being sexually harassed in university settings than men, and more than three times more likely to report being sexually assaulted', and that trans and gender diverse students (45 per cent) were more likely to have been sexually harassed in a university setting in 2016 than women and men (Australian Human Rights Commission, 2017, p. 3). The report led to the 'Respect. Now. Always' campaign, a 10-point action plan across the university sector, and student- and staff-based initiatives. Language-related issues, such as the language of consent, access to interpreters, inclusive language, and respectful use of language in the classroom and in work with research and research training, all form part of the action plan.

At the initiative of Birgit Lang, assistant dean for equal opportunity and diversity in the Faculty of Arts, University of Melbourne (2017–19), a working group came together to respond to this urgent matter of safety and respect. The authors collaborated with colleagues to produce the open access web resource *Teaching with Respect for Gender and Sexuality. Resources for Cultivating Inclusive Classrooms* (University of Melbourne, nb). Targeted at teaching staff in the Faculty of Arts, the resource includes information about the university's commitment to enabling a safe, inclusive and respectful community; statistics on the health and wellbeing of students, including LGBTQIA+ students; quick guides to sex, gender and sexuality related ideas, including preferred names and personal pronouns; information about gender-related etiquette, particularly in relation to culture and language; 'best practice' strategies for facilitating inclusive classroom interactions and learning; and online multilingual resources for lectures and the LMS.

Within a predominantly monolingual campus, awareness of the diversity of approaches to gender-just language and of the everyday translanguaging of our student cohorts continues to be low. Translanguaging, 'a transformative resemiotization process whereby language users display the best of their creativity and criticality' (Li, 2018, p. 22), unsettles dominant monolingualism. In their analysis of migrant language practice in Australia, Dryden et al. (2021, p. 3) argue that 'translanguaging safe spaces' in which the entirety of the linguistic repertoire is welcomed, thus rejecting English-only environments, 'has the potential to alleviate the anxiety that some migrants may face when trying to interact in English'. Providing multilingual resources that demonstrate the wide and complex diversity to linguistic negotiation of cis-heteronormative ideologies of gender and sexuality and offer concrete examples of how to navigate this in the languages taught (and used) on campus functions not only as a teaching resource, but also to create awareness of the importance of cultivating safe(r) spaces for our diverse student (and staff) population.

Research into queer and trans-affirmative pedagogy consistently stresses the importance of making allies within the specific institutional context where teaching and learning occur (e.g. Choudrey, 2022). In the current climate of widespread anti-trans discourse, maintaining this multilingual resource is key to raising awareness not only of the work that we do through and with language, but also of the networks of allyship we create through which safe(r) spaces can be cultivated to make way for brave stances. Like safe(r) spaces, allyship is always in a constant state of incompleteness, and requires all allies to be vigilant and mindful.

6. Conclusion

Using examples from German and Japanese, we argue that maintaining a diverse and flexible curriculum that engages with language users of a diversity of SOGIESC identities and is inclusive of LGBTQIA+ identified learners (and teachers) is key to decentring the cis-heteronormative bias of language teaching ideologies. Integrating not only linguistic but also cultural information and sociopolitical histories on the dynamics of gender expressions and discourses of heteronormativity and cisgenderism that underpin those is essential. We extend the experience of multilingual language learning to the predominantly Anglophone discourses around gender justice. Understanding what tools and resources are available from the LGBTQIA+ communities in the languages and cultures that we teach and learn on campus is integral to resource sharing and facilitating understanding. Overall, we argue that critical approaches to language education mandate an analytical re-engagement with the representation of SOGIESC, and acknowledgement of LGBTQIA+ identified learners (and teachers) in learning spaces to create a safe learning environment.

References

Abe, H. (2004). Lesbian bar talk in Shinjuku, Tokyo. In S. Okamoto & J. S. Shibamoto-Smith (Eds.), *Japanese language, gender and ideology: Cultural models and real people* (pp. 205–221). Oxford University Press.

Abe, H. (2010). *Queer Japanese: Gender and sexual identities through linguistic practices*. Palgrave Macmillan.

Abe, H. (2020). Performativity of gender in speech: Life experiences of Japanese trans women. *U.S.–Japan Women's Journal, 58*, 35–57. doi.org/10.1353/jwj.2020.0004.

Altun, M. (2023). The use of literature in language teaching: An effective way to improve language skills. *International Journal of Social Sciences and Educational Studies*, *10*(1), 195–199.

Arao, B. & Clemens, K. (2013). From safe spaces to brave spaces: A new way to frame dialogue around diversity and social justice. In L. M. Landreman (Ed.), *The art of effective facilitation: Reflections from social justice educators* (pp. 135–150). Stylus Publishing.

Arimori, J. (2020). Toward more inclusive Japanese language education: Incorporating an awareness of gender and sexual diversity among students. *Japanese Language and Literature*, *54*(2), 359–371. doi.org/10.5195/jll.2020.129.

Australian Human Rights Commission. (2017, 1 August). *Change the course: National report on sexual assault and sexual harassment at Australian universities*. humanrights.gov.au/our-work/sex-discrimination/publications/change-course-national-report-sexual-assault-and.

Banno, E., Ikeda, Y., Ohno, Y., Shinagawa, C. & Takashiki, K. (2020). *Genki: An integrated course in elementary Japanese teacher's guide* (3rd ed.). The Japan Times.

Barrett, B. J. (2010). Is 'safety' dangerous? A critical examination of the classroom as safe space. *Canadian Journal for the Scholarship of Teaching and Learning*, *1*(1). doi.org/10.5206/cjsotl-rcacea.2010.1.9.

Boostrom, R. (1998). 'Safe spaces': Reflections on an educational metaphor. *Journal of Curriculum Studies*, *30*(4), 397–408. doi.org/10.1080/002202798183549.

Britzman, D. (1995). Is there a queer pedagogy? Or, stop reading straight. *Educational Theory*, *45*(2), 151–165. doi.org/10.1111/j.1741-5446.1995.00151.x.

Callan, E. (2016). Education in Safe and Unsafe Spaces. *Philosophical Inquiry in Education*, *24*(1), 64–78.

Chiyoda City Ward. (2019). *LGBTs e no taiō ni kansuru shokuin handobukku* [Handbook for staff on supporting LGBTs].

Choudrey, S. (2022). *Supporting trans people of colour: How to make your practice inclusive*. Jessica Kingsley Publishers.

City of Vienna. (2022). *Leitfaden für geschlechtergerechtes Formulieren und diskriminierungsfreie Bildsprache* [*Guidelines for gender-inclusive language and non-discriminatory imagery*]. wien.gv.at/medien/service/medienarbeit/richtlinien/leitfaden-gender/index.html.

City of Zurich. (2022, 1 June). *Beschluss des stadtrats: fachstelle für gleichstellung, totalrevision des reglements für die sprachliche gleichstellung* [*City Council resolution: Gender equality office, comprehensive revision of the regulations on gender-inclusive language*]. Nr 465/2022. stadt-zuerich.ch/content/dam/stzh/portal/Deutsch/Stadtrat%20%26%20Stadtpraesident/Publikationen%20und%20Broschueren/Stadtratsbeschluesse/2022/Jun/StZH_STRB_2022_0465.pdf.

Cook-Sather, A. (2016). Creating brave spaces within and through student-faculty pedagogical partnerships. *Teaching and Learning Together in Higher Education, 1*(18), 1. repository.brynmawr.edu/tlthe/vol1/iss18/1.

De Vincenti, G., Giovanangeli, A. & Ward, R. (2007). The queer stopover: How queer travels in the language classroom. *Electronic Journal of Foreign Language Teaching, 4*(1), 58–72. hdl.handle.net/10453/1520.

Djavadghazaryans, A. (2020). 'Please don't gender me!' Strategies for inclusive language instruction in a gender-diverse campus community. In R. Criser & E. Malakaj (Eds.), *Diversity and decolonization in German studies* (pp. 269–287). Palgrave Macmillan.

Dryden, S., Tankosić, A. & Dovchin, S. (2021). Foreign language anxiety and translanguaging as an emotional safe space: Migrant English as a foreign language learners in Australia. *System, 101*, 102593. doi.org/10.1016/j.system.2021.102593.

Elsen, H. (2020). *Gender—Sprache—Stereotype: Geschlechtersensibilität in Alltag und Unterricht*. Narr Francke Attempto Verlag.

Endō, O. (1987). *Ki ni naru kotoba: Nihongo saikentō* [Words that bother me—a re-examination of Japanese language]. Nan'undo.

Endō, O. (1992). *Onna no yobikata no daikenkyū: gyaru kara obasan made* [Major study of terms to refer to women: From gyaru to obasan]. Sanseido.

European Parliament. (2018). *Gender-neutral language in the European Parliament*. europarl.europa.eu/cmsdata/151780/GNL_Guidelines_EN.pdf.

Fast, J. (2018). In defense of safe spaces: A phenomenological account. *Atlantis, 39*(2), 1–22. doi.org/10.7202/1064069ar.

Friedrich, M. C. G., Drößler, V., Oberlehberg, N. & Heise, E. (2021). The influence of the gender asterisk ('Gendersternchen') on comprehensibility and interest. *Frontiers in Psychology 12*, 1–11. doi.org/10.3389/fpsyg.2021.760062.

Frusciante, A. (2008). Identifying transcendence in educating for public service: Reflections on qualifying to teach as a pedagogic example. *Teaching in Higher Education, 13*(6), 679–689. doi.org/10.1080/13562510802452400.

García, B. & Van Soest, D. (1997). Changing perceptions of diversity and oppression: MSW students discuss the effects of a required course. *Journal of Social Work Education, 33*(1), 119–129. doi.org/10.1080/10437797.1997.10778857.

GLAAD, Athlete Ally, Pride House Tokyo. (2021). *Covering LGBTQ athletes at the 2020 Olympics and Paralympics: A resource for journalists and media professionals.* (In English and Japanese). pridehouse.jp/assets/img/handbook/pdf/mediaguideline_jp_v1.pdf.

Goncalves, J. (2020). 'StudentInnen, student*innen, or student_innen: How six German universities are constructing gender equitable language and increasing female linguistic and visual representation'. The University of Tennessee. Chancellor's Honors Program Projects. trace.tennessee.edu/cgi/viewcontent.cgi?article=3433&context=utk_chanhonoproj.

Gray, J. (2013). LGBT invisibility and heteronormativity in ELT materials. In J. Gray (Ed.), *Critical perspectives on language teaching materials* (pp. 40–63). Palgrave Macmillan.

Gray, J. (2016). ELT materials: Claims, critiques and controversies. In G. Hall, *The Routledge handbook of English language teaching* (pp. 95–108). Routledge.

Grenzenlos Deutsch. (n.d.) *An open access curriculum for beginning German.* Retrieved 12 January 2025, grenzenlos-deutsch.com/#gsc.tab=0.

Hofbauer, C. (2022). 'Absolut unnötig' oder, 'wichtig für Gleichstellung'?—Argumente und Motivationen für und gegen geschlechtergerechten Sprachgebrauch. Eine quantitative und qualitative Diskursanalyse ['Absolutely unnecessary' or 'essential for equality'?—Arguments and motivations for and against gender-inclusive language. A quantitative and qualitative discourse analysis]. *Wiener Linguistische Gazette (WLG) 93*, 11–51.

Holley, L. C. & Steiner, S. (2005). Safe space: Student perspectives on classroom environment. *Journal of Social Work Education, 41*(1), 49–64. doi.org/10.5175/JSWE.2005.200300343.

hooks, b. (1994). *Teaching to transgress: Education as the practice of freedom.* Routledge.

Hunter, M. A. (2008). Cultivating the art of safe space. *Research in Drama Education: The Journal of Applied Theatre and Performance, 13*(1), 5–21. doi.org/10.1080/13569780701825195.

Inoue, M. (2006). *Vicarious language: Gender and linguistic modernity in Japan.* University of California Press. doi.org/10.1525/9780520939066.

Inoue, M. (2020). Gender and language. In J. Coates, L. Fraser & M. Pendleton, *The Routledge companion to gender and Japanese culture* (pp. 40–49). Routledge.

Iversen, L. L. (2018). From safe spaces to communities of disagreement. *British Journal of Religious Education, 41*(3), 315–326. doi.org/10.1080/01416200.2018.1445617.

Japan Alliance for LGBT Legislation (Ed.). (2022). *LGBTQ reporting guidelines: From the perspective of diverse genders/sexualities* (Vol. 2). lgbtetc.jp/news/2467/.

Jugaku, A. (1979). *Nihongo to onna* [Japanese and women]. Iwanami Shinsho.

Kaufman, P. (2008). Gaining voice through silence. *Feminist Teacher, 18*(2), 169–171. doi.org/10.1353/ftr.2008.0016.

Knisely, K. A. (2020). Subverting the culturally unreadable: Understanding the self-positioning of non-binary speakers of French. *The French Review, 14*(2), 173–192. doi.org/10.1353/tfr.2020.0280.

Knisely, K. A. (2022). Gender-just language teaching and linguistic competence development. *Foreign Language Annals, 55*(3), 644–667. doi.org/10.1111/flan.12641.

Knisely, K. A. (2023). Gender-justice beyond inclusion: How trans knowledges and linguistic practices can and should be re-shaping language education. *The Modern Language Journal, 107*(2), 607–623. doi.org/10.1111/modl.12871.

Knisely, K. A. (2024). Toward trans multilingualisms: Student attitudes toward and experiences with trans linguacultures in French. *International Journal of Bilingual Education and Bilingualism, 27*(5), 643–655. doi.org/10.1080/13670050.2024.2306414.

Knisely, K. A. & Paiz, J. M. (2021). Bringing trans, non-binary, and queer understandings to bear in language education. *Critical Multilingualism Studies, 9*(1), 23–45.

Kōdō suru Kai Kiroku Henshū Iinkai (Eds.) (1999) *Kōdōsuru onnatachi ga hiraita michi: Mekishiko kara Nyūyōku e* [The path forged by Kōdōsuru onnatachi: From Mexico to New York]. Mirai-sha.

Kotoba to onna o kangaeru kai. (1985). *Kokugojiten ni mieru joseisabetsu* [Discrimination against women in national language dictionaries]. San-ichi Publishing Company.

Kretzenbacher, L. (2022). Genderneutrale sprache im Deutschen: Ja, aber wie? [Gender-neutral language in German: Yes, but how?] *Szene: Journal for Teachers of German in Australia 42*, 2–6.

l'Horizon, K. de. (2022). *Blutbuch*. Dumont-Verlag.

Lang, B. (2025). Between translanguaging and gender-justice: Teaching Kim de l'Horizon's Blutbuch in the tertiary German classroom. *Die Unterrichtspraxis/ Teaching German*. doi.org/10.1111/tger.70026.

Li, W. (2018). Translanguaging as a practical theory of language. *Applied Linguistics, 39*(1) 9–30. doi.org/10.1093/applin/amx044.

Lobin, H. (2021). *Sprachkampf: Wie die Neue Rechte die deutsche sprache instrumentalisiert* [*Language wars: How the New Right instrumentalises the German language*]. Dudenverlag.

Lunsing, W. & Maree, C. (2004). Shifting speakers: Strategies of gender, sexuality and language. In S. Okamoto & J. S. Shibamoto-Smith (Eds.), *Japanese language, gender and ideology: Cultural models and real people* (pp. 92–109). Oxford University Press.

Maree, C. (1997). Gender representation in Japanese–English dictionaries used by Japanese as-a-Foreign-Language (JFL) learners: a survey of basic verbs, basic adjectives and illustrations. *The Tōhō Gakkai Transactions of the International Conference of Eastern Studies, 42*, 83–101.

Maree, C. (2000). Kotoba no Wana no Negoshiēshon [Negotiating the trap of words]. *Gendai Shisō* (*Modern thought*), *28*(14): 212–23.

Maree, C. (2007). *Hatsuwasha no gengo sutorateji toshite no negoshiēshon (kirinukeru/ kōshō/danpan/kakeai) kōi* [Negotiation as speakers' linguistic strategy]. Hituzi.

Maree, C. (2020). *queerqueen: Linguistic excess in Japanese media*. Oxford University Press. doi.org/10.1093/oso/9780190869618.001.0001.

Moghaddam, R. (2010). Deutsch als fremdsprache mit gendergerechter didaktik? [German as a foreign language with a gender-inclusive approach?] In U. Eberhardt (Ed.), *Neue Impulse in der Hochschuldidaktik* [*New directions in university teaching*] (pp. 281–295). VS Verlag für Sozialwissenschaften.

Nagata, Y. & Sullivan, K. (2005). Hegemonic gender in Japanese as a foreign language education: Australian perspectives. In M. McLelland & R. Dusgupta (Eds.), *Genders, transgenders, and sexualities in Japan* (pp. 15–32). Routledge.

Nakamura, M. (2007). *'Onnakotoba' wa Tsukurareru* [Women's language' is culturally constructed]. Hitsuji Shobo.

Nelson, C. D. (2009). *Sexual identities in English language education: Classroom conversations*. Routledge.

Okamoto, S. & Shibamoto-Smith, J. S. (Eds.). (2004). *Japanese language, gender, and ideology: Cultural models and real people*. Oxford University Press.

Paiz, J. M. (2019). Queering practice: LGBTQ+ diversity and inclusion in English language teaching. *Journal of Language, Identity & Education, 18*(4), 266–275. doi.org/10.1080/15348458.2019.1629933.

Paiz, J. M. (2020). *Queering the English language classroom: A practical guide for teachers.* Equinox.

Paiz, J. M. & Coda, J. E. (2021). *Intersectional perspectives on LGBTQ+ issues in modern language teaching and learning.* Palgrave Macmillan.

Pfalzgraf, F. (2008). Bestrebungen zur einführung eines sprachschutzgesetzes seit der deutschen vereinigung [Efforts to introduce a language protection law since German reunification]. *German Life and Letters, 61*(4), 451–469. doi.org/10.1111/j.1468-0483.2008.00436.x.

Pöschko, H. & Prieler, V. (2018). Zur Verständlichkeit und lesbarkeit von geschlechtergerecht formulierten Schulbuchtexten [On the comprehensibility and readability of gender-inclusive textbook language]. *Zeitschrift für Bildungsforschung [Journal for Educational Research], 8,* 5–18. doi.org/10.1007/s35834-017-0195-2.

Pusch, L. (1984). *Das Deutsche als männersprache: Aufsätze und glossen zur feministischen linguistik [German as a male-dominated language: Essays and commentaries on feminist linguistics].* Suhrkamp.

Siegal, M. & Okamoto, S. (1996). Imagined worlds: Language, gender and sociocultural 'norms' in Japanese language textbooks. In N. Warner, J. Ahlers, L. Bilmes, M. Oliver, S. Wertheim & M. Chen (Eds.), *Gender and belief systems: Proceedings of the Berkeley Women and Language Conference* (pp. 667–678). Berkeley Women and Language Group.

Siegal, M. & Okamoto, S. (2003). Toward reconceptualizing the teaching and learning of gendered speech styles in Japanese as a foreign language. *Japanese Language and Literature, 37*(1), 49–66. doi.org/10.2307/3594875.

Stark, K. S. (2021). *Gendergerechte sprache im DaZ/DaF-unterricht: Bewertung und vermittlung durch DaZ/DaFLehrkräfte [Gender-inclusive language in the teaching of German as a foreign/second language: Evaluation and mediation by German teachers].* Augsburg. nbn-resolving.org/urn:nbn:de:0168-ssoar-76058-2.

Sturtzsreetharan, C. (2009). *Ore* and *omae*: Japanese men's uses of first- and second-person pronouns. *Pragmatics, 19*(2), 253–278. doi.org/10.1075/prag.19.2.06stu.

Taeubner, K. (2023). Das thema sprache ist ein sehr emotional besetztes thema. Interview mit Dr Kathrin Kunkel-Razum, Leiterin der Duden-Redaktion [Language is a highly emotionally charged topic. Interview with Dr. Kathrin Kunkel-Razum, Head of the Duden Editorial team]. *Szene: Journal for Teachers of German in Australia, 42,* 4–7.

Thomson Kinoshita, C. & Otsuji, E. (2009). Business Japanese textbooks and multifaceted studies of gender. *Japanese Language Education around the World, 19,* 49–67.

Tiller, E., Greenland, N., Christie, R., Kos, A., Brennan, N. & Di Nicola, K. (2021). *Youth survey report 2021.* Mission Australia.

University of Melbourne. (2020). *Advancing Melbourne 2030.* about.unimelb.edu.au/strategy/advancing-melbourne.

University of Melbourne (nb). *Teaching with Respect for Gender and Sexuality: Resources for Cultivating Inclusive Classrooms.* Padlet. unimelb.padlet.org/QTC/teaching-withrespect-for-gender-and-sexuality-kmuhtr6peidewse1.

Usinger, J. (2023). *Einfach können—Gendern* [*Making gender-inclusive language simple*]. Duden.

Vergoossen, H. P., Renström, E. A., Lindqvist, A. & Sendén, M. G. (2020). Four dimensions of criticism against gender-fair language. *Sex Roles, 83,* 328–337. doi.org/10.1007/s11199-019-01108-x.

Völkel, O. (2022). Queering DaF/DaZ—Queersensible zugänge für den sprachunterricht [Queering German as a foreign/second language—Queer-inclusive approaches to language education]. In A. Freese & O. Völkel (Eds.), *Gender_vielfalt_sexualität(en) im fach Deutsch als fremd- und zweitsprache* [*Gender, diversity, and sexualities in teaching German as a foreign and second language*] (pp. 88–107). Iudicium.

Wirth, K. (2010). *Der Verein Deutsche Sprache: Hintergrund, entstehung, arbeit und organisation eines deutschen sprachvereins* [*German Language Association: The background, foundation, work and organisation of a German language association*]. University of Bamberg Press.

Yoshida, M. (2018). *Negotiation of gendered language and social identities by students of Japanese as an additional language in Australian universities* [Unpublished doctoral dissertation]. University of Melbourne.

Yoshida, M. (2023). Representations of gender and sexual orientation over three editions of a Japanese language learning textbook series. *Gender and Language, 17*(2),198–221. doi.org/10.1558/genl.23358.

6

Diversifying language and culture through real-world connections: Virtual exchanges during the COVID-19 pandemic

Matt Absalom and Roberta Trapè

1. Introduction

The COVID-19 pandemic severely hindered the possibility of overseas exchange programs, particularly within the Australian university context, where international borders remained closed for an extended period. In-country experiences have long been regarded as pivotal moments for language and culture students, offering invaluable opportunities for intercultural linguistic connections and personal development. This chapter explores a series of attempts to salvage one crucial aspect of overseas exchange—the establishment of intercultural linguistic connections with peers. These attempts, initiated prior to the pandemic but gaining heightened significance during the crisis, shed light on the innovative use of virtual exchanges as a means of bridging the gap.

Our virtual exchange design places a strong emphasis on the relationship between Australian university students and Italian students from senior secondary high schools (*licei*). Several reasons underscore this decision. First, despite the virtual nature of the exchanges, we have found that a strong personal and collegial connection between educators plays a pivotal role in achieving success. Second, the distinct differences between our university and school systems present challenges when attempting to connect similar institutions, which were overcome through our university–*liceo* model. Third, the pairing of Australian undergraduate students with Italian *licei* students in their final years proves effective due to their similar ages.

Initially, our virtual exchanges involved asynchronous video exchanges using the Microsoft Flip platform (previously, Flipgrid), focusing on information exchanges around shared topics. While this approach yielded positive results, it failed to establish a strong connection among all participants. However, driven by global lockdowns and the shift to online learning, we swiftly transitioned to virtual synchronous exchanges, allowing students to manage the exchanges themselves. This chapter primarily focuses on the telecollaborative projects between Italian language students at the University of Melbourne and language students at Liceo Linguistico Adelaide Cairoli.

Drawing inspiration from the transnational model of virtual exchange for global citizenship education proposed by O'Dowd (2020), our pedagogical orientation centres on real-world language use and authentic communication. Intercultural and global citizenship approaches call for learners to collaborate with members of other cultures, instigating change in their societies or working as transnational groups to address common issues (O'Dowd, 2018). Within this framework, our virtual exchanges aim to foster students' linguistic and intercultural development through dialogical interactions, creating an open learning environment that emphasises comprehensible language.

Throughout this chapter, we provide detailed accounts of four iterations of the exchange program, spanning 2021 and 2022. We delve into the structure, implementation and outcomes of these exchanges, while also exploring student perceptions and their joint proposals for action on global issues. Additionally, we discuss the integration of virtual exchanges as a permanent fixture within our language and culture subjects, showcasing the pedagogical diversification these experiences have brought about.

In conclusion, this chapter highlights the potential of virtual exchanges for global citizenship education during times of restricted physical mobility. By capturing the successes, challenges and transformative experiences of students engaged in these exchanges, we aim to inspire educators and institutions to embrace similar initiatives, not only as temporary solutions but also as integral components of fostering global citizenship in the evolving educational landscape.

2. Key concepts

2.1. Virtual spaces as places of learning

In 'Rethinking the Virtual', Nicholas C. Burbules (2006) emphasises two fundamental ideas in relation to virtuality: the first is that 'the key feature of the virtual is not the particular technology that produces the sense of immersion, but the sense of immersion itself' (p. 37). The second develops from the assumption that the separation between the 'virtual' and the 'real' is problematic. According to this idea, any reality that we inhabit is to some extent actively filtered, interpreted, constructed or made. Therefore, the virtual should be understood 'as a context where our own active response and involvement are part of what gives the experience its veracity and meaningfulness' (p. 38). Burbules proposes his conception of the virtual through a series of steps. First, he explores four processes of engagement through which immersion happens: interest, involvement, imagination and interaction, which will prove fundamental for understanding the educational potential of virtuality. Second, he applies this conception of the virtual to a discussion of virtual space, suggesting that as virtual spaces become familiar and significant, they become virtual places.

In immersive learning experiences, the virtual, as Burbules (2006) describes it, is a very concrete way of rethinking the nature of learning spaces, 'spaces where creativity, problem-solving, communication, collaboration, experimentation, and inquiry can happen' (p. 38). The online environment is seen as a space where students spend time, interact, and do things—for example, collaborating with each other on a shared project in a shared space. The fact that they inhabit a shared space is essential for this collaboration to work. The online, networked environment supports community building and the sharing of resources and decentres the normal physical correlate of collaboration. The sense of familiarity, inhabitance and comfort students feel in virtual space, especially when this is experienced in conjunction with the familiar engagements of other students, makes virtual spaces virtual places. A place is a socially or subjectively meaningful space; it means something important to a person or to a group of people.

The elements of interest, involvement, interaction and imagination defined by Burbules actively shape our activities in space, and these activities can transform space. These activities can be collective; it is often the quality of a space as a shared space that plays a crucial role in its development into a place. Places become familiar; marked by various social conventions, they can also become a locus of community. Both the space and those inhabiting the space are changed, transformed in relation to each other. A place is a special kind of space:

> as spaces become places, there is always an element of the virtual to them (in other words, there is a quality of immersion, supported by the elements of interest, involvement, interaction and imagination).
>
> (Burbules, 2006, p. 50)

2.2. Telecollaboration, blended learning and virtual exchange

In recent decades technology seems to have become the primary means through which new (virtual) spaces of educational interactions are created. As this volume attests, there is an ongoing interest in pedagogical projects that disrupt and diversify the traditional classroom experience of teaching an additional language. Telecollaborative initiatives have developed extensively and have been implemented through joint international practices engaging groups of students located in geographically distant locations. Virtual exchange is an umbrella term used to refer to the different ways in which groups of learners are engaged in online intercultural interaction and collaboration with partners from other cultural contexts or geographical locations as an integrated part of coursework and under the guidance of educators. Recently, different models or applications of virtual exchange have emerged in the field of language education. Current debates on the economic and environmental cost of study abroad programs, as well as the challenges to physical mobility posed by the pandemic, have made virtual exchange an attractive option for institutions as they search for sustainable and low-cost models of international learning that will serve as an alternative or complement to physical mobility programs (de Wit, 2016). Post-pandemic, students and staff are now more than ever accustomed to working online.

Virtual exchange experiences are often implemented through blended learning, which consists of a mix of face-to-face and online instruction modes. The transformative affordances of blended learning to foster pedagogical shifts and student agency are well documented. As Gruba and Hinkelman (2012, p. 4) note:

> here, educators are seeking to substantially change learners from being passive receivers of information to active co-constructors of knowledge … blended approaches require the full and principled use of interactive technologies to foster agenda for transformation of learning.

Blended learning can decentre the lecturer, creating a learning environment in which the production of knowledge can be shared between the teacher and the learner; this opens up space for learners to bring their own perspectives and culture into the learning endeavour. As project designers, we set out to develop a student-centred, context-driven digital learning model. As Marsh (2012, p. 8) suggests:

> blended learning is, by its very nature, 'student-centered.' … In student-centered teaching … learning is most meaningful … when the students themselves are actively engaged in creating, understanding, and connecting to knowledge.

We were, thus, interested in developing an online learning environment that envisions learners as active meaning constructors. In this light, dialogical interaction plays a pivotal role in the design of the digital project.

Knowledge creation in digital learning environments represents another pivotal dimension of telecollaboration/virtual exchange. The aim is to create an environment where the focus is for the students not only to learn notions but also to create ideas. According to the knowledge-building tradition, learning is a spontaneous experience that happens without awareness and it is based on the information that the teacher 'vertically' transmits to the students, whereas 'knowledge creation/knowledge building is, in stark contrast, a type of deliberate, conscious action, which produces knowledge that has a public life' (Bereiter & Scardamalia, 2014, p. 35). The idea behind knowledge building applied to the classroom is that knowledge can be an experience shared by the teacher and the students that leads to the creation of ideas that can have a 'public life'—a social utility beyond the classroom. With the knowledge-building approach, the final result is obtained through the active and collaborative efforts of the teacher with the students. Students have an active role in the learning process and play a fundamental part in it.

2.3. Intercultural competence, intercultural citizenship and active citizenship

Overall, virtual intercultural exchanges aim to foster the development of both additional language skills and intercultural competence through culture-based activities. Besides promoting language learning, telecollaborative tasks need to encourage the intercultural analysis of the practices and values of the cultures of the groups involved in the virtual exchanges. For intercultural competence to be developed in virtual exchanges, intercultural sensitivity needs to be stimulated through explicit training (see Belz, 2002; Bennett, 1993; Liddicoat & Scarino, 2013). Michael Byram (1997) was one of the first researchers to define intercultural competence. He argued that when people from other languages and/or cultures interact in a social context, they contribute with what they know about their own country, but also with what they know of people from other cultures. In this sense, both knowledge and attitude are important and are affected by the processes of intercultural communication, which, in his words, refer to 'the skills of interpretation and establishing relationships between aspects of the two cultures' and 'the skills of discovery and interaction' (Byram, 1997, p. 33). In order to organise the intercultural dimension, which consists of sustaining interaction and building communication for the development of intercultural skills, we need to offer students the opportunity to grow relationships and communicative skills through the exchange of information, and help them to reflect on different ways of doing things and to be capable of accepting different views and opinions.

An ever-increasingly cited, although challenging, objective of telecollaborative projects is the development of intercultural citizenship, which envisions learners as working actively to deal with world issues (Leask, 2015), while tackling them in context-specific settings (Porto & Byram, 2015). For Porto et al. (2017, p. 237), 'there is a challenge … about how to make linguistic competence-oriented courses not only intercultural but also citizenship-oriented'. In this sense, intercultural citizenship 'integrates the pillar of intercultural communicative competence from foreign language education with the emphasis on civic action in the community from citizenship education' (Porto, 2014, cited in Trapè, 2019, p. 172).

Global or intercultural citizenship approaches 'involve learners … actually working with members of other cultures as a transnational group in order to take action about an issue or problem which is common to both societies'

(O'Dowd, 2020, p. 486). In designing the virtual exchange project, we referred to the transnational model of virtual exchange for global citizenship education proposed by O'Dowd (2020), which engages students with different and alternative worldviews within a pedagogical structure of online collaboration, critical reflection and active contribution to global society. To lay the foundations for his transnational model of virtual exchange for global citizenship education, O'Dowd used the two main models of interpretations of intercultural or global citizenship education: the Council of Europe's (2016) Framework of Competences for Democratic Culture and Byram's (2008) Framework for Intercultural Citizenship.

The concept of 'intercultural citizenship' introduced by Byram (2008) is postulated as a learning outcome to guide curriculum designers and teachers in school and higher education. It is parallel to other concepts such as 'global citizenship', 'intercultural competence' or 'cultural awareness', which are commonly used in education (Wagner & Byram, 2017). As O'Dowd (2020, p. 484) explains:

> The essential difference between global competence and global citizenship or intercultural competence and intercultural citizenship lies in the importance attributed to active engagement in society ... So, while intercultural or global competence refer to the development of knowledge, skills, attitudes and values to communicate and act effectively and appropriately in different cultural contexts, global or intercultural citizenship borrow from models of citizenship education to refer to the application of these competences to actively participating in, changing and improving society.

A key dimension of Byram's recent construct is active citizenship, which implies 'being involved in the life of one's community, both local and national' (Wagner & Byram, 2017, p. 3). In this light, intercultural citizenship is instrumental in promoting the development of language-speaking global citizens who are ready to act and interact in multilingual and international contexts, and are thus capable of exercising active citizenship (Wagner & Byram, 2017) through civic actions in their own national communities (Porto et al., 2017).

To this end, in our project, both groups of students are required to plan and carry out a civic action in their local communities; they are encouraged to become global citizens ready to interact effectively in multilingual and international contexts through active citizenship (Wagner & Byram, 2017). This is done by taking students past their comfort zone and engaging them in real-world tasks through a project that has direct relevance to their own communities. As such, the objectives of our virtual space are as follows: learning beyond the classroom walls through virtual exchange, intercultural communicative competence, working in a transnational team, motivation and engagement (meaningful learning), and community engagement and active citizenship (O'Dowd, 2021a, 2021b).

The increasingly intercultural citizenship–related dimension of online intercultural exchanges envisions learners as active global agents able to tackle world challenges (Leask, 2015). Here, telecollaborative tasks are expected to foster not only students' additional language skills and intercultural awareness but also learners' engagements with global problems tailored to local contexts:

> intercultural citizenship education … mean[s] … that learners would be encouraged to act together with others in the world and that those others would be in other countries and other languages. The purpose would be to address a common problem in the world.
> (Porto & Byram, 2015, p. 24)

2.4. Translanguaging

The design of our virtual exchange is underpinned by a translanguaging view of language education. As Li (2022, p. 1) notes, translanguaging is a:

> methodology offering a new conceptual framework that promotes a number of important analytical shifts: shift away from language as abstract codes to meaning- and sense-making; attend to a wider range of multi-semiotic resources whilst refusing to privilege particular modes and methods of meaning-making over others; approach translanguaging as an expansively integrated experience.

It is chiefly this first shift that is important in our project: the notion of students deploying their linguistic repertoires to make meaning in the communicative setting of online collaboration. The design of the virtual exchange allows students a wide degree of autonomy in structuring their interactions, with the loose prescription to try to use both languages equally. Vogel and García (2017, p. 9) remind us that, while 'much of the translanguaging that occurs in classrooms is pupil-directed', 'explicit teacher-directed pedagogical practices that leverage translanguaging' are beginning to appear. We have attempted to create an environment that promotes students' use of translanguaging for the purpose of co-designing a solution to an issue that they jointly view as important and expressing this using the two languages under instruction, namely English and Italian. Li and García (2022, p. 318) indicate that 'to leverage translanguage in education much more is needed than simply validating the students "first language"'. While we have not systematically collected data on language usage during the virtual exchange, we are aware anecdotally of students employing a broader range of linguistic resources than just English and Italian to make meaning during their interactions. This includes other shared languages such as Mandarin and Spanish, as well as non-standard varieties of English and local Italian dialects. The challenge is to make these 'translanguaging spaces ... instructionally purposeful' (Li & García, 2022, p. 321). Li and García (2022, p. 322) make the useful distinction between process and product, 'encouraging students to produce certain products in one language or another' as a response to curriculum or assessment needs. Notably, they describe formative assessment practices that 'always leverage the students' entire linguistic/semiotic repertoire to truly assess what students know and can do' (Li & García, 2022, p. 321). The design of our virtual exchange provides student participants with the freedom to exploit their full linguistic repertoires in interaction with their peers without anything other than a vague direction on language use, while their summative task asks them to channel this meaning-making into expression in the two languages being taught: Italian and English.

3. Project rationale and outline

Our initial aims in designing a virtual exchange experience arose from the desire to provide students with some continuity in the possibility of interacting with peers. For a number of years we had been collaborating on in-country connections whereby a group of University of Melbourne students would visit our host *liceo* and spend more or less a week collaborating in class. This sometimes involved homestays as well. As it was not possible to do this each year, we decided to initiate the online counterpart of this activity. Beginning with one university subject, this has now been integrated into three subjects and is a strong feature of the Italian studies program.

The earlier virtual exchanges had a straightforward focus on intercultural communication, but in 2022, with the initiative of Trapè, we made a shift towards global citizenship, the principles of which have been discussed above.

3.1. Our projects

For 2021, our attempt was to activate students' curiosity about their peers through the programmatic discussion of topics that could be considered common with a view to stimulating intercultural reflection. Due to different timeframes of our academic years (Australia: March–November, Italy: September–June), we had to work across different periods of the respective academic years, fitting in as many weeks as practicable.

Table 6.1. Virtual exchanges in 2021

May–June 2021	October–November 2021
Weekly topics	
Young people in Australia and in Italy: Relationships, aspirations, politics	Stereotypes
Free time: Music, sport, hobbies, TV, online activity	The new family
Schools and universities in Australia and Italy	Vegans/vegetarians vs carnivores
Australian and Italian 'cultures' and stereotypes	*Vivere* in Australia vs vivere in Italia
COVID-19: Impact on young people in Australia and in Italy	–

Source: Authors.

3.2. 2022

We would like to focus our attention on the virtual exchanges of 2022 as these represent our attempt to incorporate active global citizenship into the model. To begin, before students introduced themselves to their partners, they engaged in pre-virtual activities in class, which guided them in the discussions that could then commence. For example, to activate students' prior knowledge of the theme, icebreaker and brainstorming activities centred on global citizenship in face-to-face lessons and on the university/school online learning management systems (LMS). These activities were targeted to introduce key vocabulary items and/or concepts necessary for students to discuss the theme in synchronous meetings. Second, student participants were asked to consider articles and short authentic videos between 5 and 10 minutes long on questions relating to issues of global importance, such as gender equality and the disparity between men and women in different international contexts.

In their first meeting students introduced themselves and their school/university to their international partners in Australia or Italy in the dominant language of their country. As Carloni and Zuccala (2018, pp. 419–420) point out:

> task-based learning seems especially suitable to online intercultural exchanges ... In screen-based learning environments, tasks (such as problem solving, decision making, opinion-exchange, and jigsaws) can thus promote dialogical interaction focusing on real-world issues effectively.

Consequently, three main types of tasks were used in the virtual exchange: information exchange, which 'involves learners providing their telecollaborative partners with information about their personal biographies, local schools or towns or aspects of their home cultures'; comparison and analysis, which 'requires learners not only to exchange information, but also to go a step further and carry out comparisons or critical analyses of cultural products from both cultures (e.g. books, surveys, films, newspaper articles)'; and collaboration and product creation, which 'require ... learners not only to exchange and compare information but also to work together to produce a joint product or conclusion' (O'Dowd & Waire, 2009, pp. 175, 178).

In their second meeting students discussed articles and videos uploaded to the university/school LMS. The task was to read and watch the materials individually, and to discuss them within the class face-to-face and with the students' respective international partners online.

In the remaining meetings with their international partners, students reflected on the creation of a transnational group whose aim was to consider issues related to global citizenship and plan civic action. During the meetings, the students, in dyads or triads, discussed and made plans to collaboratively create a multimodal presentation on how they were developing their civic action. Communication and collaboration among the students led to the creation of a product planned and realised by each set of students. Students selected the digital technologies they wanted to use to create their multimodal presentations and, once they were finished, they uploaded them to the respective LMS. All learners involved in the online intercultural exchanges watched the presentations created by the other students. The presentations were also discussed in face-to-face lessons. The final discussion was organised in the form of a group-to-group video conferencing session (involving whole groups of students in Italy and in Australia). The development of intercultural, citizenship-focused exchange in the final phase of the project took students out of their comfort zone and engaged them in real-world tasks. The students' final presentations and the discussion were assessed.

After seeking others' perspectives and advice, the students proposed change and acted together to instigate change in their local communities (Byram, 2008; O'Dowd, 2020). The objectives were to promote the analysis of the chosen issue, to enhance dialogical interaction in the target language, and to foster intercultural competence and intercultural citizenship. We assisted students during in-class face-to-face activities in considering the value systems underlying Italian and Australian cultural practices in relation to issues related to global citizenship. To foster intercultural competence in the digital learning environments we worked in class to 'involve … learners in moving between cultures and reflecting on their own cultural positioning and the role of language and culture within it' (Liddicoat & Scarino, 2013, p. 117). Students' voices, experiences and background knowledge are central to discussing topics within an intercultural framework; students are encouraged to examine phenomena and experience their own cultural situatedness while seeking to enter into the cultural worlds of others. It requires an act of engagement in which learners compare their own cultural assumptions, expectations, practices and meanings with those of others, recognising that these are formed within a cultural context that is different to their own (Scarino, 2014, p. 391). As O'Dowd (2018, p. 11) notes:

> Video conferencing was seen as developing students' abilities to interact with members of the target culture under the constraints of real-time communication and also to elicit, through a face-to-face dialogue, the concepts and values which underlie their partners' behaviour and their opinions.

However, emails and messaging via WhatsApp and other social media were employed to both send and receive much more detailed information on the two cultures' products and practices as seen from the partners' perspective. In the classroom, the students' learning was continuously supported by guided reflections concerning the intercultural encounters and questions made possible by the virtual exchange. The online meetings and other means of exchange and collaboration increased the students' exposure to Italian/English; fostered the development of their interactional skills and fluency in the target language; allowed them to experience authentic language use, enabling access to meaningful interactions; fostered students' active learning, increasing their motivation, agency and autonomy; and cultivated active citizenship.

Table 6.2 shows the details provided to University of Melbourne students regarding the virtual exchange undertaken at the beginning of 2022.

Table 6.2. Virtual exchanges in 2022

Details of virtual exchange from University of Melbourne LMS
Progetto Pavia-Melbourne
*Scambio virtuale	Virtual exchange*
*Italian Studies, University of Melbourne, Australia	Liceo Linguistics Adelaide Cairoli, Pavia, Italia*
Ogni studente avrà un/a partner internazionale nell'altro paese con cui si vedrà online una volta alla settimana per 4 settimane per discutere degli seguenti argomenti	Each student will have an international partner in the other country, who she/he will meet **once a week online (4 weeks)** to talk about the following topics.
Lo scambio virtuale consisterà di	The virtual exchange will consist of:
• Scambio linguistico — **parlerete sia in inglese che in italiano** durante lo scambio. Si suggerisce un minimo di 20 minuti in ciascuna lingua durante ogni incontro (almeno 40 minuti)
*Language exchange — **you will speak both English and Italian** during the exchange. We suggest at least 20 minutes in each language during each encounter (at least 40 minutes)*
• Scambio intercultural — **ascoltandovi a vicenda e comunicando**, metterete a confronto **culture diverse** per poterle valutare **in modo critico**. Certo che conoscerete meglio l'Australia e anche l'Italia!
*Intercultural exchange — **listening to each other and communicating**, you will compare **different cultures** and **think critically** about them. You will certainly get to know Australia, and also Italy, better!*
*Idea centrale	The central idea*
Siamo consapevoli di **questioni globali** quali cambiamento climatico, migrazione, cause di povertà e mancata parità tra uomini e donne?	*Are we familiar with **global issues** such as climate change, migration, causes of poverty and equality between men and women?*
La competenza globale secondo il Programme for International Student Assessment (PISA) si definisce come **una competenza multidisciplinare che implica la capacità di:**
Global competence** is defined in the Programme for International Student Assessment (PISA) as **a multidimensional capacity that encompasses the ability to:
• **esaminare** questioni di rilievo locale, globale e culturale	*examine issues of **local, global and cultural significance***
• **capire** e apprezzare **la prospettiva e il punto di vista altrui**	*understand and appreciate **the perspectives and worldviews of others***
• **interagire in modo aperto e appropriato attraverso culture diverse con esiti positivi**	*engage in open, appropriate and **effective interactions across cultures***
• e **prendere iniziative** che portano al **benessere** e allo **sviluppo sostenibile** collettivi	*and **take action** for collective **wellbeing and sustainable development*** (OECD, 2021).

Questioni globali | Global issues:
- salute climatica e riscaldamento globale | *climate change and global warming*
- salute mondiale (per es. epidemie) | *global health (e.g. epidemics)*
- migrazione (spostamento dei popoli) | *migration (movement of people)*
- conflitti internazionali | *international conflicts*
- fame o malnutrizione in diverse parti del mondo | *hunger or malnutrition in different parts of the world*
- cause di povertà | *causes of poverty*
- parità tra donne e uomini in diverse parti del mondo | *equality between men and women in different parts of the world.*

Date | Dates

Per la prima settimana (cioè quella della pausa didattica), usate Flip per creare la vostra presentazione. Visitate flip.com e usate questo Join Code: xXXXxxXX

Per capire come usare Flip, visitate help.flip.com/hc/en-us

Per le settimane successive, dovete organizzare almeno un incontro online ogni settimana con il tuo/la tua partner durante il quale parlate dell'argomento della settimana. La tabella seguente indica i gruppi - mandatevi una mail per cominciare a organizzarvi.

For the first week (the week of the teaching break), use Flip to create your introductions. Go to flip.com and enter this Join Code: xXXXxxXX

To understand how to use Flip, visit help.flip.com/hc/en-us

For the following weeks, you need to organise at least one meeting online with your partner each week during which you talk about the week's topic. The following table will show the groups - send each other an email to start organising yourselves.

Gruppi | Groups

…

Programma | Program

Pausa didattica

Postate il vostro video su Flipgrid | *Post your video on Flipgrid*

Settimana 8:

Primo incontro — fissate date e orari per i vostri incontri | *First meeting — decide with your international partner dates and time of your meetings*

- Ci presentiamo/*Introduce yourself*
- Ti senti 'cittadina/o del mondo'? Che significa per te?/*Do you feel like a 'world citizen'? What does it mean for you?*

Settimana 9

- L'Australia e l'Italia e l'educazione alla cittadinanza globale | *Australia and Italy and global citizenship education*
- Commenta gli articoli con la/il tua/o partner internazionale | *Comment on the articles with your partner*
- Qual è la questione globale che conosci meglio? Quella che ti interessa di più? | *Which global issue do you know best? Which one interests you the most?.*

www.aics.gov.it/news/2018/20618/

www.ilsole24ore.com/art/ocse-gli-studenti-italiani-sono-cittadini-globali-parole-ma-non-fatti-ADukJcx

theconversation.com/australian-students-say-they-understand-global-issues-but-few-are-learning-another-language-compared-to-the-oecd-average-168073

Settimana 10
Quali azioni potresti intraprendere nella tua comunità che potrebbero contribuire a uno sviluppo più sostenibile? | *What sorts of actions could you take in your community that would contribute to sustainable development?*
Confronto Melbourne Pavia | *Compare Melbourne Pavia*
Settimana 11:
Possiamo trovare un'azione comune? | *Can we find a common action?*
Pianificare video/presentazione/leaflet su azione di cittadinanza attiva | *Plan a video/presentation/leaflet/etc. on an action of active citizenship*
Settimana 12
Realizziamo video/presentazione insieme al/la tuo/a partner su azione di cittadinanza attiva | *Create video/presentation/leaflet/etc. with your partner on an action of active citizenship*
SWOT-VAC
Tutti insieme su Zoom | *All together online on Zoom*
Assessment
This project will be assessed via the remaining two small online assessments (week 8 and week 12) and in the final exam.
• In your blog, I want you to include **a dedicated reflection** on the sorts of things you discover through your interactions with your partner in line with the ideas immediately above — this can be in Italian or English or a mix. This will be considered along with your reading reflections in week 9 and week 11. For me to consider your reflections, you need to have published a Flip video in the first week of the project. • On the final exam, there will be an explicit section in which you will be asked to describe what you've shared and learnt during the exchange along with any particular language aspects that came out.

Source: Authors.

As Table 6.2 shows, students were able to focus on topics of immediate interest to them. Similarly, the product they made could take any form that they chose. Students selected topics that ranged from global warming to a comparison of experiences of catcalling, sustainability and rubbish collection, food and food waste, water contamination and LGBTQIA+ issues, just to name a few. Figures 6.1–6.3 are examples of the presentations produced during the virtual exchange. Students mostly opted for a bilingual approach, combining the use of Italian and English in different ways. Figures 6.1 and 6.3 compare the two lived experiences of the participants but arrive at a common solution. Figure 6.2 shows an approach that emphasises issues common across both international contexts.

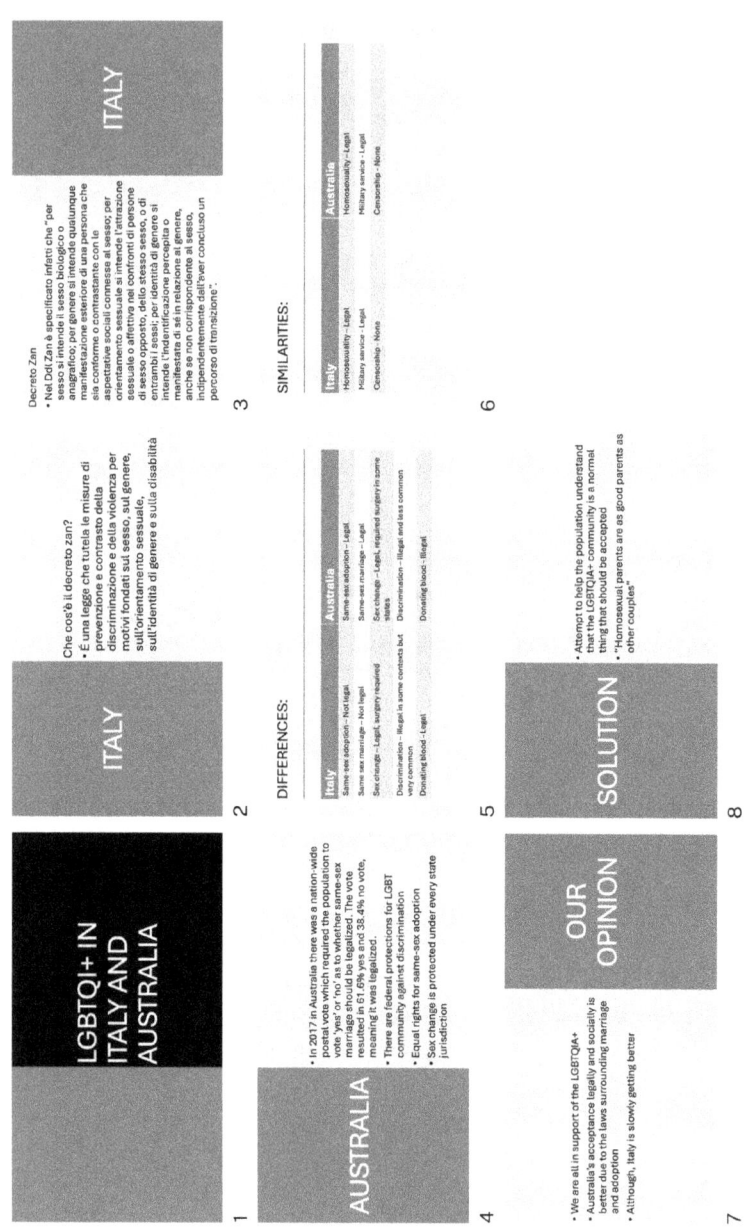

Figure 6.1. LGBTQI+ in Italy and Australia

Source: Authors.

Figure 6.2. The education of citizenship
Source: Authors.

Figure 6.3. Catcalling in Melbourne and Milan
Source: Authors.

3.3. Student responses to the virtual exchange

The analysis of student perceptions has shown positive results and learners' appreciation of the experience. In their comments on the LMSs and in class, students noted linguistic and cultural improvements as the project's main benefit. With regards to the perception of linguistic improvement, students referred to the virtual exchange as helping them with vocabulary, grammar, fluency and pronunciation.

All the learners appreciated the opportunity to practise the target language. Some students underlined the importance of understanding culture when learning a language. Learning how to communicate effectively with native speakers within an intercultural framework has emerged as one of the key assets of the virtual exchange.

However, feedback has also highlighted some critical issues. In this respect, students maintain that virtual exchange can often be too time-consuming and that it is important that it be assessed with appropriate weighting, rather than just being an add-on. Students suggested that the discussion of the topics to be addressed in the final video meeting with all participants should be refined. Developing this discussion would assist with consolidating students' understanding of the topics studied.

What students appreciated most in this virtual exchange was the possibility of working together on a common action of active citizenship, which they could see could have a relevant application in their community.

3.4. Students' comments on the virtual exchange

Examining the reflective comments of the Italian students involved in the virtual exchange reveals that the broad aims of the project appear to have been successful. In Table 6.3, excerpts from students' comments are organised according to several overarching themes: being/becoming a global citizen, big issues, similarities, need for change, learning about self to learn about others, language gains, a new friendship. The full statements can be found in Appendix A.

These comments reveal a broad and deep engagement with issues over the course of the virtual exchange. They also demonstrate that students are successfully mediating an intercultural relationship through language use that extends along a continuum of formality. It seems to us reasonable to suggest that framing a virtual exchange experience around notions of global citizenship can inspire students to transcend limited transactional communication to achieve authentic interactions that simultaneously build language and (inter)cultural competence. While a focus on global issues might seem limiting, in some sense, it actually frees the students from the embarrassment of having to try to find common ground on which to build their nascent relationship while at the same time providing fertile ground for stimulating exchanges. It is also sufficiently malleable to adapt to most pedagogical endeavours, making it transferable and sustainable.

Table 6.3. Italian students' comments

Theme	Comment
Being/ becoming a global citizen	• I am achieving the goal of being a global citizen of only a half of the world. In fact, my whole culture is based on the western part of the planet and almost nothing on the eastern one. I realised how our worldview is totally Western-centric. For this, to become global citizens we really need to know more about the different parts of the whole world. (G) • We agreed that the people who study one or more foreign languages are more likely to open up to global issues. (F) • The adjective that suits her best is for certain cosmopolitan and I would say that not only for her origins but mostly for her ability to adapt to different realities by making different places in the world her home. For me she is the perfect example of a global citizen … I was born in Italy and I actually lived in the same place where my parents had grown up. (E) • Me and my partner have found solutions to all these problems and summarized them into a presentation so that everyone can look and try to help the world. (A) • I learned that the basis of global competence must be mutual respect, understanding different cultures, and also trying to create a coexistence in the name of peace and collaboration for a better world. (G2)
Big issues	• We spent most of the time on … gender equality. (G) • I also hope Italian society will became more multicultural, including foreign people instead of cutting them out because of their origins. (F) • We're both interested in women empowerment in entrepreneurial activities … we found a way to put all these three key topics together. We decided to create a food blog called 'Eat, cook, be organic' in order to share low waste recipes, connect with other cultures and promote examples of sustainability and women empowerment. (F) • The environment must be respected and each of us should do what we can to improve it, such as simply recycle, reduce pollution using alternative and non-polluting means of transport, and also improve the soul of your city by making it greener, planting trees and plants that produce oxygen and improve the quality of the air we breathe. (G2) • No poverty and Zero Hunger. (F2)
Similarities	• Made us understand how two countries as far away as Australia and Italy have the common problem regarding the mental closure of their people. (G) • For example, she appeared astonished when she learned that I'm not planning to be mother in the future, and that I don't have much faith in marriage. However, I tried to clarify my opinions justifying and explaining that they are not [immovable] decisions. Eventually, this discussion helped me to open my mind in order to understand her thoughts, which are not really far from mine. Moreover, we both found a common ground talking about the difficulties we experienced as women as the phenomenon of catcalling. (G) • I enjoyed meeting someone who lives on the other side of the world and even though we were born in different countries, I found out we have something in common. (F2)

Theme	Comment
Need for change	• This project made me understand how both our countries have many difficulties concerning all the topics proposed and for this we must act quickly in order to change the situation. (G) • We should all learn how to do a correct waste collection and help the environment as much as possible. (A)
Learning about self to learn about others	• M told me she was surprised of the low numbers of foreign languages' Australian learners, and she could only explain this phenomenon by the expendability of English language. The article by 'Il sole 24 ore' astonished me as well. Honestly, I didn't expect Italian girls and boys to be global citizens in words, but not in facts. (F) • Something that surprised me was that the percentage of people who suffer from hunger in Australia is much less than the percentage in Italy. This makes me think that the government still needs to do a lot of work to improve the poor condition of a huge number of people in my country. (F2)
Language gains	• My English knowledge has improved and I'm happy I have managed to overcome my uncertainties in speaking foreign languages. (F) • In this second intercultural exchange I obviously had the opportunity to practice my language in an informal way, by talking about light topics or interests, but also in a more 'formal' one, as we talked mainly about profound topics that I don't often consider. (E) • I really enjoyed this experience, I was worried about the language but it was not a problem. We managed to distribute enough time both to speak in Italian and to speak in English and a few times as the Italian or English vocabulary were a bit more difficult we changed them into easier words or we even tried to explain them. This experience was really helpful, interesting and enjoyable. I learned many new words and some Australian slang like 'reckon', it's another way to say 'I think'. The thing I liked the most was the fact that the meetings didn't seem forced but natural and pleasant because we always found some cultural aspects to talk about despite the age difference. (G2) • I also learnt new vocabulary such as lippy, brekkie and colloquial expressions like 'To cost big bikkies'. (F2)
A new friendship	• I have gained a friend who has helped me in this journey through global issues. M has been really accommodating, presenting her experiences with kindness and enthusiasm. (F) • At a general level, it was a very beautiful and interesting experience because talking about common themes reduced the distance between Italy and Australia. (A)

Source: Authors.

4. Conclusion and future directions

With a return to open borders and the resumption of international travel, in-country exchange has begun again. This does not spell the end of virtual exchange, which offers certain affordances that traditional exchange cannot. Virtual exchange can be integrated into whole subjects/classes without the cost constraints of traditional in-country experiences, thus providing a potentially more equitable solution for all students, particularly for cases in which all students do not have the means to travel. Finding the right collaboration in the target country is imperative, which might involve considering what could be viewed as a mismatch: in our case, university and *liceo* connections. In our experience, a virtual exchange based on strong collegial connections between educators will guarantee the best success. The introduction of virtual exchanges has taken on a viral nature for us and led to the diversification of our pedagogical programs. As one student aptly noted: all language programs should include a virtual exchange.

References

Belz, J. A. (2002). Social dimensions of telecollaborative language study. *Language Learning & Technology, 6*(1), 60–81. doi.org/10125/25143.

Bennett, J. M. (1993). Cultural marginality: Identity issues in intercultural training. In R. M. Paige (Ed.), *Education for the intercultural experience* (pp. 109–135). Intercultural Press.

Bereiter, C. & Scardamalia, M. (2014). Knowledge building and knowledge creation: One concept, two hills to climb. In S. C. Tan, H. J. So & J. Yeo (Eds.), *Knowledge creation in education* (pp. 35–52). Springer. doi.org/10.1007/978-981-287-047-6_3.

Burbules, N. C. (2006). Rethinking the virtual. In J. Weiss et al. (Eds.), *The international handbook of virtual learning environments* (pp. 37–58). Springer. doi.org/10.1007/978-1-4020-3803-7_1.

Byram, M. (1997). *Teaching and assessing intercultural communicative competence*. Multilingual Matters.

Byram, M. (2008). *From foreign language education to education for intercultural citizenship: Essays and reflections*. Multilingual Matters. doi.org/10.21832/9781847690807.

Carloni, G. & Zuccala, B. (2018). Blending Italian 'down-under': Toward a theoretical framework and pragmatic guide for blending tertiary Italian language and culture courses through Skype-enhanced, pre-service teacher-centred tele-collaboration. *LEA: Lingue e letterature d'Oriente e d'Occidente, 7*, 405–445. doi.org/10.13128/LEA-1824-484x-24408.

Council of Europe. (2016). *Competences for democratic culture: Living together as equals in culturally diverse democratic societies*. Council of Europe Publishing. rm.coe.int/16806ccc07.

de Wit, H. (2016). Internationalisation and the role of online intercultural exchange. In R. O'Dowd & T. Lewis (Eds.), *Online intercultural exchange: Policy, pedagogy, practice* (pp. 192–208). Routledge.

Gruba, P. & Hinkelman, D. (2012). *Blending technologies in second language classrooms*. Palgrave Macmillan. doi.org/10.1057/9780230356825.

Leask, B. (2015). *Internationalizing the curriculum*. Routledge.

Li, W. (2022). Translanguaging as a political stance: Implications for English language education. *ELT Journal, 76*(2), 172–182. doi.org/10.1093/elt/ccab083.

Li, W. & García, O. (2022). Not a first language but one repertoire: Translanguaging as a decolonizing project. *RELC Journal, 53*(2), 313–324.

Liddicoat, A. J. & Scarino, A. (2013). *Intercultural language teaching and learning*. Wiley-Blackwell. doi.org/10.1002/9781118482070.

Marsh, D. (2012). *Blended learning opportunities for language learners*. Cambridge University Press.

O'Dowd, R. (2017). Online intercultural exchange and language education. In S. L. Thorne & S. May. (Eds.), *Language, education and technology* (3rd ed.) (pp. 1–12). Springer. doi.org/10.1007/978-3-319-02237-6_17.

O'Dowd, R. (2018). From telecollaboration to virtual exchange: state-of-the-art and the role of UNI Collaboration in moving forward. *Journal of Virtual Exchange, 1*, 1–23. doi.org/10.14705/rpnet.2018.jve.1.

O'Dowd, R. (2020). A transnational model of virtual exchange for global citizenship education. *Language Teaching, 53*(4), 477–490. doi.org/10.1017/S0261444819000077.

O'Dowd, R. (2021a). Virtual exchange: Moving forward into the next decade. *Computer Assisted Language Learning, 34*(3), 209–224. doi.org/10.1080/09588221.2021.1902201.

O'Dowd, R. (2021b). What do students learn in virtual exchange? A qualitative content analysis of learning outcomes across multiple exchanges. *International Journal of Educational Research, 109*, 101804. doi.org/10.1016/j.ijer.2021.101804.

O'Dowd, R. & Waire, P. (2009). Critical issues in telecollaborative task design. *Computer Assisted Language Learning, 22*(2), 173–188. doi.org/10.1080/09588220902778369.

OECD. (2021). *Education at a glance 2021: OECD indicators*. OECD Publishing. doi.org/10.1787/b35a14e5-en.

Porto, M. (2014). Intercultural citizenship education in an EFL online project in Argentina. *Language and Intercultural Communication, 14*(2), 245–261. doi.org/10.1080/14708477.2014.890625.

Porto, M. & Byram, M. (2015). A curriculum for action in the community and intercultural citizenship in higher education. *Language, Culture and Curriculum, 28*(3), 226–242. doi.org/10.1080/07908318.2015.1087555.

Porto, M., Houghton, S. A. & Byram, M. (2017). Intercultural citizenship in the (foreign) language classroom. *Language Teaching Research, 22*(5), 484–98. doi.org/10.1177/1362168817718580.

Scarino, A. (2014). Learning as reciprocal, interpretative meaning-making: A view from collaborative research into the professional learning of teachers of languages. *The Modern Language Journal, 98*(1), 386–401. jstor.org/stable/43651767.

Trapè, R. (2019). Building empathy and intercultural citizenship through a virtual exchange project. *Le Simplegadi, 17*(19), 167–180. doi.org/10.17456/SIMPLE-136.

Trapè, R. (2020). Developing global citizenship through real-world tasks—a virtual exchange between North American university students and Italian upper-secondary school students. In M. Hauck & A. Müller-Hartmann (Eds.), *Virtual exchange and 21st century teacher education: short papers from the 2019 EVALUATE conference* (pp. 147–155). Research-publishing.net. doi.org/10.14705/rpnet.2020.46.1140.

Vogel, S. & García, O. (2017). Translanguaging. *Oxford research encyclopedia of education*. doi.org/10.1093/acrefore/9780190264093.013.181.

Wagner, M. & Byram, M. (2017). Intercultural citizenship. In Y. Y. Sim (Ed.), *The international encyclopedia of intercultural communication* (pp. 1–6). Wiley. doi.org/10.1002/9781118783665.ieicc0043.

Appendix A

G (V)

We preferred to dedicate more time to the path of citizenship, which had been proposed to us, telling our opinions.

We started our exchange asking what the word 'world citizen' means to us. We shared the idea that the languages are the bases of a true citizen who can live in a modern world. Exploring this topic, I personally reflected on the fact that I am achieving the goal of being a global citizen of only a half of the world. In fact, my whole culture is based on the western part of the planet and almost nothing on the eastern one. I realised how our worldview is totally Western-centric. For this, to become global citizens we really need to know more about the different parts of the whole world. For example, V is learning two languages: Japanese and Italian, indeed. Moreover, we discussed about the multicultural aspect of our cities. If compared to Melbourne, Pavia doesn't offer many opportunities to explore foreign cultures. However, V seemed interested by our Cultural City Twinning we made with Spain, France, Finland, and Germany. This topic managed to reveal numerous needs that young people have both in Australia and in Italy regarding the meeting with new countries.

During the first meeting we had the opportunity to talk about the global citizenship education, as well. First, I've immediately started thinking about the subject of Civic Education, imagining it was also a subject of study in Australian schools. V explained to me that in Australia students are aware of global issues, but a real subject dedicated to them doesn't exist. In fact, these topics are only mentioned in English class or language classes. This lack of education in the topic, which is also present in Italy despite the hours of Civic Education, has made us reflect on it. For this reason, it will be the key idea of our project. For example, V didn't know anything about the 2030 Agenda and she discovered this program thanks to one of the articles we had to read. Analysing them, we both found that the Italian and English [articles] are spectacular. In fact, these articles made us understand how two countries as far away as Australia and Italy have the common problem regarding the mental closure of their people.

Overall, V and I have mostly agreed on all the global topics. However, the issue we spent most of the time on was gender equality and that is why we decided to base our project on it. Probably, V understood how much I care for this critical issue and she decided to indulge me. The exchange of views was interesting since she has views which are different from mine. In my opinion, sometimes my positions seemed to be slightly exaggerated to her. For example, she appeared astonished when she learned that I'm not planning to be mother in the future, and that I don't have much faith in marriage. However, I tried to clarify my opinions justifying and explaining that they are not [immovable] decisions. Eventually, this discussion helped me to open my mind in order to understand her thoughts, which are not really far from mines. Moreover, we both found a common ground talking about the difficulties we experienced as women as the phenomenon of catcalling. Discussing in this way with V made me feel close to her and that's why it is the part I enjoyed most.

The exchange with V … Discussing the issues which afflict the world with a completely foreign person was definitely a particular way to know her. Despite this, I think that this project helped us to face with other opinions which are not always similar to ours. In addition to it, this project made me understand how both our countries have many difficulties concerning all the topics proposed and for this we must act quickly in order to change the situation.

F (M)

My international partner is M … Talking about global competence and global citizenship, we agreed that the people who study one or more foreign languages are more likely to open up to global issues. It was interesting to see the differences and the similarities between our perceptions of these issues … Subsequently, I tried to be sympathetic and put myself in her shoes in order to understand her choice. In addition, we are both keen on cooking and I got really amazed when she showed me some pictures of vegan recipes she prepared. Food and sustainability were one of the most furthered analysed themes. We have both described our food habits, agriculture, meat industry, organic standard, and rules in our countries. In this aspect, the PCTO (Percorsi per le Competenze Trasversali e per l'Orientamento [Pathways for Transversal Skills and Orientation]) work helped me a lot to give her a whole vision of the situation in Italy. Furthermore, she got really [struck] when I told her how mafia has contaminated the environment through illegal dumps. Then, she wanted to know more about it, and I told her something about Giovanni Falcone.

Another topic we discussed was migration. I realised Australia is a good example of integration and multiculturality. It was interesting to see the dichotomy between that general statement and what was told in *The Conversation*'s article. M told me she was surprised of the low numbers of foreign languages' Australian learners, and she could only explain this phenomenon by the expendability of English language. The article by 'Il sole 24 ore' astonished me as well. Honestly, I didn't expect Italian girls and boys to be global citizens in words, but not in facts. Maybe that's because I spend most of my time at school and my perception is that there, we are conscious of global citizenship. I also hope Italian society will became more multicultural, including foreign people instead of cutting them out because of their origins.

Another 2030 agenda's goal that caught our attention was gender equality. I am personally really into it as I enjoy reading about female figures who helped to give women a voice. In particular, we discussed about Bebe Vio as M had read about her at the university. We're both interested in women empowerment in entrepreneurial activities, too. Finally, we found a way to put all these three key topics together. We decided to create a food blog called 'Eat, cook, be organic' in order to share low waste recipes, connect with other cultures and promote examples of sustainability and women empowerment. We created a Google presentation and a Canva presentation about our common action, hoping at least it will be appreciated in the future.

I have learnt a lot from this experience. Even though I have been busier in May, I tried to put effort in the presentation and to benefit from this exchange. My English knowledge has improved and I'm happy I have managed to overcome my uncertainties in speaking foreign languages. Moreover, I have gained a deeper knowledge of global citizenship. To be honest, I think this cultural exchange is one of the virtuous behaviours we should adopt to achieve the 2030 agenda goals. In fact, trying to see the world through another person's eyes is a good way to connect with other cultures and take common actions to make the world better. Last but not least, I have gained a friend who has helped me in this journey through global issues. M has been really accommodating, presenting her experiences with kindness and enthusiasm.

E (S)

In this second intercultural exchange with the University of Melbourne my partner was S. One of the most fascinating features of my partner is in fact her childhood; she has lived and visited several countries around the world including the United Arab Emirates, where she grew up. Due to this interesting life the adjective that suits her best is for certain cosmopolitan and I would say that not only for her origins but mostly for her ability to adapt to different realities by making different places in the world her home. For me she is the perfect example of a global citizen and that's why I found [it] very interesting talking about this type of topic with her, as we live in two completely different ways. Meanwhile she is characterized by such an articulated past, I was born in Italy and I actually lived in the same place where my parents had grown up.

However, when we started to discuss some differences in our educational systems we found that the roles were reversed: while in my Italian school I am offered a range of projects and activities outside of the usual curriculum to expand my knowledge in environmental matters but also foreign culture, in Australia that does not happen. It is precisely for this reason that the article that struck me the most was that of 'ilsole24ore', the one entitled 'Italian students are global citizens in words but not in acts'. Objectively the school I attend raises the awareness of students on various global issues but at the same time I feel that this cultural involvement ends within the school walls. Despite this openness in my education world, I don't think I can define myself as a global citizen right now and that's because the interest that I have in learning more about other cultures is partially [materialized] in my everyday life. As the same journalist who wrote the article says, very often young people like me believe that to feel and define as global citizens it's just travelling to other countries, when in reality this expression conveys a much broader meaning. On the other hand, while I believe I am a global citizen in theory but not in practice, S experiences the opposite situation. In fact, if we look at the requirements of a cosmopolitan, we will find the description of a person without prejudice and very open-minded, characterized by an interest in other cultures or by the ability to adapt to countries and environments atypical of their daily life. All characteristics, as I have already said, that belong to my partner who can therefore be defined as a global citizen in practice but not in theory. In fact, S told me that the only extracurricular activities based on these themes are those offered by the language courses, so the only classes in which the interest in [others'] realities is the first requirement to attend them.

To sum up, thanks to this experience, I was able to deal with a person who, despite some similarities in character, is quite different from me. I think it was this particular thing that made our meetings even more interesting and different from my first experience, in which I found a partner that was on the same wavelength as me. In this second intercultural exchange I obviously had the opportunity to practice my language in an informal way, by talking about light topics or interests, but also in a more 'formal' one, as we talked mainly about profound topics that I don't often consider. This was the detail that I appreciated the most, being able to escape from the stress of the last days of school and the last tests by calmly discussing my opinion with a stranger on the other side of the world that shares her opinion with me.

To conclude, I'm really thankful for this experience and I'd love to have the opportunity to take part in it again.

A (L)

My international partner's name is L. The general theme we were given was the global citizenship which can be understood thanks to the knowledge of all the global problems. Through each of our meetings we have discussed and analyzed these issues pointing out the ones we considered the most dangerous. We analyzed the following problems:

- Global warning and recycling: the wastes produce pollution, for that reason they are a real cost and both economical and human resources are needed for their treatment to fix the damage they cause at the environment. We should all learn how to do a correct waste collection and help the environment as much as possible.
- Equality between men and women in different parts of the world: we think it's a very important condition because all the human beings should receive equal treatments, resources, and opportunities despite their gender. It's a global right that must be improved.
- Causes of poverty: unfortunately, there are still people who live in a condition of poverty, failing [to] satisfy their own primary needs [such] as having a house, accessing ... hospital treatments, and having an education.

- Global health: last years were [marred] by the pandemic which made us more vulnerable and, in the meantime, united [us] in searching to win COVID. We all should pay attention to our personal hygiene and do the vaccines because it's a responsibility act for ourselves, for the others and for the fragile subjects.

Me and my partner have found solutions to all these problems and summarized them into a presentation so that everyone can look and try to help the world. To analyze the points above, as well as having viewed the material uploaded to google classroom, me and L did some internet research … We have managed to meet us four times via Zoom meetings of one hour each (usually on Saturday morning). The communication went very well because we took in consideration all the appointments of the other, finding a common day for our meetings.

At a general level, it was a very beautiful and interesting experience because talking about common themes reduced the distance between Italy and Australia pointing out the need of good actions to be real global citizens.

G2 (S2)

My international partner for the Pavia–Melbourne exchange was S2 … During these weeks we have discussed many topics: we addressed all those mentioned on classroom, mainly we talked more about the differences that exist between Italy and Australia, also about the COVID current situation and the political one, but at the beginning to get to know each other better we talked about our families, our hobbies, our personalities and then we focused on preparing the presentation 'Global Citizenship'.

I really enjoyed this experience, I was worried about the language but it was not a problem. We managed to distribute enough time both to speak in Italian and to speak in English and a few times as the Italian or English vocabulary were a bit more difficult we changed them into easier words or we even tried to explain them. This experience was really helpful, interesting and enjoyable. I learned many new words and some Australian slang like 'reckon', it's another way to say 'I think'. The thing I liked the most was the fact that the meetings didn't seem forced but natural and pleasant because we always found some cultural aspects to talk about despite the age difference.

Thanks to this experience, as well as improving my level of English and being more fluent in the language, I also deepened my skills in the cultural field, I learned that the basis of global competence must be mutual respect, understanding different cultures, and also trying to create a coexistence in the name of peace and collaboration for a better world.

My partner and I thought that we should start first of all from trying to be good citizens, and this concept is certainly easier to extend it to the whole world, regardless of the religion, society and culture of each of us. It would be enough to respect more the environment around us, something that all the citizens of the world have in common. The environment must be respected and each of us should do what we can to improve it, such as simply recycle, reduce pollution using alternative and non-polluting means of transport, and also improve the soul of your city by making it greener, planting trees and plants that produce oxygen and improve the quality of the air we breathe. Reading the articles posted on classroom we learned many notions that we did not know before, such as the 2030 agenda goal that seems to be far away but is not. We also reflected a lot on the article 'Il Sole 24 ore' where in my opinion in our society, it's common to associate Italian people with the adjective 'mammoni'. I recognize that aspects of this idea is true since Italians have strong relationships with their family and cultural customs. This characteristic undoubtedly creates a [sense] of comfort associated with our culture, but closes us off from the rest of the world. Due to the globalized state of our modern society, it is automatically assumed that we are accepting and understanding of different cultures. However, I still find that aspects of the Italian society has not changed and remained racist. Through the extremist culture of adolescents that suggests that proving social predominance is another form of racism. Therefore, it is difficult to compare to other societies that have already passed this step.

F2 (L)

My partner's name is L … We spoke about global citizenship and the differences between Italy and Australia in handling this issue. We exchanged opinions about many different topics connected also to the Agenda 2030. In particular we dealt with the first two points: No poverty and Zero Hunger. Something that surprised me was that the percentage of people who suffer from hunger in Australia is much less than the percentage in Italy. This makes me think that the government still needs to do a lot of work to improve the poor condition of a huge number of people in my country. I learnt that everyone can contribute to reducing hunger in the world starting from doing what we can as individuals. We can make our voice be heard protesting peacefully against the government indifference, helping charities by making even small donations. Helping others can be very rewarding.

What I found really surprising was the fact that only a small number of students in Australia study a foreign language. I feel that even if English is a language spoken worldwide, learning another language can enrich everybody's lives as it allows you to broaden your horizon and it may also help you understand other cultures better.

Apart from the topics on global citizenship we had a chance to discuss everyday situations. For instance we talked a lot about COVID-19 and how we lived lockdown both in Italy and Australia. During this second exchange I also learnt new vocabulary such as lippy, brekkie and colloquial expressions like 'To cost big bikkies'.

I enjoyed meeting someone who lives on the other side of the world and even though we were born in different countries, I found out we have something in common.

7

Designing for adult language learning in a robot-assisted language learning context

Grace Yue Qi, Yuping Wang and Nian-Shing Chen

1. Introduction

There is a consensus that digital technology has become an integral part of language acquisition and pedagogy. From computer-mediated communication to augmented, virtual and mixed reality, researchers have demonstrated the affordances and effectiveness of technology that enhances the experience of language learners and teachers (Klimanova, 2021). However, as noted in a large body of literature (Flavin, 2012), the disruptive potential of technology has not been maximised to empower pedagogy that is appropriate for facilitating learning both inside and outside classrooms (Reinders et al., 2022). In the context of higher education, for example, universities have promoted the use of uniformised digital platforms and technological tools as strengthening student–teacher interaction, student engagement and the overall tertiary learning experience (Flavin, 2012). However, integrating digital technology into teaching and learning alone does not necessarily lead to effective teaching and learning. This is partly because, often, technology is adopted for its own sake and teaching with it is not positioned in clear pedagogical goals or strategies. In other words, digital technology is often employed to facilitate reproducing existing pedagogical approaches rather transforming or innovating them (Aljawarneh, 2020; Fry & Love, 2011; Margaryan et al., 2011; Rapanta et al., 2021). This trend is still relevant today, although some studies have reported practices transformed by capitalising on the affordances of enabling technologies, such as mobile technology (Lan & Tam, 2022; Stockwell, 2021), virtual reality (VR) (Lan, 2021) and robotic technology (Cheng et al. 2021).

The Australian tertiary sector has witnessed growing diversity in learning needs in different language learning environments. This diversity reflects the consequence of multifaceted globalisation and mobility—that is to say that everything and everyone, including language and culture, are mobile and fluid in real and virtual spaces (Benson, 2021; Kramsch, 2009). In this sense, finding ways to diversify learning opportunities and strategies becomes vital for frontline educators to meet individual learners' needs. One possible way is to engage digital technologies in language education, which seems to have become a norm amid the COVID-19 disruption. Building teachers' content and pedagogical knowledge to (continually) explore methodological innovations is essential (Qi, 2021). What is missing, though, is the lens of design for learning, which acknowledges that learning cannot be designed, but can be designed *for* (Goodyear & Dimitriadis, 2013). In considering teaching as a design science (Laurillard, 2012) that is multidimensional from a temporal perspective, design is part of the pre-active form of teaching and can be regarded as a type of planning, conceived as 'the intelligent centre of the whole teaching–learning lifecycle' (Goodyear, 2015, p. 32). Further, design often includes a process of (re)design based on the interactive forms of teaching (facilitation of learning in the formal educational setting with teachers and peers), the post-active forms of teaching (evaluation, reflection and assessment) and the analysis of data collected for subsequent design decisions (Goodyear & Dimitriadis, 2013). As Shuell (1986, p. 429) noted, 'what the student does is actually more important in determining what is learned than what the teacher does'. In other words, students possess agentive power to capitalise on learning potential in the process of task performance. It is essential for teachers to nurture this power through task design and facilitation—that is, to develop their capacity to design good learning tasks and to clearly communicate task specifications to students (Goodyear, 2015). The concept of design for learning foregrounds teaching as a design science and a moral activity that:

> intentionally shapes what other people do, in order to help them learn, and later in turn shapes their future actions, capabilities, dispositions, ways of comprehending themselves and the world, and so on.
>
> (Goodyear, 2015, p. 27)

Since design for learning is vital for transformative practices, this calls for the repositioning of *teachers-as-designers*.

This chapter draws on the nuances of disruption and diversification in language education and illustrates a design pattern developed in a pilot study. It is argued that the concept of design for learning must be integrated into computer-assisted language learning (CALL) and technology-enhanced language learning (TELL), leveraging the capacity of researchers, teachers and instructional designers and technological affordances to ultimately achieve transformative pedagogical practice. As exemplified in our case study, which pilots a robot-assisted language learning (RALL) task informed by research, a design-based practice that incorporates technology is urgently needed in Australian tertiary language programs and beyond. This is an essential first step for design for learning to become an integral part of tertiary language programs, reshaping student understandings of language learning and helping them to experience languages in new ways (Darvin & Norton, 2017; Norton, 2013).

2. CALL/TELL: Digital technology as an impetus for disruption

CALL/TELL research has experienced exponential growth and has explored various aspects of language teaching and learning. Gillespie (2020) presented the most researched and under-researched topics covered by 777 articles published in highly ranked CALL journals between 2006 and 2016. He found that writing, computer-mediated communication (CMC), vocabulary and teacher education were among the most active areas, whereas pedagogy, games and blended learning were the least active topics. CALL pedagogy, despite a temporarily strong focus in the 2016 literature, remains under-explored over the years. As Gillespie (2020) noted, most research focused on language skills, alongside vocabulary, grammar and CMC. Conversely, research into advanced language learning and integration of language, culture and context in learning and teaching was significantly lacking. Another synthesis review article, by Chen et al. (2021), investigated CALL research trends by drawing from 1,295 articles published over a 25-year period ending in 2020. Also focusing on prestigious journals in the field, their findings revealed that the development of mobile-assisted language learning, blended learning and project-based learning has attracted the most interest. VR and virtual world games, the mixed use of mobile and other applications in various contexts, and the integration of digital multimodality into project-based learning have also drawn attention from researchers and educators.

Both review studies revealed that CALL is a growing area of research. It has gone beyond 'the search for and study of the computer applications in language teaching and learning' (Levy, 1997, p. 1) and moved towards the exploration of the diversity of computer technology used in and integrated into 'a language learning context' (Hubbard, 2009, p. 2). The refreshed definition of CALL research by Hubbard (2009) considers not only 'the development and use of technology applications in language teaching and learning' (Levy & Hubbard, 2005, p. 143), but also 'learners learning language in any context with, through, and around computer technologies' (Egbert, 2005, p. 4). We share Hubbard's (2009) definition of CALL and make connections with what language learners do for their learning today: CALL has been part of their life and they now 'have greater control over choices of what, why, where and when they learn' (Sun, 2021, p. 1061).

However, not all teachers are tech-savvy, and they are often constrained by technology accessibility and affordances in the learning context (Sun, 2021). Face-to-face instruction therein remains a key and preferred teaching mode, with digital technology employed as an add-on tool for communications and collaborative learning in schools (Goldie, 2016). Even teachers who have envisioned the benefit of digital technology for learning appear reluctant to try CALL/TELL in most cases (Biesta et al., 2015).

During the global pandemic, when teaching online became an unprecedented norm, teachers were forced to find ways of adapting pedagogical approaches, with the necessary support of digital technology (Le et al., 2022). A number of studies have brought teacher agency to the fore to explore language teachers' emergency response to online teaching. Ashton (2022) examined the agency of four secondary school teachers in New Zealand and called for teacher professional development programs to better prepare teachers for different kinds of teaching environments in response to increasing demands in day-to-day teaching. Exploring teacher agency in a Chinese university teaching context, Chen's (2022) study highlighted the important dynamics between digital affordances and teacher agency under pandemic situations. Her study offered some helpful teaching strategies, including better supporting students to understand task instructions by deconstructing and modelling task procedures in advance, and allowing for multiple submissions to lower the stakes of testing and to nurture students' self-learning. Both studies have reinforced that teachers' consistent exploration, practice, evaluation and reflection are crucial to better position themselves to positively cope with digital stress and to build confidence in using digital technology in teaching practice (Chen, 2022).

The aftermath of the pandemic has bolstered the growth of CALL/TELL, but it cannot guarantee transformative pedagogical practice. To effectively integrate technology into language teaching/learning, with the aim of innovating and transforming learning, rather than reproducing traditional teaching practices, as Flavin (2012) warned, it is time for CALL/TELL researchers and language teachers to rethink and redesign contemporary learning experiences that learners desire (eBeetham & Sharpe, 2013, 2020). Egbert et al. (2018) identified eight major gaps in CALL research, including a lack of information and understanding about implementing CALL tasks on a day-to-day basis in language classrooms. They urged CALL scholars to pay specific attention to how language teachers plan, implement, assess and think about CALL tasks both inside and outside the classroom, throughout the curriculum and school year, and how the process may affect learning progress and outcomes. This holistic approach to focusing on the process of CALL is essential to ensure optimal development and integration of CALL, which can significantly enhance the quality of language teaching and learning outcomes if teachers are supported throughout the design and implementation process (Rienties et al., 2018).

3. Design for learning in CALL and RALL

3.1. Design for learning in CALL research and practice

Connecting CALL to the theoretical concepts and approaches of design for learning could potentially address Egbert et al.'s (2018) concern that more CALL research is required to explore language teachers' design, implementation and assessment process, and to relate that process to students' learning progression and outcomes. Integrating CALL and design for learning requires 'a shift of design thinking from the traditional design-as-final products to design-as-ongoing process' (Sun, 2021, p. 1066). Several studies have looked into the needs and challenges of preparing future language teachers for evolving educational contexts and have advocated for more research and practice in forming teachers-as-designers (Colpaert, 2010; Kuure et al., 2016; Mor & Mogilevsky, 2013; Qi et al., 2023).

Associated with teachers-as-designers, research has focused on interventions aiming to support teaching with technology. One well-known example is the technology, pedagogy and content knowledge (TPACK) framework developed by Mishra and Koehler (2006), which guides reflective practice on the equal relationship between technology, pedagogy and content as teachers create designs for learning (Rolf, 2021). However, undertaking reflective practice grounded in TPACK does not necessarily lead to good design, because design prioritises teachers' ability to create and share their designs, with the emphasis on learners, the context and processes of learning (Law et al., 2017). Similarly, Puentedura's (2014) SAMR model (substitution, augmentation, modification and redefinition) also consistently emphasises teachers using technology as a means of examining what they can and should do. While this focus allows teachers to progress through the hierarchy from substitution and augmentation to modification and redefinition, learning is highlighted as a product rather than as a process (Hamilton et al., 2016). Critical accounts of both TPACK and SAMR have highlighted the dynamic nature of teaching and learning with technology. As Koehler et al. (2014) noted, it is imperative for teachers to understand the relationships between teaching, technology and learning for nurturing students' growth and achievement across space and time. According to Goodyear and Dimitriadis (2013), design for learning is a practical strategy, but also needs to be theorised, taking into account questions such as 'who is doing the learning, why do they learn, and what do they learn and how do they learn?' These questions encompass the three main components of design for learning: 1) design of the task, 2) design of the physical architecture and 3) design of the social architecture for learning (Carvalho & Goodyear, 2013).

In considering teaching as design and teachers-as-designers (Goodyear, 2015; Goodyear & Yang, 2009; Laurillard et al., 2013), it is important that teacher-designers are encouraged to learn from and build on the work of others to inform decisions they make in their design. This is often achieved through teachers sharing teaching ideas and good practices. Specifically, teachers are expected to develop knowledge and skills of design that have a positive impact on sharing, exchanging, discussing and improving their educational processes (Ghislandi & Raffaghelli, 2015). To achieve this, it is necessary to develop a structured, systematic design approach in a common, simple and accessible design language (Sun, 2021). This design approach helps to bridge the proximity in testing, expanding understanding of the problem and finding ways of handling the problem; and support collaboration and meaningful conversations among instructional designers, researchers, and teacher-designers in the design process to achieve a shared goal. Alexander et al. (1977) suggested a patterns-based approach—or, put simply, design patterns. The benefits of implementing Sun's (2021, p. 1064) design patterns include that they act as a 'design tool', mediate 'concise and accurate communication' among stakeholders in the design process, 'disseminate expert knowledge to novice[s]' and offer 'reusable solutions to commonly occurring problems at the very heart of sustainability of design' (see Avgeriou et al., 2003; Frizell & Hubscher, 2008; Goodyear, 2005).

Design patterns are adopted to support e-learning (Goodyear, 2005), but they have not yet been widely used in CALL/TELL. Sun (2021) adopted the pattern by Alexander et al. (1977)—including problem, context and solution, and added pedagogical underpinning as the fourth dimension (Chatteur et al., 2010; Laurillard, 2012)—in developing her online Chinese language courses at a New Zealand university. She argues that pedagogical underpinning indicates pedagogical patterns that are powerful for teacher-designers for not only narrating a sequence of teaching–learning activities, but also for relating and mapping them to pedagogical principles. Her creation of the fourth dimension is also inspired by Goodyear's (2005) modelled design patterns in which design experience, educational values and research-based ideas are highlighted. When aiming for effective designs, according to Chatteur et al. (2010), it is crucial to embed pedagogical theories, case studies and teaching strategies and tactics.

Sun (2021) chose a number of design tasks that captured the pedagogy and learning principles informed by her design for learning. Adopting the format of the e-learning pedagogy-embedded pattern (Chatteur et al., 2010), she incorporated six sequential components into her design pattern:

1. context
2. problem
3. literature search for solution (pedagogical theories, case studies, teaching strategies and tactics)
4. solution
5. consideration of other patterns
6. references (presentation of literature used in the design).

Most worthwhile, as Sun (2021) noted, was her experience as a teacher-designer in the process of design. The design patterns developed in her research gave her flexibility and space for reflection and improvements over time:

> I felt that I was constantly prompted to reflect and connect pedagogical values and principles to the design patterns. I also found that the reflection was extremely helpful, e.g., it helped explain why some tasks had worked better or been favoured more by students. I also felt inadequate in trying to understand the pedagogical principles behind some of the tasks, and it was a valuable learning experience to research the related literature.
>
> (Sun, 2021, p. 1078)

Sun's design patterns and her reflective account provide us with a holistic view embracing different models to inform effective pedagogical solutions foregrounded by the concept of design for learning. Keeping the sequence of problem, context and solution, we focus on the pedagogical underpinning of each of the three components. We also need to expand the pattern by adding diversification as a new component to emphasise our commitment to accommodating diverse learning needs. In addition, ongoing reflective practice is critical for learning designers as they progress through each step of the design process, following the design pattern and informed by practices from the classroom. We unpack the development of our design pattern below.

3.2. Considerations of design for learning in RALL

Despite growing academic interest in RALL, particularly in the context of young learners (Vogt et al., 2017), to our knowledge, few researchers have engaged with RALL as an emerging subfield of CALL/TELL and design patterns. Most studies in RALL have highlighted design-based research (DBR) as a widely accepted qualitative research approach, highlighting collaborations between researchers, practitioners and instructional designers (Belpaeme et al., 2018). The DBR approach poses a series of design principles, procedures and practices, mostly through various iterations of tests and refinements, that ensure that the design is constantly informed by the results of such tests (Cheng et al., 2021). Consequently, DBR allows and encourages a collaborative process of design, involving practitioners and researchers, to co-develop educational interventions to bridge the theoretical research and educational practice (Getenet, 2019). Cheng et al. (2021) were one of the very first teams looking at learning design in RALL for young learners. As a collaborative team consisting of language teachers, instructional designers, and educational technologists and researchers, they created and designed an authoring system of robots and tangible objects. This authoring system enabled young learners to experience a scenario-based interactive language learning environment. Their system design and development process included four cycles, each lasting 18 weeks. Each cycle was constructed in four phases: needs analysis, system prototyping, system evaluation, and improving system functionalities and usability. A fifth phase, reflection, was added after all four cycles were completed. Their study revealed the following key findings:

1. Cross-disciplinary expertise is required, and factors concerning children's language and cognitive development, child–robot interactions, and hardware and software design and evaluation should all be considered in a comprehensive design framework.
2. The design team needs to consider effectiveness-related issues to mitigate usability concerns, including what is the effective setting for learners, in their case, for child–robot interaction.
3. For child–robot effective interaction, the tablet should be smaller in size and attached to the robot's hand or belly to avoid distraction.

Notwithstanding the difference in target learners, these results are worthy of note for our design patterns approach.

Focusing on adult learners learning Chinese as an additional language, we—as a group of researchers, language teachers and instructional designers—were inspired to work towards tasks designed to cater for different learning needs. Our design approach—adopting a socially embodied robot—emphasises RALL as a viable means of facilitating adult learners' language practice in a real-life context. This is especially important when learners' opportunities and resources for acquiring and using the language they are learning are constrained, even in a multilingual and multicultural society such as Australia.

4. The study

Informed by design for learning, this study developed a design pattern specifically for guiding RALL design. Through this pattern, we designed a multimodal language learning task for adult learners to complete, with the support of a suite of emerging technologies, including a robot, a tablet and tangible objects. This task focused on facilitating our intermediate-level learners (second year) to acquire a Chinese sentence structure, the ba-construction, in a real-life context. It was evaluated by five participant learners in a Chinese language class at an Australian university. We received institutional human ethics approval to proceed with the pilot study in 2021. Five participant learners, two females and three males aged between 20 and 25, volunteered for the study. They were the only five learners enrolled in the intermediate-level Mandarin course offered for non-heritage learners at this university. The following two sections explain how we developed a RALL design pattern and how this design pattern was implemented and evaluated.

4.1. Developing a RALL design pattern

As illustrated in Figure 7.1, our design pattern comprises four components, *context*, *problem*, *solution* and *diversification*, together presenting an overarching view of the design stages. Specifically, *context* refers to the situated design for learning, focusing on task overview and organisation; *problem* highlights why educational interventions are necessary; and *solution* presents the task designed for learning intervention. Instead of seeing the pedagogical underpinnings as an additional dimension, our design pattern allows teachers-as-designers to elicit details by inquiring into, and reflecting on, how targeted goals can be reached in each component, and incorporating context-dependent pedagogical values, factors and theories with evidence and visions (Goodyear, 2005). Additional factors such as people, things, place, information, ubiquitous technologies, space and time are considered in the reflection process (Benson, 2021). Following the solution stage, our design pattern presents pedagogical suggestions at the *diversification* stage to help diversify the design, potentially involving design modifications. Diversification is a featured component of our design pattern. Based on the research-informed piloting, the diversification stage provides space for ongoing (re)design that considers learners' evolving learning needs (Goodyear, 2015) and is centred around design for learning.

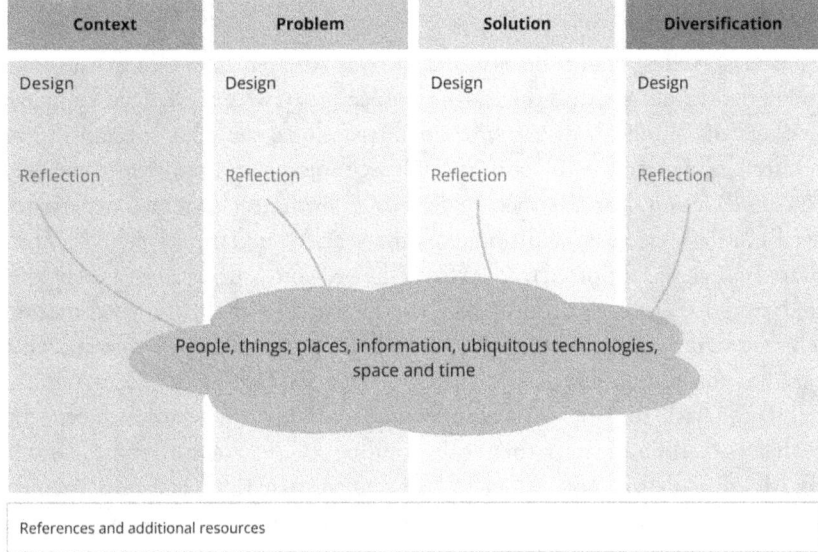

Figure 7.1. A design pattern for teachers designing for adult language learning at university
Source: Authors.

4.2. Implementing and evaluating the RALL design pattern

The design pattern discussed above can be further illustrated with reference to the design process of the pilot study (see Table 7.1). Aiming to evaluate the validity and effectiveness of the design pattern, the pilot study adopted a combination of qualitative and quantitative research approaches and involved a research team comprising two language teachers-as-designers and instructional designers, and five adult learners as the participants. Primary data gathered from the participants, who were enrolled in an intermediate Chinese course in an Australian university, include their responses to pre- and post-study surveys and their group discussions upon completing a learning task. The research and design teams undertook reflections throughout the design process, drawing on their observation of the participant learners taking part in the task and individual recounts of their experience. Descriptive statistics and thematic analysis were employed to analyse the data collected from the learner participants and reflective notes shared by the research team.

4.2.1. Context

Context specifies where the task design was situated, the role of the class teacher and students, and the learning objectives. Two experienced language teachers of Chinese worked with an instructional designer specialising in research and practice on educational technology to brainstorm the key challenges adult learners face in learning. Both teachers had experience teaching Chinese as an additional language at Australian universities. They shared the view, supported by data from the pre-study survey discussed below, that students generally found the ba-construction challenging to master. This is mainly because there is no equivalent English structure that students can draw on or that teachers can refer to when explaining the construction. While the basic sentence structure seems to be straightforward, subject – ba – object – verb, indicating the result or influence of an action, most learners find it difficult to know when to use this construction. Learners become even more confused when encountering variations of this construction. In view of these difficulties, the research team decided to create real-life contexts for students to use the ba-construction, hoping to enhance their awareness of when and how to use it appropriately.

4.2.2. Problem

Part of a typical design approach, taking advantage of the practical experience of the two language teachers, is to see the problem as 'a symptom of some larger problem' (Goodyear, 2015). The account of both teachers at the initial brainstorming sessions initiated the *problem* dimension in the design pattern, identifying areas that needed educational interventions corresponding with research findings and visions. These suggested the need for enabling technologies to help solve the *problem*, given the constraint of class time, the feature of the ba-construction in using the language for communications and the need for technologies enabling multimedia as resources in support of learning.

A pre-design survey was administered to understand students' general view of the difficulty level of the ba-construction and self-assessment of their acquisition of the construction after they had learnt it during the semester. The questions in the survey were multiple-choice, created by the research team based on the two language teachers' experience and student feedback received in previous years of teaching. The questions aimed to capture a quick and spontaneous assessment of student understanding and mastery of the ba-construction. The research team sought external validation of the survey questions from experts. The students were asked to provide their perception of the difficulty level of the ba-construction and identify support that could potentially help them acquire the construction. Four of the five students highlighted ways that could support them to confidently acquire the ba-construction. They nominated having more practice using the ba-construction in 'scenario-based activities with others in class', or in 'a real-life situation', as the most favourable approaches. One student added other possibilities, such as 'having more translation exercise' and 'receiving more explanation about the use of the ba-construction'. Another student, who specifically indicated that the ba-construction was difficult to learn, wanted to 'practise using the ba-construction in a real-life situation'. According to one student, the ba-construction 'is not too difficult and not too easy. [I] understand most of the time but still need help sometimes.'

Based on the teachers' feedback, the pre-study survey results and the research team's assessment of the affordance of the authoring system developed by Cheng et al. (2021, see below), we created a 'Making Dumplings' task design as a *solution* to the problem. This *solution* presents a research-informed, data-based task design and evaluation process, supported by the research team's ongoing reflection.

4.2.3. Solution

At the *solution* stage, our RALL design adopted an authoring system developed by Cheng et al. (2021) to facilitate task completion in an immersive Mandarin learning context. This system enables interaction between the learner, a robot named Kebbi, a tablet and tangible objects with barcodes attached. An example of such an interaction is presented in Figure 7.2. In this task design, Kebbi is a human-like social agent, facilitating the making and cooking of dumplings by two students. Each pair, with one student acting as head chef and the other as sous chef, carefully listens to Kebbi's step-by-step instructions about how to make dumplings and scans the barcode of each food ingredient and piece of kitchenware using a barcode reader. The scanning of the barcodes provides the learners with hands-on experience of using the ba-construction, as it enables Kebbi's recognition of the learners' moves. Following Kebbi's instruction, the head chef tells the sous chef what to do and how to do it step by step in Chinese. The system also allows learners to ask Kebbi to repeat an instruction that they fail to understand (see the interactions between the learners and Kebbi in Figure 7.2). The tablet is used to provide extra help with students' understanding of the robot's speech by displaying images and texts. The task enables students to listen to the robot, speak with their peers and Kebbi in Chinese (English may also be used) and handle real objects, creating a real-life context for making dumplings. The task design process following the proposed design pattern is presented in Table 7.1.

Figure 7.2. An excerpt of learner-robot interactions
Source: Authors.

7. DESIGNING FOR ADULT LANGUAGE LEARNING IN A ROBOT-ASSISTED LANGUAGE LEARNING CONTEXT

Table 7.1. The task design process for making dumplings

Context	Problem	Solution	Diversification
This pattern support students practising the use of ba-construction in a real-life context, 'Making Dumplings', with a robot and IoT-based toys (or, if possible, ingredients and kitchenware required for dumpling making).	Chinese language learners in the tertiary setting have struggled to efficiently develop proficiency due to limited input and practice opportunities in and beyond classroom (Wang & Qi, 2018). *How can technology help create an environment allowing for embodied and situational learning experience?*	Adopt Cheng et al.'s (2021) authoring system with a robot, IoT-based toys (in this case, food ingredients and kitchenware for dumplings making), and a tablet, through which the learners listen to the robot's instructions and work with the robot and their peers to accomplish the task of 'Making Dumplings'. The tablet, displaying learning content, highlights key information in Chinese characters to support the task completion. The robot, called Kebbi, performs as a human-like teaching aid, facilitating learning and interacting with learners with body and facial movements. Each food ingredient and piece of kitchenware used for making dumplings is tagged with a specific barcode. Using the barcode reader to scan ingredients and kitchenware, learners follow Kebbi's guidance and the learning content displayed on the tablet. Do so, they will end up having dumplings made, cooked and eaten as the indication of accomplishing the task (see Figure 7.3).	Teachers are encouraged to use this design for learning beyond the class time, either on campus or online. By setting up one set of the authoring system (a robot, a tablet and IoT-based toys), students can come and practise individually, or pair up/team up and practise with their study partner/s. It is also possible that students co-design a modified task with the teachers-as-designers: for instance, making a sandwich, a cup of coffee/tea, or something related to their life experience, for their best interest and learning needs.
Students work in pairs along with the robot, Kebbi, in one-week class times.	Ba-construction, non-translatable in English, commonly used in the transitive event, in which an agent performs some actions that affect an entity, is one of the most challenging grammatical structures for learners of Chinese (Yang, 2020). *How can this complex construction be learnt and mastered?*		
Teachers set up the classroom. They also provide a brief before the practice, casual/informal feedback for improvements wherever possible, and a debrief after each pair completes the practice.	It is crucial for learners to develop autonomy and ownership for an enhanced learning experience with digital technologies. Text-based materials, even with the support of mobile devices or other emerging technologies, have proven to be less attractive to learners who are more in favour of a multimedia program (Kuo, 2015), allowing for engagement, embodiment and interactivity, including human–robot interactions.	Teachers are involved in designing the task by drafting a task script, including learning contents (words, phrases and sentences) for making dumplings, and instructional language for the robot to perform in facilitating the task undertaking sequentially. After converting the task script to a coding script, several rounds of testing and refinements are played out before formally launching the task for learning.	
The ongoing practice encourages students to practise more in other potential contexts to apply and use ba-construction as well as reflect and make improvements in communications.			

161

Context	Problem	Solution	Diversification
Reflection on the role of teachers in design and facilitation; the collaborative task design process with various expertise; students' needs.	**Reflection** on the ideas to address the multifaceted issues arising, including integrating technology into language education for an enhanced learning experience.	**Reflection** is vital at the solution stage, where language teachers, instructional designers and technical specialists work collaboratively to test and refine the design. With students' feedback on their learning experience, the design team's reflection focuses on their observation, improvements and the possibility of diversifying the design in response to various learners' needs.	**Reflection** among the task design team is necessary. The focus can be on two aspects: design and implementation, taking into account students, their learning experience (individual, in pairs/groups), their language development, their interactions with Kebbi (the robot) and the tablet, user-friendliness of ubiquitous technologies in the task, learning environment for the task, spatial-temporal effects and other issues arising from the design team and student feedback.

Source: Authors.

4.2.4. Diversification

Diversification, the final stage in the design process, provides an avenue for language teachers-as-designers to rethink and reconsider possibilities of redesigning the task for different learning needs. This includes inviting the class tutor to help diversify the design for learners needing more practice out of class, and having students, as co-designers, design new tasks that are of interest to them in real-life contexts. Our developed design pattern can serve as a useful guide, enriching diversification by facilitating either personalised or collaborative learning. It is crucial to consider various levels of diversity carefully. This may include accommodating different learning contexts and environments, as well as acknowledging the varying levels of language proficiency and experiences with language and culture.

4.2.5. Evaluation of the task design

During the design process, multiple tests took place, followed by rounds of refinement of the design, particularly the technical part, led by the instructional designer/researcher, as well as volunteer learners of Chinese at other institutions. The five students who completed the pre-study survey piloted the task with the authoring system installed, as shown in Figure 7.3. The design team observed the process together with the class tutor. Observation notes were recorded by the team, incorporating students' interactions with the robot and their peers, and issues arising throughout the process. Upon completion of the task, an informal group discussion took place, and a post-study survey was distributed onsite to gather students' immediate feedback on their experience.

Figure 7.4 presents selective findings from the post-study survey in which 32 statements (Appendix 1) were provided for students to indicate their agreement from 1 (strong disagreement) to 5 (strong agreement). The statements were created based on the knowledge of the research team and their observations of the rounds of testing undertaken before the piloting. They were reviewed by external researchers who have knowledge of Chinese teaching and learning. Students indicated their level of consensus regarding the positive experience they had with the designed task. Specifically, they believed that the task provided them with a culturally immersive learning experience and allowed them to simultaneously listen to the robot, speak much more Chinese using the ba-construction and engage in the hands-on practice of making real dumplings. Most importantly, they strongly agreed that, after this task, they knew the ba-construction better and felt more confident using it. In terms of interactions with the robot, they showed a positive attitude towards the robot's clear instructions that were easy for them to follow while accomplishing the task. The task was designed in such a way that it not only encouraged the students to reproduce the ba sentences spoken by Kebbi in a meaningful context but also prompted the students to paraphrase the sentences they heard from Kebbi when interacting with their partner. Students' overall experience of learning Chinese in this task was satisfactory. However, they also pointed out a few challenges they experienced in the task, for example, the lack of familiarity with certain key vocabulary items needed for completing the task, as pointed out by two participants, even though the vocabulary needed for the task had been taught in advance (mean = 2.80, standard deviation = 1.30). Although, overall, it was a positive experience for the students, the activity was challenging, as multiple actions were happening almost simultaneously: the students had to listen to the robot, understand its instructions, relay the instruction to their partner while scanning the objects needed for each step and performing the required actions, such as washing and cutting chives (see Figure 7.2) (mean = 3.8, standard deviation = 0.45).

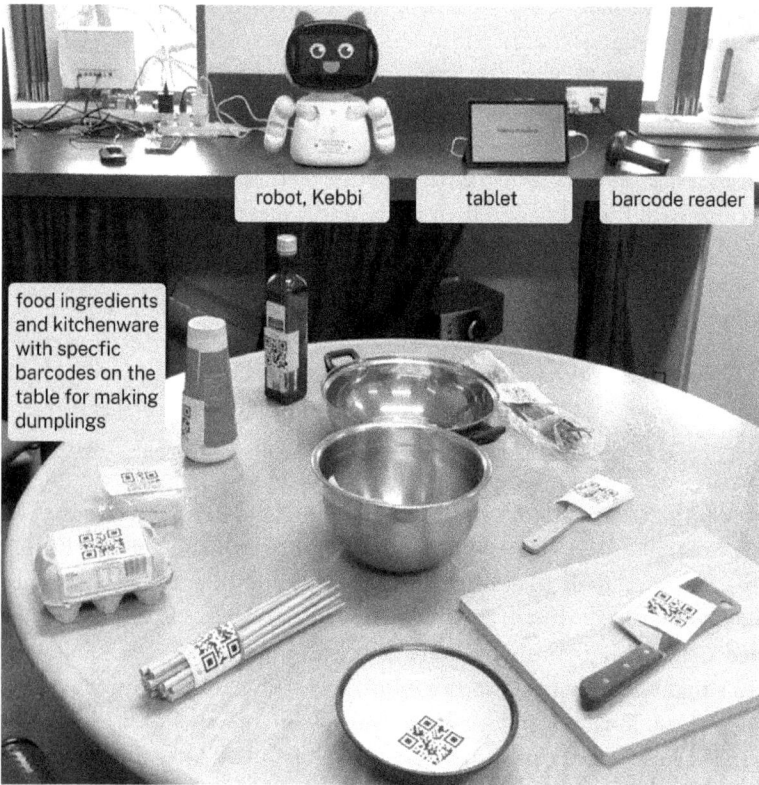

Figure 7.3. Making dumplings with a robot, a tablet and tangible objects (food ingredients and kitchenware)

Source: Authors.

7. DESIGNING FOR ADULT LANGUAGE LEARNING IN A ROBOT-ASSISTED LANGUAGE LEARNING CONTEXT

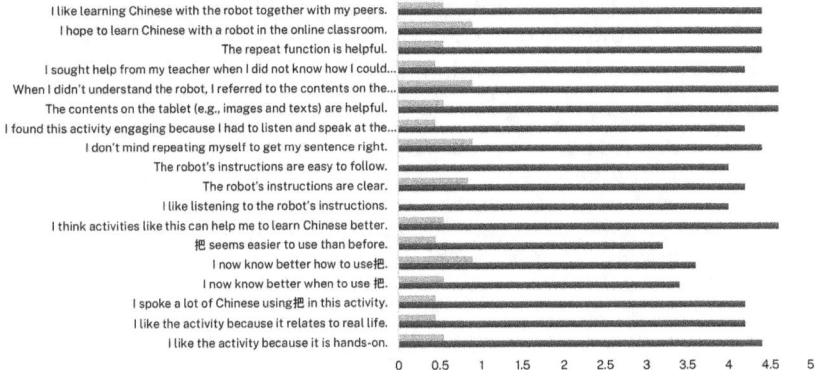

Figure 7.4. Students' positive perceptions of statements incorporated in the post-study survey
Note: Mean and standard deviation presented.
Source: Authors.

4.2.6. Reflections

The research and design teams shared reflective notes on LINE, a social media platform, the day after the students completed the task in class. Figure 7.5 demonstrates some of the key interactions between language teachers-as-designers and the instructional designer on LINE. The design team acknowledged the challenges students encountered as indicated in their post-study survey (see Figure 7.4).

A week later, the research team gathered again on Zoom to reflect more deeply and critically on their observations, particularly of students' experiences, and discuss possible improvements to the task design. The discussion focused on two aspects: task design and implementation. A thematic analysis of the Zoom interactions among the design team revealed concerns over the task design, including the necessity of using a tablet for supporting learners' understanding, speech detection issues and the robot's performance in the task operation. Although students found the tablet helpful for displaying images and texts that provided extra support for comprehension, the design team was reluctant to positively appraise this tool, reflecting instead on the fundamental purpose of the task. One of the teachers asked: 'what was the task for? are we focusing on students' language development or their [use] of the ba-construction for communications?' The team felt that the tablet, while beneficial in terms of improving students' understanding of the content, could be a distraction, diverting them from concentrating on listening, and delaying their response to the robot and performance of actions required to

165

complete the task. Part of the solution, the instructional designer suggested, was to reconsider the role of each device and its functionality in alignment with the purpose of the intervention that the task aimed to achieve.

We observed that students found it hard to say the sentences following Kebbi's instructions, especially with the longer sentences. Two possible reasons for this: 1. They were not familiar with the vocabulary and got stuck with the words so Kebbi wouldn't accept that. 2. They did not listen to Kebbi carefully for the first time and relied on reading the sentences from the tablet. This also slowed them down.

One thing I am not sure is sometimes the students said things almost perfectly but Kebbi still didn't accept them. This is the most frustrating thing to the students. I think Google Home is more tolerant about different accents in English speeches.

Thanks for sharing the photos. And Yes I learned a lot from observing students' behaviours and obstacles. Will think about how to improve our APP design from the technical perspective. You and [the other teacher-as-designer] could think about how to improve paper script design to avoid or work around some of the challenges students facing.

Thanks [instructional designer] for conducting this activity with [University] students. It's a great success and the students ate all the dumplings they made! Kebbi behaved admirably well except she found it hard to understand aussie accent. [...] Both the class tutor and the students commented on the fast speed of Kebbi speaking.

Figure 7.5. The design team's immediate reflection, shared on the social media platform LINE
Source: Authors.

As the design team pointed out, this meant rethinking 'what might be the preferred way for learners to learn or practice'. The students involved in the task found the digital content on the tablet useful. It supported their learning, as the images of food ingredients and kitchenware and words spoken by the robot helped their comprehension of the task requirements. However, others might prefer practising with the robot only so that the robot becomes a more social, human-like figure. The chosen design was expected to support individual learners' engagement in the task and bridge the gap for students progressing towards interacting with other people for meaningful and effective communication in various contexts. Our team's critical discussion, reflecting on the design and implementation of the task and inquiring into each component of the design pattern, is fundamental to theorising the design for future learning. This practice-informed research demonstrates teaching as a design science, in which research evidence and aims are taken into account to revamp students' situated activity (Goodyear, 2015).

Students also mentioned seeking support from their class tutor when they encountered difficulties in accomplishing the task. The design team responded to this feedback by raising concerns about:

> how might the class tutor think about their involvement in our RALL task? what about other teachers if they attempt to adopt our task for their learners and learning environments and contexts?

This reflection prompted consideration of the role of class tutors and potential pedagogical approaches in support of task design, as well as students' ability to learn the content and apply it in real-life contexts. The two language teachers discussed the potential engagement of class tutors in the next round of the task redesigning process to better tailor the design to meet students' needs more effectively. Both suggested that the interaction between the students and the robot should receive more attention in task design at the diversification stage.

The language teachers also reflected on their roles in the research-led design process. Similar to Sun (2021), one of them reflected:

> I don't know if I am a learning designer as the literature suggests. I know I am a teacher and a learning facilitator caring for my students' learning progress and performance. I have to admit, though, this task design process with my fellow teacher and instructional designer helped me realise my accountability and professional identity in language education. I enjoyed brainstorming with my team members and came up with creative ideas that eventually became our creation of learning resources for students. Working along with the established design pattern provided me with a fresh insight into what learning design means to me, our team and students. Our collaborative process with the design team brings so much inspiration for me to carry on as a teacher, a facilitator, a researcher and possibly a designer.

Here we see this language teacher becoming aware of the multiple roles she had taken on in language education. Although her devotion to her role as a designer was emerging, she valued the experience of engaging with her fellow teacher and the instructional designer in the task design process. It might seem presumptuous for a teacher to claim a new professional identity after having a positive experience. Yet this teacher was clearly aware of, and had considered the possibility of, having a new identity added to her other roles in her professional life in the foreseeable future (Ashton, 2022). Her growing sense of being a teacher-designer was seeded in, evolving through and situated in (ongoing) collaboration with her fellow teacher-researcher and instructional designer-researcher.

5. Discussion and conclusion

Drawing on the design patterns for CALL/TELL (Sun, 2021), we developed a design pattern consisting of four sequential stages for a RALL task design—context, problem, solution and diversification. Within each stage, our design pattern enabled us to identify, explore and discuss possible design ideas and pedagogical underpinnings, alongside ongoing reflection, considering people, things, information, place, ubiquitous technologies, space and time in a sustainable, sequential manner. Our creation of the design pattern reflects design for learning in principle, highlighting language teachers-as-designers who are encouraged to explore ways in which they can design for students' personalised and collaborative learning (Goodyear, 2015).

Piloting the task design with five students facilitated our further examination of the validity and effectiveness of the design pattern developed in this study. As confirmed by the students, the dumpling-making task allowed learners to fully engage in hands-on task completion in a real-life setting, mobilising their listening and speaking skills as well as grammatical knowledge about the ba-construction.

In addition, closely examining the task design process enabled the two language teachers to develop their awareness of, and strengthen their confidence in, their teacher-as-designer identity and capacity. Their agentic actions in taking the lead in designing, testing, refining and piloting the task, and observing and reflecting on the process of design and implementation, demonstrated that digital competence is one of the key design competencies needed for effective task design in RALL (Rolf, 2021). At the stage of diversification, we considered students' feedback and the potential involvement of class tutors in task design refinement, as our design approach regards students as co-designers in the design process (see Table 7.2). In fact, we regard such refinements as an ongoing endeavour, enabling us to work towards the best possible design and implementation of learning tasks to meet the needs of learners in different learning contexts. This could involve multiple rounds of testing, feedback from learners and language professionals, and ongoing reflections from the research and design teams.

The design pattern developed in this study can be adapted by language teachers, instructional designers, researchers and students. It can be tailored to suit individual design needs and should be used as a springboard to embrace different ideas (Cross, 2023; Rolf, 2021). According to Goodyear and Dimitriadis (2013), the success of design for learning depends on the work of language teachers-as-designers, other professionals and learners. Learners who engage in the implementation of the design provide the design team with more understanding of their learning needs for better (re)design. This highlights that design for learning involves adaptation and fine-tuning, and that ongoing reflection is vital throughout the process. Collaboration is crucial. A collaborative and reflective design for the learning process is particularly important for RALL, as RALL tasks are often multimedia and multimodal, requiring the concerted efforts and expertise of a skilled research team. This collaborative process emphasises knowledge sharing and building that is also centred around a community of practice (Wenger, 1998). As Carvalho and Yeoman (2019, p. 22) note:

> successful collaborations of this nature depend on the materialisation and subsequent spatial orientation of information and ideas relevant to the task, and an ability to communicate and work with others to identify potential design solutions and converge on a single 'good' as opposed to 'correct' solution.

Our attempt at task design is consistent with this view, centring on human agency, language teachers-as-designers and students; utilising the support of instructional designers and researchers; and interacting with ubiquitous technologies in the constantly evolving arena of spatial-temporal language learning. We acknowledge that having such a strong learning design team is a luxury often unattainable in real life. However, our findings indicate a growing need for such a team to narrow or bridge the gap between what is needed in teaching and learning and what technological affordances we can tap into to meet such needs. Not every teacher is tech-savvy, and not every technical expert has a good knowledge of classroom needs.

We also acknowledge that there are limitations in this study, as data generated from one task design and one round of task implementation with a small number of student participants cannot be generalised. However, this study provides useful insights into how a design pattern can be developed that supports language teachers in designing for personalised and/or collaborative learning. Although our pilot study took place in a classroom setting with a small number of participants and under the supervision of the class tutor, the same or similar tasks and the RALL environment could be scaled in different ways and at different levels. For example, the task environment can be replicated in a computer lab where a number of robots and tangible objects can be installed. Students could complete the task with the robot and their peers outside class time (that is, in their own time without the supervision of the class tutor). The recent development of generative AI unleashes endless opportunities for RALL task design to be executed beyond the confines of the classroom and classroom times.

Finally, our design pattern, drawing on the literature and expanded in our RALL task design, should be seen as an iterative process that has the potential to inform any task design undertaken by language educators. Focusing on classroom learning task design at a tertiary level, this case study provides a starting point for examining how design for learning can be implemented in RALL task design, and how this process can help language teachers to become confident designers for learning. We see language teachers as learning designers by the nature of their profession; however, they need ongoing support and collaboration with instructional designers and RALL researchers to effectively integrate design for learning into their day-to-day design practice.

Acknowledgements

This research was supported by the National Science and Technology Council, Taiwan, under project numbers MOST 111-2410-H-003-028-MY3 and 109-2511-H-003-053-MY3. This work was financially supported by the Institute for Research Excellence in Learning Sciences of National Taiwan Normal University from the Featured Areas Research Center Program within the framework of the Higher Education Sprout Project by the Ministry of Education in Taiwan.

References

Alexander, C., Ishikawa, S., Silverstein, M., Jacobson, M., Fiksdahl-King, I. & Angel, S. (1977). *A pattern language*. Oxford University Press.

Aljawarneh, S. A. (2020). Reviewing and exploring innovative ubiquitous learning tools in higher education. *Journal of Computing in Higher Education*, *32*(1), 57–73. doi.org/10.1007/s12528-019-09207-0.

Ashton, K. (2022). Language teacher agency in emergency online teaching. *System*, *105*, 102713. doi.org/10.1016/j.system.2021.102713.

Avgeriou, P., Papasalouros, A., Retalis, S. & Skordalakis, M. (2003). Towards a pattern language for learning management systems. *Educational Technology & Society*, *6*(2), 11–24. jstor.org/stable/jeductechsoci.6.2.11.

Beetham, H. & Sharpe, R. (Eds.). (2013). *Rethinking pedagogy for a digital age: Designing for 21st century learning*. Routledge.

Beetham, H. & Sharpe, R. (Eds.). (2020). *Rethinking pedagogy for a digital age: Principles and practices of design* (3rd ed.). Routledge.

Belpaeme, T., Vogt, P., van den Berghe, R., Bergmann, K., Göksun, T., de Haas, M., et al. (2018). Guidelines for designing social robots as second language tutors. *International Journal of Social Robotics*, *10*(3), 325–341. doi.org/10.1007/s12369-018-0467-6.

Benson, P. (2021). *Language learning environments: Spatial perspectives on SLA*. Multilingual Matters. doi.org/10.21832/BENSON4900.

Biesta, G., Priestley, M. & Robinson, S. (2015). The role of beliefs in teacher agency. *Teachers and Teaching*, *21*(6), 624–640. doi.org/10.1080/13540602.2015.1044325.

Carvalho, L. & Goodyear, P. (Eds.). (2013). *The architecture of productive learning networks*. Routledge.

Carvalho, L. & Yeoman, P. (2019). Connecting the dots: Theorising and mapping learning entanglement through archaeology and design. *British Journal of Educational Technology*, *50*(3), 1104–1117. doi.org/10.1111/bjet.12761.

Chatteur, F., Carvalho, L. & Dong, A. (2010). Embedding pedagogical principles and theories into design patterns. In P. Goodyear & S. Retalis (Eds.), *Technology-enhanced learning: Design patterns and pattern languages* (pp. 183–199). Brill. doi.org/10.1163/9789460910623_012.

Chen, M. (2022). Digital affordances and teacher agency in the context of teaching Chinese as a second language during COVID-19. *System*, *105*, 102710. doi.org/10.1016/j.system.2021.102710.

Chen, X. L., Zou, D., Xie, H. R. & Su, F. (2021). Twenty-five years of computer-assisted language learning: A topic modelling analysis. *Language Learning & Technology*, *25*(3), 151–185. hdl.handle.net/10125/73454.

Cheng, Y.-W., Wang, Y., Yang, Y.-F., Yang, Z.-K. & Chen, N.-S. (2021). Designing an authoring system of robots and IoT-based toys for EFL teaching and learning. *Computer Assisted Language Learning*, *34*(1–2), 6–34. doi.org/10.1080/09588221.2020.1799823.

Colpaert, J. (2010). Elicitation of language learners' personal goals as design concepts. *Innovation in Language Learning and Teaching*, *4*(3), 259–274. doi.org/10.1080/17501229.2010.513447.

Cross, N. (2023). *Design thinking: Understanding how designers think and work* (2nd ed.). Bloomsbury Publishing.

Darvin, R. & Norton, B. (2017). Identity, language learning, and critical pedagogies in digital times. In J. Cenoz, D. Gorter & S. May (Eds.), *Language awareness and multilingualism* (3rd ed.). doi.org/10.1007/978-3-319-02240-6.

Egbert, J. (2005). *CALL essentials: Principles and practice in CALL classrooms*. TESOL.

Egbert, J. L., Shahrokni, S. A., Zhang, X., Yahia, I. A., Borysenko, N., Mohamed, A. F. S., Herman, D., et al. (2018). Planning for future inquiry: Gaps in the CALL research. *International Journal of Computer-Assisted Language Learning and Teaching*, *8*(2), 39–59. doi.org/10.4018/IJCALLT.2018040103.

Flavin, M. (2012). Disruptive technologies in higher education. *Research in Learning Technology*, *20*, 102–111. doi.org/10.3402/rlt.v20i0.19184.

Frizell, S. S. & Hubscher, R. (2008). Using design patterns to support e-learning design. In L. Lockyer, S. Bennett, S. Agostinho & B. Harper (Eds.), *Handbook of research on learning design and design objects: Issues, applications and technologies* (pp. 144–166). IGI Global.

Fry, N. & Love, N. (2011). Business lecturers' perceptions and interactions with the virtual learning environment. *International Journal of Management Education*, *9*(4), 51–56.

Getenet, S. (2019). Using design-based research to bring partnership between researchers and practitioners. *Educational Research*, *61*(4), 482–494. doi.org/10.1080/00131881.2019.1677168.

Ghislandi, P. M. M. & Raffaghelli, J. E. (2015). Forward-oriented designing for learning as a means to achieve educational quality. *British Journal of Educational Technology*, *46*(2), 280–299. doi.org/10.1111/bjet.12257.

Gillespie, J. (2020). CALL research: Where are we now? *ReCALL*, *32*(2), 127–144. doi.org/10.1017/S0958344020000051.

Goldie, J. G. S. (2016). Connectivism: A knowledge learning theory for the digital age? *Medical Teacher*, *38*(10), 1064–1069. doi.org/10.3109/0142159X.2016.1173661.

Goodyear, P. (2005). Educational design and networked learning: Patterns, pattern languages and design practice. *Australasian Journal of Educational Technology*, *21*(1). doi.org/10.14742/ajet.1344.

Goodyear, P. (2015). Teaching as design. *HERDSA Review of Higher Education*, *2*, 27–50. herdsa.org.au/herdsa-review-higher-education-vol-2/27-50.

Goodyear, P. & Dimitriadis, Y. (2013). *In medias res*: Reframing design for learning. *Research in Learning Technology*, *21*, 1–13. doi.org/10.3402/rlt.v21i0.19909.

Goodyear, P. & Yang, D. F. (2009). Patterns and pattern languages in educational design. In L. Lockyer, S. Bennett, S. Agostinho & B. Harper (Eds.), *Handbook of research on learning design and learning objects: Issues, applications and technologies* (Vol. 1, pp. 167–187). IGI Global.

Hamilton, E. R., Rosenberg, J. M. & Akcaoglu, M. (2016). The substitution augmentation modification redefinition (SAMR) model: A critical review and suggestions for its use. *TechTrends*, *60*(5), 433–441. doi.org/10.1007/s11528-016-0091-y.

Hubbard, P. (Ed.) (2009). *Computer assisted language learning: Critical concepts in linguistics*. Routledge.

Klimanova, L. (2021). The evolution of identity research in CALL: From scripted chatrooms to engaged construction of the digital self. *Language Learning & Technology*, *25*(3), 186–204. hdl.handle.net/10125/73455.

Koehler, M. J., Mishra, P., Kereluik, K., Shin, T. S. & Graham, C. R. (2014). The technological pedagogical content knowledge framework. In J. M. Spector, M. D. Merrill, J. Elen & M. J. Bishop (Eds.), *Handbook of research on educational communications and technology* (pp. 101–111). Springer. doi.org/10.1007/978-1-4614-3185-5_9.

Kramsch, C. (2009). *The multilingual subject*. Oxford University Press.

Kuo, J. Y. (2015). Cognition-based multimedia classifier learning. *CASLAR, 4*(1), 23–45. doi.org/10.1515/caslar-2015-0002.

Kuure, L., Molin-Juustila, T., Keisanen, T., Riekki, M., Iivari, N. & Kinnula, M. (2016). Switching perspectives: From a language teacher to a designer of language learning with new technologies. *Computer Assisted Language Learning, 29*(5), 925–941. doi.org/10.1080/09588221.2015.1068815.

Lan, Y.-J. (2021). Language learning in virtual reality: Theoretical foundations and empirical practices. In Y.-J. Lan & S. Grant (Eds.), *Contextual language learning: Real language learning on the continuum from virtuality to reality* (pp. 1–21). Springer. doi.org/10.1007/978-981-16-3416-1_1.

Lan, Y.-J. & Tam, V. T. T. (2022). The impact of 360° videos on basic Chinese writing: a preliminary exploration. *Educational Technology Research and Development, 71*, 539–562. doi.org/10.1007/s11423-022-10162-4.

Laurillard, D. (2012). *Teaching as a design science: Building pedagogical patterns for learning and technology*. Routledge.

Laurillard, D., Charlton, P., Craft, B., Dimakopoulos, D., Ljubojevic, D., Magoulas, G., Masterman, E., Pujadas, R., Whitley, E. A. & Whittlestone, K. (2013). A constructionist learning environment for teachers to model learning designs. *Journal of Computer Assisted Learning, 29*(1), 15–30. doi.org/10.1111/j.1365-2729.2011.00458.x.

Law, N., Li, L., Herrera, L. F., Chan, A. & Pong, T.-C. (2017). A pattern language based learning design studio for an analytics informed inter-professional design community. *Interaction Design and Architecture(s), 33*, 92–112. hdl.handle.net/1783.1/88860.

Le, V. T., Nguyen, N. H., Tran, T. L. N., Nguyen, L. T., Nguyen, T. A. & Nguyen, M. T. (2022). The interaction patterns of pandemic-initiated online teaching: How teachers adapted. *System, 105*, 102755. doi.org/10.1016/j.system.2022.102755.

Levy, M. (1997). *Computer assisted language learning: Context and conceptualization*. Oxford University Press.

Levy, M. & Hubbard, P. (2005). Why call CALL 'CALL'? *Computer Assisted Language Learning, 18*(3), 143–149. doi.org/10.1080/09588220500208884.

Margaryan, A., Littlejohn, A. & Vojt, G. (2011). Are digital natives a myth or reality? University students' use of digital technologies. *Computers & Education, 56*(2), 429–440. doi.org/10.1016/j.compedu.2010.09.004.

Mishra, P. & Koehler, M. J. (2006). Technological pedagogical content knowledge: A framework for teacher knowledge. *Teachers College Record, 108*(6), 1017–1054. doi.org/10.1111/j.1467-9620.2006.00684.x.

Mor, Y. & Mogilevsky, O. (2013). The learning design studio: Collaborative design inquiry as teachers' professional development. *Research in Learning Technology, 21*. doi.org/10.3402/rlt.v21i0.22054.

Norton, B. (2013). *Identity and language learning: Extending the conversation.* Multilingual Matters.

Puentedura, R. (2014, 20 February). Learning, technology, and the SAMR model: Goals, processes, and practice. *Ruben R. Puentedura's Weblog: Ongoing thoughts on education and technology.* hippasus.com/rrpweblog/archives/2014/06/29/LearningTechnologySAMRModel.pdf.

Qi, G. Y. (2021). COVID-19 underlines the importance of learning languages via emerging technologies. *Melbourne Asia Review, 7*. doi.org/10.37839/MAR 2652-550X7.16.

Qi, G. Y., Sun, S. Y. H. & Carvalho, L. (2023). Designing for diversity in Aotearoa/New Zealand Chinese language classrooms. *Language Teaching Research.* doi.org/10.1177/13621688231167933.

Rapanta, C., Botturi, L., Goodyear, P., Guàrdia, L. & Koole, M. (2021). Balancing technology, pedagogy and the new normal: Post-pandemic challenges for higher education. *Postdigital Science and Education, 3*(3), 715–742. doi.org/10.1007/s42438-021-00249-1.

Reinders, H., Lai, C. & Sundqvist, P. (Eds.). (2022). *The Routledge handbook of language learning and teaching beyond the classroom.* Routledge.

Rienties, B., Lewis, T., McFarlane, R., Nguyen, Q. & Toetenel, L. (2018). Analytics in online and offline language learning environments: The role of learning design to understand student online engagement. *Computer Assisted Language Learning, 31*(3), 273–293. doi.org/10.1080/09588221.2017.1401548.

Rolf, E. (2021). *Teachers as designers: Analyses of pedagogical patterns and their use.* Stockholm University. su.diva-portal.org/smash/record.jsf?pid=diva2%3A1602 928&dswid=-3647.

Shuell, T. (1986). Cognitive conceptions of learning. *Review of Educational Research, 56*(4), 411–436. doi.org/10.3102/00346543056004411.

Stockwell, G. (2021). Living and learning with technology: Language learning with mobile devices. *English Teaching, 76*, 3–16. doi.org/10.15858/engtea.76.s1.202109.3.

Sun, S. Y. H. (2021). Using patterns-based learning design for CALL tasks. *Computer Assisted Language Learning, 34*(8), 1061–1084. doi.org/10.1080/09588221.2019.1657902.

Vogt, P., De Haas, M., De Jong, C., Baxter, P. & Krahmer, E. (2017). Child–robot interactions for second language tutoring to preschool children. *Frontiers in Human Neuroscience, 11*, 73. doi.org/10.3389/fnhum.2017.00073.

Wang, Y. & Qi, G. Y. (2018). Mastery-based language learning outside class: Learning support in flipped classrooms. *Language Learning & Technology, 22*(2), 50–74. doi.org/10125/44641.

Wenger, E. (1998). *Communities of practice: Learning, meaning, community*. Cambridge University Press.

Yang, Y. (2020). Acquisition of the Mandarin ba-construction by Cantonese learners. *Macrolinguistics, 8*(1), 88–104. doi.org/10.26478/ja2020.8.12.6.

Appendix A: Post-activity survey on learning experience with the robot

Your experience with the robot in practising 把. Please indicate the level of your agreement with each of the following statements. 1 = strongly disagree and 5 = strongly agree.

1. I like the activity because it is hands-on.
2. I like the activity because it relates to real life.
3. I spoke a lot of Chinese using 把 in this activity.
4. I now know better when to use 把.
5. I now know better how to use 把.
6. 把 seems easier to use than before.
7. I still think 把 is difficult after the activity.
8. I think activities like this can help me learn Chinese better.
9. I like listening to the robot's instructions.
10. The robot's instructions are clear.
11. The robot's instructions are easy to follow.
12. The robot's instructions are hard to follow because there were lots of words I did not know.

13. I did not understand the robot's instructions because it spoke very fast.
14. I don't mind repeating myself to get my sentence right.
15. I like speaking after the robot (following the robot's instructions) because I could be sure my sentences were correct.
16. I didn't mind when the robot didn't understand me.
17. When I did not understand the robot, I touched the robot's head to ask it to repeat what it had said.
18. I found the activity challenging because I had to listen, speak and act at the same time.
19. I found this activity engaging because I had to listen, speak and act at the same time.
20. The contents on the tablet (e.g. images and texts) are helpful.
21. When I didn't understand the robot, I referred to the contents on the tablet for clarification.
22. The contents on the tablet (e.g. images and texts) should be displayed on the robot's face.
23. When I didn't know what I should do in the activity, I sought help from my teammate.
24. I sought help from my teacher when I did not know how to proceed with the activity.
25. The repeat function is helpful.
26. The robot spoke too fast to follow.
27. Making real dumplings helped me understand 把 better.
28. I hope to have more rounds of the same activity.
29. I hope to learn Chinese with a robot outside the classroom.
30. I like learning Chinese with the robot together with my peers in class.
31. I hope to learn Chinese with the robot by myself in my own time.
32. Robot-assisted Chinese learning has great potential.

8

'It wasn't like getting up in front of the class to speak': Promoting L2 motivation and reducing L2 speaking anxiety through a podcasting project

Riccardo Amorati, Elisabetta Ferrari and John Hajek

1. Introduction

One of the major difficulties facing language learners—especially those at the elementary or intermediate level—is gaining confidence in communicating in the L2. Oral activities are those most generally associated with a sense of anxiety and inadequacy on the part of students. These negative feelings can have a detrimental impact on the overall enjoyment of their learning experience (see Kim, 2009; Young, 1990). For this reason, it is important to diversify language curricula by proposing and evaluating novel activities that are sensitive to 'the overwhelming presence of anxiety that foreign language classroom learning incurs' (Kim, 2009, p. 154). It is also important to present activities that have a direct positive influence on students' overall motivation and foster their engagement, that is, their active participation and involvement in academic tasks (Mercer & Dörnyei, 2020).

This chapter presents a student-centred, project-based activity developed at the University of Melbourne, which aims to increase student motivation and reduce the anxiety normally associated with speaking activities, while also contributing to a diversification of the language curriculum. The activity is included in an intermediate Italian studies subject and consists of the production of podcasts in Italian on topics chosen by students. The project also incorporates the use of student-generated content (SGC), as these podcasts are used in class by students as a starting point for listening comprehension activities and class discussions. Selected podcasts are also submitted to the Australian national radio station SBS Italian, which broadcasts fully in Italian for an Italian-speaking audience in Australia and potentially elsewhere.

In this chapter, we first present the project and explain two key methods underpinning its structure, namely project-based learning (PBL) and the use of SGC. We then review previous scholarship on L2 motivation (Deci & Ryan, 1985; Dörnyei, 1994, 2001; Lambert et al., 2017), and language anxiety (Gkonou, et al., 2017; Kim, 2009) that informed its design. Finally, we present the results of a study that aimed to 1) examine the effect of the project on students' motivation, and to 2) explore whether it was effective in reducing levels of anxiety normally experienced during traditional oral presentations.

2. Project design: Capitalising on PBL and the use of SGC

As noted above, the project incorporates PBL and SGC, with both methods associated with a shift from a teacher-centred to a learner-centred curriculum (see Brown, 2003). In a traditional teacher-centred pedagogy, the teacher has full control over the learning process, and, thus, has complete authority in the choice of teaching materials and their delivery. In contrast, a learner-centred pedagogy aims to provide opportunities for students to shape their own learning experiences by giving them more freedom in the choice of learning content and by promoting cooperative and authentic activities in which the teacher takes the role of a facilitator (Brown, 2003).

PBL is a teaching method that fosters content and skill acquisition through group activities aimed at the creation of a final product that holds meaning for students and that has real-world relevance (Buck Institute of Education, 2022; Larmer et al., 2015). Based on group work and self-directed learning, PBL contributes to a decentring of pedagogical practices (see Mergendoller et al., 2006). There is a wealth of literature on the benefits of PBL on motivation, student engagement, learner autonomy and self-regulation, as well as on the acquisition of skills, such as problem-solving, communication and collaboration (see Stefanou et al., 2013; Stoller, 2006; Supe & Kaupuzs, 2015). PBL has been incorporated in various courses on offer in the Italian studies program at the University of Melbourne. For instance, upper-intermediate students of Italian work on the design and production of a theatre project as part of their assessment (Absalom, 2017, 2021) and advanced students are supported in the creation and self-publishing of a short storybook in Italian (Amorati & Hajek, 2021).

As noted previously, the project-based activity presented in this chapter consists of the production of a podcast. There is a developing body of literature on the use of podcasting in language classes in different contexts, such as Anglophone countries, Malaysia and Nigeria (see Martín & Beckmann, 2011; Mbah et al., 2013; Samperi Mangan, 2008; see also Amorati et al., 2022; Ferrari et al., 2024; Hasan & Hoon, 2013). Generally, students perceive podcasts as very motivating—they are both an authentic listening source and a popular media genre (Martín & Beckmann, 2011). As we have observed elsewhere (Amorati et al., 2022), an additional benefit of podcasts is that they are characterised by a colloquial and informal style, which is generally appealing for students (Edirisingha et al., 2007).

A considerable novelty of the podcast project in comparison to other activities on offer in our Italian program and to those reported in the literature on podcasting (e.g. Martín & Beckmann, 2011; Samperi Mangan, 2008) is that it combines PBL (with students working on the creation of a podcast entirely in Italian) with the use of SGC, as the podcasts created by students are used in class as teaching materials. As noted previously, the use of SGC stands in contrast to current approaches to L2 task design, which are generally reliant on teacher-generated content. It is argued that the inclusion of SGC as part of the project contributes to decentring pedagogical practices, in that it is students who choose the topics and then create the content for assessment and class discussion, not teachers. By giving students more agency in topic choice and in materials to be included in the syllabus, and by encouraging group work and independent learning, it is also hoped that their motivation will increase (see Section 3). SGC has, in fact, a clear influence on students' motivation. Lambert's (1997, 2004) research suggests that reusing student-produced content in later stages of a project or series of sequential tasks has a positive impact on students' learning progression and contributes to their investment in the learning process. Additionally, there is evidence that learner-generated tasks have greater positive effects on students' motivation and performance than teacher-generated tasks (Lambert et al., 2017).

In terms of structure, as we have discussed elsewhere (Amorati et al., 2022; Ferrari et al., 2024), the project, which spans a 12-week semester, consists of three parts. The first part (generally weeks 2–4) includes the 'experiential phase': students are exposed to podcasts through listening comprehension activities and familiarise themselves with their genre-specific conventions. They are also assigned resources to improve their pronunciation and intonation. Students then choose their own groups and are presented with the 'challenge': creating a five-minute podcast for a real audience on a topic of their choice relating, for instance, to their experience as students, to Italian cultural events in Melbourne or worldwide (see Ferrari et al., 2024, for an overview of topics chosen over the years).

In the second part (weeks 5–9), students work in groups on their podcast script and are required to submit it one week before recording, so that they can have sufficient time to rehearse the corrected version before the recording. As part of the feedback on the first script, students receive grammatical corrections and may also receive queries or requests to make additional changes to their script, following an authentic review process. In normal circumstances, the recording is done in a professional studio located at the University of Melbourne with the help of their teacher and a sound engineer. Considerable time is allocated for each recording session to allow extra time for retakes and feedback on various aspects of students' pronunciation, fluency and overall language skills. The feedback aims to improve the quality of the recorded performances, emphasising clear articulation and pronunciation as well as expressive and authentic intonation. One week after the recording, students are required to submit a personal reflection in which they contemplate their individual contributions to the project, reflect on the skills they have learnt and assess their group's collaborative dynamics. While peer evaluations are not formally integrated into the project in its current design, this reflection provides an opportunity for students to critically examine their group's collaboration. During the COVID-19 pandemic, when online delivery was the norm, students were required to work on the project entirely online and were responsible for recording the podcast themselves. No other structural change was deemed necessary, so it can be said that the shift to online teaching did not cause any significant disruptions to its delivery.

In the third part (weeks 10–12), the podcasts are played in class and are used as part of listening comprehension activities and as a starting point for class discussions on the topics presented. This means that in the last three weeks of the semester, discussion centres on topics chosen by students.

In terms of assessment (see also Ferrari et al., 2024), students receive a mark and feedback on:

- their first podcast script (use of language, vocabulary and structure, research and data collection)
- the final recording (accuracy and pronunciation during voice recording, coherence and teamwork as per the final recording)
- the reflection submitted at the end of the activity.

As mentioned earlier, students also receive real-time feedback on their pronunciation and intonation during the recording session, aimed at enhancing the quality of the final podcast.

3. Diversifying the language learning experience: Enhancing motivation and alleviating language anxiety

In this section, we present scholarship on two key areas that informed the design of the project (see Ferrari et al., 2024, for a general overview of its theoretical underpinnings), namely scholarship on L2 motivation and language anxiety.

3.1. Motivating students and increasing their engagement in L2 learning

In the design of the project we drew upon previous scholarship on motivational teaching practice (Dörnyei, 2001) and engagement (Mercer & Dörnyei, 2020). Scholars in this area agree that motivation and engagement tend to increase if the activities presented are varied (that is, contain different components that include different skills), include elements of novelty for students, are meaningful and cater to students' interests.

As Lambert et al. (2017) note, allowing students to personalise their work based on their interests and life experiences clearly contributes to improving their engagement with language use and their affective response to the task(s) at hand. It is argued that enabling students to learn a language while developing their interests is particularly important in the Australian university context, where students pursue language studies alongside a range of other disciplines, and are therefore likely to have different interests and expectations regarding the content to be covered in L2 classes (see also Amorati et al., 2022).

One of the primary goals of the project was to enable students to develop intrinsic motivation—that is, the drive to engage in tasks or activities that are perceived as personally relevant, are deemed satisfying in themselves and involve some degree of challenge (see Noels, 2001). Intrinsic motivation is considered to be more effective than extrinsic motivation, which is instead driven by the fulfilment of externally imposed obligations and can often fade when these obligations cease to exist (Noels, 2001, 2009; Noels et al., 2003). Dörnyei (1994, 2001) notes that intrinsic motivation should be fostered in language classes by encouraging students' autonomy in learning whenever possible and by including activities on topics of interest to students. In the podcast project, we aim to foster the development of intrinsic motivation by giving creative freedom to students regarding both the topics of the podcast (which become topics of class discussion in the latter part of the course, see Section 2) and the organisation of the group work. It is also hypothesised that the presence of a real audience and the real-world relevance of the project can help make learning more meaningful and satisfying for students and, thus, impact their sense of accomplishment and overall engagement with the task at hand.

3.2. Reducing language anxiety in oral activities

The design of the project also draws upon research addressing issues of student anxiety in second language acquisition. Language anxiety is a term used to refer to the feeling of apprehension and, in the most severe cases, even fear, in contexts and situations where language students are asked to communicate in their L2 (Dewaele, 2007; Gkonou et al., 2017). As noted previously, oral activities and oral assessments conducted in class, such as classroom presentations or tasks involving unrehearsed speaking, are generally considered by students to be anxiety inducing (Kim, 2009; Young, 1990; see also Gregersen & MacIntyre, 2014). Fear of oral presentations can have an overall negative effect on learning progression as well as student experience (Grieve et al., 2021). Foreign language anxiety is also more common in teacher-centred contexts, where power differentials are often marked and students may fear being judged (Dewaele et al., 2019).

Anxiety about oral presentations or public speaking is not a phenomenon only restricted to language learning (see Grieve et al., 2021, for a broader perspective), but it is particularly relevant to second language users, due to the fact that they generally have less control over 'what they say in the target language, how they say it and what image of themselves they project' (Amorati & Venturin, 2021, p. 39), particularly at lower levels of proficiency.

There is general agreement that language anxiety can be reduced by creating and fostering community building in the L2 classroom, as well as by presenting activities that are more sensitive to students' sources of anxiety, particularly regarding oral testing (see Gregersen & MacIntyre, 2014). For this reason, we decided to replace the more traditional oral class presentations with a more complex project that tests both writing and oral skills. In fact, there is evidence that PBL can contribute to alleviating language anxiety and to improving students' willingness to communicate in the L2, mostly because it encourages collaboration and the sharing of responsibilities and tasks (see Miguel & Carney, 2022).

4. An empirical study: Methodology

To examine various aspects related to the mechanics of the project and its effect on students' learning, we conducted a mixed-methods study. The data collected via a questionnaire eliciting both quantitative and qualitative responses from the 2018 and 2019 on-campus cohorts (n = 24) and from the 2020 and 2021 online cohorts (n = 10) are complemented by those obtained via semi-structured interviews with on-campus respondents (n = 7). The rationale for focusing on students from different academic years and, consequently, different modes of study is that one of our goals is to evaluate whether the project retained its effectiveness in the transition to online teaching. It should also be noted that the online and on-campus cohorts had the same instructors, so no differences in aspects like class management or teaching style were expected to affect students' motivation and language anxiety, which are constructs influenced by contextual factors (Dewaele, 2007; Dewaele et al., 2019; Mercer & Dörnyei, 2020; Noels, 2009).

Both questionnaire and interview respondents were asked various questions regarding their attitudes towards the project and its components (for example, what they enjoyed or did not enjoy about it, what benefits it had for them, whether they liked working collaboratively and listening to their podcasts in class, how it compared to a more traditional oral presentation as an assessment method, what skills they developed, what problems they encountered, etc.). Online students were also asked if they enjoyed the project as an online activity and if they liked being able to talk about topics of immediate relevance in their podcast, such as their experience during the pandemic. In this chapter, due to our research focus, we report only on data related to the impact of the project on students' motivation and language anxiety, and evaluate whether considerable differences were present in the experiences of on-campus and online students. Our goal is to examine whether the project was perceived as motivating and whether it was successful in reducing the level of anxiety typically associated with class presentations.

Due to space limitations, the reader is referred to Amorati et al. (2022) and Ferrari et al. (2024) for a detailed overview of the design of the study, of the research materials (questionnaire and interview guidelines), as well as of the demographic and study-related characteristics of the on-campus sample. Similarly to on-campus respondents, the online sample consisted of students enrolled in different degrees (like arts, music and science), with a predominance of arts students. All online students were female and were mostly in the 18–25 age bracket. They were all domestic students with one exception.

The qualitative data collected via the questionnaire and the interviews were analysed using the software NVivo 12 by means of general content analysis principles (Dörnyei, 2007; O'Leary, 2010). First, descriptive codes and subcodes were identified both deductively (in light of the topics targeted in the study) and inductively (unanticipated codes that emerged from the data) by performing a line-by-line coding of the data. After the first coding process was completed, four themes were found to subsume the previous descriptive codes. These will be used to present the data in the findings. Quantitative data were analysed using descriptive statistical procedures.

5. Findings and discussion

In this section, quotations from on-campus and online students are marked with the abbreviations OC and OL, respectively. Extracts from interview data are labelled with INT. It should also be noted that the percentages included in the tables are rounded to non-decimals. Because of this, in one instance (Table 8.2, item 2), percentages do not add up perfectly to 100 per cent.

5.1. Impact of the project on motivation

As noted previously, the analysis of the data revealed that four highly interconnected factors contributed to students' motivation. They are displayed in Figure 8.1. In the next sections, we focus on each factor separately.

Figure 8.1. Factors contributing to students' motivation
Source: Authors.

5.1.1. Freedom in topic choice and self-directed learning

Our qualitative findings were very encouraging. Most students, both from the on-campus and online cohorts, reported enjoying the project. Enjoyment was often linked to freedom in creative production: students appreciated being given the opportunity to focus on a topic of their choice that they perceived as personally relevant. They also valued the chance to engage in self-directed learning. These aspects are clearly illustrated in the quotations below:

> Being able to choose a topic [was the most enjoyable aspect of the project] … Having the opportunity for free learning permitted me to find a topic that was directly relevant to me.
>
> (OC)

> I really enjoyed that the project was self-directed, and we could choose the topic ourselves.
>
> (OC)

> I enjoyed having the ability to have a lot of control over what I was producing as well as … to extend my learning beyond the textbook.
>
> (OC)

> There wasn't [sic] too many rules so we had freedom to play around and have fun with it [the script].
>
> (OL)

Freedom in creative production meant that many participants viewed the project as conducive to the creation of a personally relevant finished product rather than simply as an academic assignment. This finding is in keeping with previous studies showing that having students personalise their work based on their interests and life experiences contributes to their engagement and overall motivation for L2 learning (Dörnyei, 2001; Lambert et al., 2017; Mercer & Dörnyei, 2020).

5.1.2. Novelty and challenge

Students also enjoyed the project because it was unlike any other assessment that they had completed before. In keeping with Dörnyei's (2001) and Mercer and Dörnyei's (2020) observations about motivational teaching practices (see Section 3), we found that the inclusion of novel elements had a positive impact on students' motivation and general level of classroom engagement. Several questionnaire respondents cited the project's 'novelty' as a reason for their enjoyment of the activity:

> It was nice to do something a bit different for an assessment. This was far more fun than just doing a presentation in class, probably because it was novel to pretty much everyone.
>
> (OC)

> The fact that we were doing something different was very motivating.
>
> (OC)

> It was exciting and different.
>
> (OL)

> The multi-dimensional and real-world assessment was a fantastic experience.
>
> (OL)

As can be seen in Figure 8.2, most participants across cohorts also enjoyed the project, as they considered it an enjoyable challenge. Students were, in fact, expected to oversee all aspects related to script creation and podcast production and were given considerable freedom in organising a complex and multi-step project.

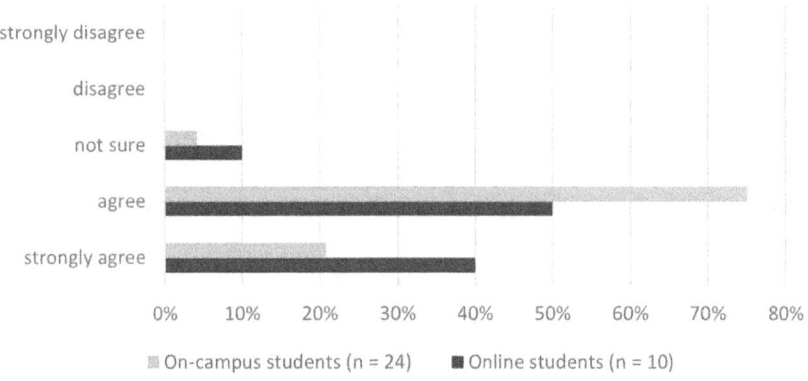

Figure 8.2. The project as a challenging experience
Source: Authors.

Working on tasks that represent a positive challenge has a clear impact on student motivation (Deci & Ryan 1985) and encourages a deeper engagement with the learning process (Lambert et al., 2017).

5.1.3. Tangible accomplishment and meaning

Another aspect contributing to motivation was the fact that the project entailed the production of a meaningful finished product that students could call their own and could share with others. The quantitative data reported in Table 8.1 show that most respondents from both the on-campus and online cohorts agreed or strongly agreed that the project was rewarding and allowed them to use their language skills to produce something tangible.

Table 8.1. The project as a rewarding experience and as an example of project-based learning

Items	Strongly agree		Agree		Not sure		Disagree		Strongly disagree	
	OC	OL	OC	OL	OC	OL	OC	OL	OC	OL
1) The podcast project was a rewarding experience	**54%**	**70%**	38%	30%	8%	0%	0%	0%	0%	0%
2) The podcast project allowed me to use my language skills to produce something tangible[1]	**67%**	50%	25%	**50%**	8%	0%	0%	0%	0%	0%
Total	OC (n = 24) OL (n = 10)									

Notes: Data from on-campus (OC) and online (OL) students. The most selected responses for each sample group are in bold.
Source: Authors.

As can be seen, online students had particularly positive attitudes towards the project, with 70 per cent strongly agreeing that it was rewarding. The opportunity to work collaboratively was especially welcome due to the isolation experienced during the pandemic-related lockdown period:

> The podcast project really allowed me to get to know a small group of people well, which meant I could connect more online.
>
> (OL)

For these students, the project not only represented an opportunity for social/peer interaction after the shift to online teaching, but also gave them a chance to use Italian more meaningfully to discuss topics immediately relevant to them and their own experience(s) during the pandemic, with

---

[1] Please note that the data reported for on-campus students related to this item are also discussed in Amorati et al. (2022), in which the focus is on the acquisition of L2 skills.

many podcasts focusing on these themes in 2020 and 2021. Students generally enjoyed the opportunity to bring their lived experience into the classroom and share it with others while also completing an academic assignment and improving their language skills:

> I really enjoyed talking about the COVID situation at the time with my group because there was so much to talk about since we were literally right in the middle of it. I liked the fact that we were talking about something so relevant and highlighting the difficulties and/or surprising benefits of the pandemic on our studies.
>
> (OL)

As the qualitative data demonstrate, the fact that the project had the production of a podcast with a clear audience in mind as its ultimate goal made it more significant for students, pushing them to put more effort into the final product. As Lambert et al. (2017, p. 667) note:

> the meaning that tasks have for learners is crucial as it will determine the degree to which they are willing to become personally invested in the performance of a task in terms of devoting their time, talents, and energy into its performance.

This is clearly reflected in our data:

> The desire to produce the podcast to a high standard was stronger as I was representing myself in a different way, not simply demonstrating language skills.
>
> (OL)

The results presented so far show that the project contributed to the development of intrinsic motivation. As noted in Section 3, intrinsic motivation denotes the desire to perform an activity in which the person is interested, and which involves some degree of challenge. An additional characteristic of this type of motivation is the sense of satisfaction and reward associated with the completion of a meaningful task (Deci & Ryan, 1985).

5.1.4. Real audience and conversational language

Table 8.2. The use of language as part of the project and its link to the Italian presence in Melbourne

Items	Strongly agree		Agree		Not sure		Disagree		Strongly disagree	
	OC	OL	OC	OL	OC	OL	OC	OL	OC	OL
1) Creating and recording a podcast enabled me to use the language in a real way	**42%**	**60%**	**42%**	40%	8%	0%	8%	0%	0%	0%
2) The podcast project allowed me to use Italian in a more authentic way beyond the classroom[2]	33%	**60%**	**54%**	20%	8%	0%	4%	20%	0%	0%
3) The podcast project made me reflect on the Italian presence in Melbourne	**42%**	**50%**	**42%**	10%	12%	20%	4%	20%	0%	0%
Total	OC (n = 24) OL (n = 10)									

Notes: Data from on-campus (OC) and online (OL) students. The most selected responses for each sample group are in bold.
Source: Authors.

If we look at the first two items in Table 8.2, it can be seen that participants from both the on-campus and online group mostly agreed or strongly agreed that creating and recording a podcast prompted them to use Italian for a real purpose (item 1) as well as to use it more authentically beyond the classroom (item 2), for instance, to research topics of interest for a real audience. Once again, no important differences were found between the on-campus and online groups.

As we have noted elsewhere (see Amorati et al., 2022), students also appreciated learning about more colloquial forms of Italian. Many students noted how the discursive style required to make their podcast more engaging prompted them to familiarise themselves with colloquial Italian phrases as well as with the use of discourse markers and filler words that are not generally required in other, more formal academic assignments:

---

2 Please note that the data reported for on-campus students related to item 1 and 2 are also discussed in Amorati et al. (2022), where the focus is on the acquisition of L2 skills.

> I wrote my script, so it forced me to write in a new style that I had not previously written in Italian before. Since most of our Italian writing is just paragraphs/essays in assignments.
>
> (OC)

In line with previous studies (Martín & Beckmann, 2011; Moreno-López et al., 2017; Samperi Mangan, 2008), these findings indicate that podcasting has the benefit of diversifying the linguistic input presented to students (see Amorati et al., 2022, for further discussion on this).

The qualitative responses reveal that students identified a diverse audience for their podcasts: 1) Italian speaking family and friends they shared their project with; 2) other students in the Italian class (as part of the final part of the project including the use of SGC); and 3) a community of Italian speakers, both in Melbourne and in Australia. Over the years in which the project has been offered, many podcasts have focused on events related to the Italian community in Melbourne (for example, cultural festivals and events, exhibitions by Italian artists, etc.). This may explain why several students strongly agreed or agreed that the project made them more aware of the Italian presence in Melbourne, as can be seen in Table 8.2 (item 3).

The inclusion of student-generated podcasts as part of classroom activities also appeared to be particularly appreciated. Listening to other groups' podcasts not only enabled students to learn about new topics, but also to find out more about their classmates, with these activities contributing to community building as well:

> I really enjoyed listening to the other groups' recordings: they were really fun and involved novel topics and approaches. [I] was impressed by the talents and abilities of the students in our course! This was very encouraging.
>
> (OC)

> I was mostly amazed by how much effort everyone put in; and by how good they sounded.
>
> (OC)

> I really loved this part. It was so interesting to see how other people took the same criteria and came up with something completely different. It was also just nice to share with each other.
>
> (OL)

> [I] loved [listening to other groups' podcasts]. I got to learn more about my classmates. Perhaps mostly it was the opportunity as … we do not see content from our classmates often. So to be able to receive this amount of information in an easy-to-access way that required little time invested was simply a gift.
>
> (OL)

The use of SGC is often tied up with concerns about linguistic perfection and adequate models, as content produced by students is likely to include errors or forms that deviate from native norms. These concerns were reflected in the comments of some students, who emphasised their preference for native-produced listening sources. Others, however, pointed out that content produced by their peers was effective because it was more understandable, as it included linguistic structures and a vocabulary range shared by all students in the course. The two statements below exemplify these trends:

> [Listening to other students' podcasts] was good. However, because our accents are not refined (mine included!) I thought it would be better to listen to a native speaker for listening practice.
>
> (OC)

> Since we are mostly at the same language level, it was fairly easy to understand the vocab and grammar structures they have used.
>
> (OL)

The findings presented in this section suggest that SGC has considerable benefits and should be included in the curriculum as a means of expanding and diversifying the materials presented, as it contributes to improved student motivation. However, students' comments also point to the importance of retaining more traditional listening activities that incorporate materials produced by native speakers. This is done in the first part of the project, where students are exposed to podcasts produced for an Italian audience.

5.2. Impact of the project on language anxiety

Figure 8.3 displays students' ratings regarding the level of anxiety that they experienced while recording the podcast script as opposed to what they would experience during a more traditional oral presentation.

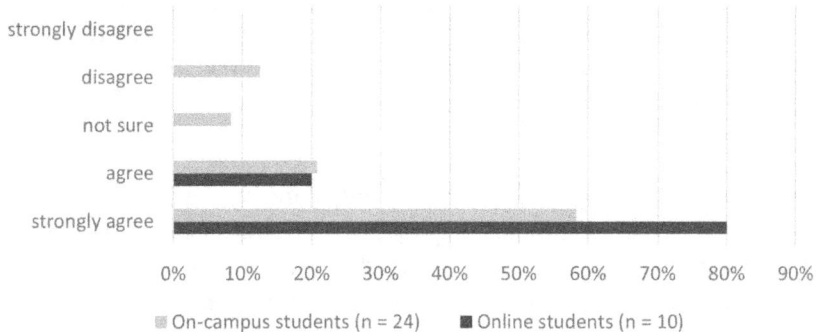

Figure 8.3. The level of anxiety experienced in comparison to a class presentation
Source: Authors.

It can be seen that most respondents from both groups strongly agreed that they felt less stressed recording the podcast than doing a class presentation. These findings were supported by the qualitative data:

> It was enjoyable to have something collaborative and not so stressful like an oral presentation.
>
> (OL)

> It wasn't like getting up in front of a class, it was more interesting because doing an oral presentation in front of a class is kind of boring and also ... I would be even more nervous for it ... whereas I wasn't as much for it.
>
> (INT)

Students experienced lower levels of anxiety recording a podcast because they had the opportunity to rehearse the script at length and re-record difficult sentences or individual words in case of mistakes during the recording session. Feedback received from the teacher or from other students during the recording session was perceived as more meaningful, as the goal was to create a better finished product rather than simply completing an academic assignment. Students were also working with their group rather than in front of the whole class, so the feedback was received in a fairly 'save-face' environment. These trends are illustrated in the following quotations:

> [Recording the script in the recording studio] was an interesting experience. We had more than one chance to go. It was far more relaxing than delivering presentation in front of a class. In the end, we would have a nice podcast recording to keep.
>
> (OC)

> For the oral [presentation] you can try, but you only have one chance [to pronounce something correctly], but with the podcast we were stopping and starting and making sure that everyone pronounced correctly.
>
> (INT)

Instead of standing in front of the class and taking on the role of a teacher by giving a class presentation, the project contributes to a decentralisation of teaching and learning practices: students work on the podcast and receive feedback outside the classroom, and the finished product—which incorporates feedback and editing—is then presented to the rest of the class and used for class activities.

In their qualitative responses, students referred to an increase in their speaking confidence, which mostly resulted from the sense of accomplishment about a final product that could be shared with and enjoyed by others (Lambert et al., 2017). In addition, as noted previously, many students reflected critically about conventions of colloquial Italian and received feedback from their teachers and peers during the project, with all aspects contributing to an increase in their general self-confidence as L2 speakers.

6. Conclusion

The data presented clearly show that the project contributes to diversifying the language curriculum while also decentring teaching practices by placing learners, their interests and their work at the centre of the learning process. The project also offers a novel experience for students with the potential of increasing their motivation and alleviating their L2 anxiety. No major differences were found in the experiences of on-campus and online students, or in their perceptions of the impact of the project on their motivation and anxiety. This suggests that the project can be successfully implemented both in person and online.

As noted previously, the project was found to have a direct positive effect on students' intrinsic motivation for four main reasons:

1. It enables students to engage in self-directed learning and choose a topic that is relevant to them
2. It is novel and different from any other activity that students have engaged with before at university, and is perceived as a positive challenge

3. It entails the creation of a meaningful finished product that students can call their own and that can be showed to and enjoyed by others
4. It has a real audience and enables students to acquire a better understanding of spoken Italian.

These findings reflect the effectiveness of the integration of PBL and SGC in the classroom. While SGC should not be the only linguistic input learners are exposed to, our data show that students enjoyed listening to their peers' podcasts, with these activities contributing to improving community building in the classroom and allowing them to have more control over the topics included in the curriculum.

Our findings also indicate that students perceived the project as less anxiety inducing than class presentations. The opportunity to rehearse the script and correct mistakes during the recording phase, the feedback received while being engaged in a joint effort in a face-saving environment, and the collaborative nature of the project appeared to be the key elements associated with lower levels of anxiety, in keeping with previous research on the benefits of PBL (see Miguel & Carney, 2022). Our research provides some insights for future iterations of the project and paves the way for its adaptation for other languages in Australia or elsewhere.

References

Absalom, M. (2017). The theatre project: From critical analysis to collaborative action—using Dario Fo's *Non tutti i ladri vengono per nuocere* in the teaching and learning of Italian. *Spunti e Ricerche, 31*, 12–19 spuntiericerche.com/index.php/spuntiericerche/article/view/626.

Absalom, M. (2021). Il teatro per insegnare l'italiano [Using theatre to teach Italian]. In Rubino, A., Tamponi, A. R. & Hajek, J. (Eds.), *L'italiano in Australia: Prospettive e tendenze nell'insegnamento della lingua e della cultura* [*Italian in Australia: Perspectives and trends in the teaching of language and culture*] (pp. 187–201). Franco Cesati Editore.

Amorati, R., Ferrari, E. & Hajek, J. (2022). Podcasting as project-based learning and its effect on the acquisition of linguistic and non-linguistic skills. *Language Learning in Higher Education, 12*(1), 7–28. doi.org/10.1515/cercles-2022-2036.

Amorati, R. & Hajek, J. (2021). Fostering motivation and creativity through self-publishing as project-based learning in the Italian L2 classroom. *Foreign Language Annals, 54*(4), 1003–1026. doi.org/10.1111/flan.12568.

Amorati, R. & Venturin, B. (2021). 'I command thee thou shalt speak': Understanding and counteracting foreign language anxiety in the classroom. *Ricerche di Pedagogia e Didattica. Journal of Theories and Research in Education, 16*(3), 39–57. doi.org/10.6092/issn.1970-2221/12350.

Brown, K. L. (2003). From teacher-centered to learner-centered curriculum: Improving learning in diverse classrooms. *Education, 124*(1), 49–54.

Buck Institute of Education. (2022). *Golden standards for PBL: Essential project design elements*. PBL Works. pblworks.org/what-is-pbl/gold-standard-project-design.

Deci, E. L. & Ryan, R. M. (1985). *Intrinsic motivation and self-determination in human behavior*. Plenum. doi.org/10.1007/978-1-4899-2271-7.

Dewaele, J. M. (2007). The effect of multilingualism, sociobiographical, and situational factors on communicative anxiety and foreign language anxiety of mature language learners. *International Journal of Bilingualism, 11*(4), 391–409. doi.org/10.1177/13670069070110040301.

Dewaele, J. M., Magdalena, A. F. & Saito, K. (2019). The effect of perception of teacher characteristics on Spanish EFL learners' anxiety and enjoyment. *The Modern Language Journal, 103*(2), 412–427. doi.org/10.1111/modl.12555.

Dörnyei, Z. (1994). Motivation and motivating in the foreign language classroom. *Modern Language Journal, 78*(3), 273–84. doi.org/10.2307/330107.

Dörnyei, Z. (2001). *Motivational strategies in the language classroom*. Cambridge University Press. doi.org/10.1017/CBO9780511667343.

Dörnyei, Z. (2007). *Research methods in applied linguistics*. Oxford University Press.

Edirisingha, P., Rizzi, C., Nie, M. & Rothwell, L. (2007). Podcasting to provide teaching and learning support for an undergraduate module on English language and communication. *Turkish Online Journal of Distance Education, 8*(3), 87–107.

Ferrari, E., Amorati, R., Hajek, J. (2024). Teaching Italian through podcasting: Pedagogical rationale, implementation and student evaluation of the podcast project 'Dagli inviati sul campus'. In G. Guarnieri, G. (Ed.), *The art of teaching Italian* (pp. 135–152). Georgetown University Press. doi.org/10.2307/jj.8816158.12.

Gkonou, C., Daubney, M. & Dewaele, J. M. (Eds.). (2017). *New insights into language anxiety: Theory, research and educational implications*. Multilingual Matters. doi.org/10.21832/9781783097722.

Gregersen, T. & MacIntyre, P. D. (2014). *Capitalizing on individual differences: From premise to practice*. Multilingual Matters. doi.org/10.21832/9781783091218.

Grieve, R., Woodley, J., Hunt, S. E. & McKay, A. (2021). Student fears of oral presentations and public speaking in higher education: A qualitative survey. *Journal of Further and Higher Education*, *45*(9), 1281–1293. doi.org/10.1080/0309877X.2021.1948509.

Hasan, M. M. & Hoon, T. B. (2013). Podcast applications in language learning: A review of recent studies. *English Language Teaching*, *6*(2), 128–135. doi.org/10.5539/elt.v6n2p128.

Kim, S. Y. (2009). Questioning the stability of foreign language classroom anxiety and motivation across different classroom contexts. *Foreign Language Annals*, *42*(1), 138–157. doi.org/10.1111/j.1944-9720.2009.01012.x.

Lambert, C. (1997). Motivation and personal investment in the learning process. *Journal of Nanzan Junior College*, *24*, 55–88.

Lambert, C. (2004). Reverse-engineering communication tasks. *ELT Journal*, *58*(1), 18–27. doi.org/10.1093/elt/58.1.18.

Lambert, C., Philp, J. & Nakamura, S. (2017). Learner-generated content and engagement in second language task performance. *Language Teaching Research*, *21*(6), 665–680. doi.org/10.1177/1362168816683559.

Larmer, J., Mergendoller, J. & Boss, S. (2015). *Setting the standard for project-based learning*. Association for Supervision and Curriculum Development.

Martín, M. D. & Beckmann, E. A. (2011). Simulating immersion: Podcasting in Spanish teaching. In B. R. Facer & M. Abdous (Eds.), *Academic podcasting and mobile assisted language learning: Applications and outcomes* (pp. 111–131). IGI Global. doi.org/10.4018/978-1-60960-141-6.ch007.

Mbah, E. E., Mbah, B. M., Iloene, M. I. & Iloene, G. O. (2013). Podcasts for learning English pronunciation in Igboland: Students' experiences and expectations. In L. Bradley & S. Thouësny (Eds.), *20 Years of EUROCALL: Learning from the past, looking to the future. Proceedings of the 2013 EUROCALL Conference, Évora, Portugal* (pp. 183–187).

Mercer, S. & Dörnyei, Z. (2020). *Engaging language learners in contemporary classrooms*. Cambridge University Press. doi.org/10.1017/9781009024563.

Mergendoller, J. R., Markham, T., Ravitz, J. & Larmer, J. (2006). Pervasive management of project-based learning: Teachers as guides and facilitators. In C. Evertson, C. M. Weinstein & C. S. Weinstein (Eds.), *Handbook of classroom management: Research, practice, and contemporary issues* (pp. 583–615). Routledge. doi.org/10.4324/9780203874783.

Miguel, E. & Carney, W. (2022). Foreign language acquisition anxiety and project-based learning in collaborative L2 instruction: A case study. *Theory and Practice in Language Studies, 12*(1), 1-6. doi.org/10.17507/tpls.1201.01.

Moreno-López, I., Ramos-Sellman, A., Miranda-Aldaco, C. & Gomis Quinto, M. T. (2017). Transforming ways of enhancing foreign language acquisition in the Spanish classroom: Experiential learning approaches. *Foreign Language Annals, 50*(2), 398–409. doi.org/10.1111/flan.12267.

Noels, K. A. (2001). New orientations in language learning motivation: Toward a contextual model of intrinsic, extrinsic, and integrative orientations and motivation. In Z. Dörnyei & R. Schmidt (Eds.), *Motivation and second language acquisition* (pp. 43–68). University of Hawai'i.

Noels, K. A. (2009). The internalization of language learning into the self and social identity. In Z. Dörnyei & E. Ushioda (Eds.), *Motivation, language identity and the L2 self* (pp. 43–65). Multilingual Matters.

Noels, K. A., Pelletier, L. G., Clément, R. & Vallerand, R. J. (2003). Why are you learning a second language? Motivational orientations and self-determination theory. *Language Learning, 53*(S1), 33–64. doi.org/10.1111/1467-9922.53223.

O'Leary, Z. (2010). *The essential guide to doing your research project*. Sage.

Samperi Mangan, J. (2008). Podcasting and iPod in teaching and learning Italian language, culture and literature: A research study at Université de Montréal. In E. Occhipinti (Ed.). *New approaches to teaching Italian language and culture: Case studies from an international perspective* (pp. 210–224). Cambridge Scholars.

Stefanou, C., Stolk, J. D., Prince, M., Chen, J. C. & Lord, S. M. (2013). Self-regulation and autonomy in problem- and project-based learning environments. *Active Learning in Higher Education, 14*(2), 109–122. doi.org/10.1177/1469787413481132.

Stoller, F. (2006). Establishing a theoretical foundation for project-based learning in second and foreign language contexts. In G. H. Beckett & P. Chamness Miller (Eds.), *Project-based second and foreign language education: Past, present, and future* (pp. 19–40). Information Age.

Supe, O. & Kaupuzs, A. (2015). The effectiveness of project-based learning in the acquisition of English as a foreign language. *Society, Integration, Education. Proceedings of the International Scientific Disciplines, 2*, 210–218. www.researchgate.net/publication/277887431_The_Effectiveness_of_Project_-Based_Learning_in_the_Acquisition_of_English_as_a_Foreign_Language.

Young, D. J. (1990). An investigation of students' perspectives on anxiety and speaking. *Foreign Language Annals, 23*(6), 539–553. doi.org/10.1111/j.1944-9720.1990.tb00424.x.

9

No tickets required! Interactive virtual tours and virtual environments in the study of Italian language and culture

Elisabetta Ferrari and Mitch Buzza

1. Introduction

This chapter offers an overview of two distinct virtual reality (VR) projects and their application in two undergraduate Italian subjects. These projects, designed and developed by the authors at the University of Melbourne, aim at diversifying content delivery and enhancing student learning experience and engagement through the use of a virtual learning environment (VLE). Both projects have been created using available resources in addition to authentic historical material and have been inserted into the curricula of two subjects, taught in Italian, that focus on the study of the historical and cultural period from the Italian unification (1861) to the end of World War II (1945). The projects not only give students a new approach to understanding this historical period, but also offer the opportunity for language immersion, which has the potential to improve listening and comprehension skills. Additionally, as will be discussed in this chapter, this approach implements diversified pedagogical practices within the subjects' curricula to enhance student participation and motivation.

The first project, *Dal Foro Romano al Foro Italico* (From the Roman Forum to the Foro Italico), was realised using a non-immersive interactive video and a 360° virtual tour achieved using exports from Google Earth, Google Streetview and H5P Interactive Video. The virtual tour allows students to explore the architectural features of two distinct areas of Rome that were built during the Fascist dictatorship (1922–43) to better understand the connection between Fascist propaganda and architecture. The virtual tour is accessible to students on their own computer or tablet. Offering a voiceover narration in Italian and interactive links to deepen their understanding, it creates pathways for individual learning. The second project, *La Spedizione dei Mille* (The Expedition of the Thousand), consists of an immersive VR 360° video that is accessible via the use of Oculus Quest headsets or as an immersive video on tablets or computers. This virtual tour recreates part of the voyage undertaken by the so-called 'Expedition of the Thousand' in Italy in 1860–61 that led to the unification of the nation. It also includes a voiceover narration using extracts of diaries compiled by volunteers who participated in the expedition.

The first project was conceived during the context of a worldwide pandemic that limited our ability to travel and experience firsthand different cultures and languages. Initially, the project was designed to give students the opportunity to experience virtual travel during a period when actual travel was not possible, as Australia had closed its borders. The shift undertaken by many tertiary institutions to online and/or dual delivery teaching modes and content during COVID-19 highlighted the need to increase the use of new learning environments capable of stimulating students' engagement and deeper connection with topics studied. This shift in teaching and learning, which involved long periods of online delivery and working from home, forced many in the higher education sector to quickly become solo video producers, composing video backgrounds, optimising lighting and sound, and modifying speaking delivery for pace and energy. These are, in fact, the foundation blocks of regular video production, and it quickly became apparent that we, as instructors, needed more variety than the talking head/webcam style production available to most people. One positive result that emerged from this disruptive period is that it has prompted many in the sector to rethink teaching outputs and diversify modes of delivery. The second project was, in fact, the result of this synergy and was created from the desire to continue to offer students the opportunity to experience different perspectives in studying traditional material. With the easing of restrictions and the return to on-campus teaching, the first project continued to be used successfully as an effective tool to diversify content delivery.

In this chapter we offer a review of existing scholarship that focuses on the use of VR in the classroom setting and its theoretical foundation, while also highlighting the diversity of applications and degree of interactivity/immersion that can be achieved. We then provide a detailed description of the two projects, their technical realisation and required equipment. We also offer an overview of the structure and implementation of the VR content and related activities, and discuss the engaging learning opportunities these projects can offer to language students. Finally, preliminary informal student feedback on the two projects is discussed to demonstrate the effectiveness of their use. We also provide some suggestions on the application of these tools in other educational or cultural contexts.

2. Literature review

2.1. VR and virtual learning environments as pedagogical tools

VR technology and tools have been extensively used in various commercial and gaming sectors (for example, Second Life, Open Simulator, etc.). However, it is now increasingly common to see the use of VR as a VLE in teaching and learning. This, in turn, has generated a plethora of research in computer-assisted language learning (CALL) focused on the evaluation of these tools on a pedagogical level (Lin & Lan, 2015). Among early VR adopters in the first part of the new millennium, Second Life, in particular, proved to be an engaging tool for language learning applications. It was embraced by various language institutes (e.g. Instituto Cervantes, Goethe Institute) for its immersive features, which are able to recreate a virtual space for education, interaction and exchange (Coppola, 2016). Second Life has now been superseded by newer technologies adapted for educational purposes; however, one relevant key observation from the research concerned the disconnect between the potentiality of such programs and the way in which they were utilised by language teachers. Teachers tended simply to transfer, into these virtual worlds, activities and methodologies used in a traditional language setting, without taking advantage of the virtual dimension and opportunities available (Panichi & Deutschmann, 2012). Physical/spatial, affective/creative and social/communicative/cognitive dimensions are vital in the use of 3D worlds and need to be considered when adapting virtual environments for educational purposes (Coppola, 2016; Panichi & Deutschmann, 2009).

The use of VR applications in language teaching has also been studied for its ability to provide students with a more realistic engagement, not only with the content of their subjects, but also with their overall learning experience. Scholarly literature on VR and experiential learning underlines the pedagogical benefits of the use of the former in the classroom context (e.g. Chittaro and Ranon, 2007; Lin & Lan, 2015; Pilgrim & Pilgrim, 2016). VR can be used and applied with different degrees of virtual participation (through avatars, headsets, interactive spaces, etc.) and in many different contexts (gaming, entertainment, medical and science fields, education, etc.). VR provides an immersive tool that can enhance students' experience and interaction, and facilitate the learning of difficult concepts through firsthand visualisation that is not achievable in more traditional learning environments (Amara et al., 2023).

Two important features observed in the use of VR are immersion and interaction. These can be developed through a learner-centred approach (Lan, 2020; Schwienhorst, 2002). In particular, immersion through virtual motion has been found to be beneficial in the learning of additional languages as it enhances verbal memory in an environment perceived as true-to-life (Repetto, 2014). Moreover, VR has been studied for its ability to position learners in a situated experiential education environment in consideration of the fact that, while offering immersion and interaction with space and other people, it also provides a complex experience (Schott & Marshall, 2018). 'Complexity', considered in pedagogical terms, is identified as one of the key elements in student learning objectives, as it enables the development of critical thinking skills by exposing students to intricate and challenging problems (Schott & Marshall, 2018). This is in line with foundation studies centred on situated activity and cognition theories of learning (Lave, 1988; Lave & Wenger, 1991) that focus on positioning the learning process in the 'real world' to provide meaningful experiences and promote knowledge acquisition.

Further, the use of VR applications within the teaching curriculum constitutes an optimal framework to engage in experiential learning while also creating an opportunity for students to develop digital literacy skills. Experiential learning encourages learning by doing in an attempt to shift the focus of the student from a passive role (visualising and listening) to an active participatory role (Jackson, 2015; see also Bonwell & Eison, 1991; Kolb, 1984).

2.2 VR as a form of multimodal delivery

Research demonstrates that the use of diversified teaching approaches in both content and delivery, with a focus on learner-centred activities and experiential learning, is essential for successful outcomes, especially in language learning (Bhattacharjee, 2015; Lan, 2016). Digital technologies are key tools for a range of modalities and media as they allow meaning to be conveyed through various communication resources (Magnusson & Godhe, 2019). It follows that VLE offers the opportunity for engagement in the study of a language and diversification of teaching delivery (Coppola, 2016).

A multimodal approach was central to the design and teaching format of the Italian subjects under consideration in this chapter. Teaching delivery for these subjects had originally been conceived following the traditional lecture and seminar class format. By interposing content assimilation in different formats and styles, while still linking these to the rest of the program, students are given the opportunity to differentiate their learning experience and approach to learning. The aim is to diversify the content delivery of lecture-style classes that are usually offered in person and recorded for students who are unable to attend. Lectures are not counted as part of students' attendance hurdle requirements; consequently, in-person attendance is very low. It is common knowledge that one of the major challenges faced by Australian universities is a lack of student attendance at face-to-face lectures when recordings are made available. Additionally, students tend to listen, only partly, to recorded content as observed in statistics from online student lecture access.

There has long been debate over the effectiveness of the lecture as a teaching method (French & Kennedy, 2017). Notwithstanding this, it is now recognised that the lecture format is changing and becoming increasingly interactive (e.g. French & Kennedy, 2017; Palaima, 2014). Research shows that it is essential to implement a range of teaching methods that create an alternative to standard lectures and that take into consideration our changing educational environments (French & Kennedy, 2017).

In the case of the two Italian subjects considered here, a multimodal approach was achieved by interposing other teaching delivery styles that complemented the VR activities. Students were given access to an object-based learning (OBL) lab to consult primary sources from the university library special collection, enabling them to analyse, firsthand, a range of authentic material and exposing them to a different kind of immersive approach in their studies.

3. Analysis of content and technical details of the two VR projects presented

3.1. Overview of projects

The two VR projects presented in this chapter were created as teaching and learning material to be included in the curricula of two Italian subjects—ITAL10002/20008 Italian 4 and ITAL20001 Italian Cultural Studies B—offered at the University of Melbourne to post-beginners and second-year advanced students of Italian. The two projects were designed as VLEs. Their goal is to enhance students' experiential and active learning, immersion and participation in the approach of language material—key concepts for successful language learning (Lan, 2020). Additionally, the inclusion of VR projects in the subject curriculum contributes to diversifying teaching approaches and complements other styles of content delivery. Both projects foster immersion in the study of the language: while they are both offered in Italian for students enrolled at an advanced level, students at post-beginner level take part in the first project in Italian and have a choice of Italian or English for the second project, depending on their listening abilities.

It is important to note that, although the focus on language learning is prominent, it does not constitute the main learning outcome; one of the major aims is to achieve a competent historical and cultural understanding of the period analysed. This aspect places these projects in a slightly different position to traditional VR use within language teaching and learning. Research shows that, in the teaching and learning of additional languages, VR has predominantly been used as a successful tool to improve and develop students' language skills (vocabulary, pronunciation, syntax, etc.) and understanding of some contemporary cultural aspects (Berti, 2019; Chen, 2016; Figueroa et al., 2022). The use of VR in these two projects enables students to delve deeply into a historical context through evocative immersion in the places, sentiments and forces that shaped the period.

The curricula of the two subjects in question are structured over a 12-week semester (with four contact hours weekly for post-beginners and 2.5 for advanced students, respectively). The curricula focus on the study of the historical and cultural period from Italian unification to the end of World War II. Although the content is similar for the two subjects, the language of instruction and material is tailored according to subject level. Students attend diverse class styles (seminars, lectures and OBL laboratories) where they are given the historical, social and cultural context necessary to discuss and analyse different kinds of primary and secondary sources. The use of OBL, in particular, allows students to analyse authentic primary sources (made available from the university library special collection) and view historical documents firsthand. Texts studied to analyse the historical period cover a wide range of genres, from primary sources in Italian (diaries, extracts from novels or short stories, manifestos, etc.) to secondary sources in English and Italian (academic articles on contextual topics). Importantly, the subjects are also devoted to the investigation of visual arts (painting, artefacts, etc.) and the artistic elements used in the representation of the historical periods covered. Students enrolled at post-beginner level attend, in addition, a one-hour weekly language workshop aimed at improving grammar and oral/aural skills, focusing on a range of topics related to Italian culture.

The two VR projects were created with the assistance of the Faculty of Arts eTeaching Unit at the University of Melbourne. This unit, like those in many tertiary institutions, supports staff to create and deploy digital teaching assets with various hardware and software—from standard learning management system (LMS) websites (like Canvas) to large-scale web tools (Padlet, H5P, Feedback Fruits and others) and teaching videos (Kaltura, Echo360, Zoom). In recent years, the demand for new teaching methodologies has seen increased experimentation by eTeaching units in the university sector, with new forms of production, such as 360° video and cameraless, low-code/no-code video production, particularly using free-to-use and open-source tools.

The two projects outlined here offer two different kinds of VR applications. VR use can be distinguished as immersive, which usually refers to the use of a VR headset or Oculus Rift, or non-immersive or desktop VR in a 3D environment (Lan, 2020). Following this categorisation, the first project (From the Roman Forum to the Foro Italico) can be defined as a non-immersive VR application, whereas the second (The Expedition of the

Thousand) represents a fully immersive VR experience. The choice of two different VR applications reflects the desire to diversify the ways in which students experience and interact with material made available to them.

3.2. Project 1: *Dal Foro Romano al Foro Italico* (From the Roman Forum to the Foro Italico)

For the first project we designed and developed a non-immersive interactive video and a 360° virtual tour of two distinct areas of Rome (EUR and Foro Italico). Both areas of Rome were built during the Fascist dictatorship and are representative of the way in which the regime used architecture and urban spaces for propagandistic purposes, while also highlighting the paradigm of rationalist architecture merged with elements of classical Roman Empire. For this reason, the virtual tour departs from the Colosseum (within the Roman Forum), moving from the centre of Rome to the southern part of the city where the suburb EUR is located. Various buildings of the EUR complex are then virtually visited to highlight architectural features and stylistic elements. Images vary, from aerial shots to frontal and interior shots of the buildings visited (Palazzo dei Congressi, Palazzo degli Uffici, Palazzo della Civiltà Italiana), to outside spaces and other areas. The virtual tour then continues to the north side of the city towards the Foro Italico, offering an overview of this sports complex and its architectural style, statues and use of symbols. The virtual tour concludes by taking the viewers back to the Colosseum, demonstrating the visual correlation between the architecture of ancient Rome and the use of classical elements within the architecture of the two other areas visited.

The video is five minutes and 10 seconds long and contains five break points where students can choose to pause the virtual tour and access various interactive links. This allows students to further analyse and research specific aspects of the sites visited (Figures 9.1 and 9.2). Links include 2D recorded videos (in Italian), academic articles and YouTube videos (in English or Italian). These extra resources represent further contextual and informative material to help in the understanding of the virtual tour elements and are in line with the material used during the rest of the subject programs.

The goal of the virtual tour is not only to give students an engaging learning experience but also to immerse students in the country of their studies from afar. Additionally, the tour gives students an approximation of the spatial aspect of the city and an appreciation of spatial distances, dimensions and the scope of the area.

Figure 9.1. The beginning of the VR non-immersive video tour (Project 1)
Source: Authors.

Figure 9.2. Example of a virtual tour break and interactive links (Project 1)
Source: Authors.

With this first project, through the use of non-immersive VR, we wanted to create a virtual tour experience for students using resources already available while also retaining the element of authenticity in the teaching material (Lan, 2020). Additionally, we wanted to achieve an experience that was cost-neutral and/or cost-effective; thus, it was important to be able to create a virtual tour that did not necessitate filming on location (for example, with a 360° 3D camera—a popular use of interactive VR in education). Therefore, rather than make a video slideshow from still images and a voiceover, we decided to break new ground and combine three web-based tools to make a 'no-camera' video, but with all the movement and dynamism of real camera moves, such as drone shots, pans, tilts and zooms. We then proceeded to weave through some interesting links, pop-ups, text and music for higher engagement and impact. Finally, a voiceover narration was added in specific parts of the tour to guide viewers through the principal locations of the journey.

The project was achieved using exports from Google Earth, Google Streetview and H5P Interactive Video. This is quite an innovation, as video exports from Google Earth Studio were, until fairly recently, only available to network broadcasters with expensive licensing fees; it is really only since 2019 that it has become a viable product for this kind of purpose (it is now a free, cloud-based, 3D animation tool, exporting up to 4K resolution in 2D and 360° formats without any copyright restriction). Additionally, major cities like Rome are sumptuously rendered, as they have been extensively scanned in 3D for Google's mapping services. This allowed us to use dramatic drone shots to simulate, for example, a flight at high speed from the Colosseum and around EUR and then to the Foro Italico. At ground level in Rome, Google Streetview (using iStreetView software) gave us the choice of thousands of 360° spherical panoramas, and allowed us to simulate pans, tilts and zooms at the various locations featured in the virtual tour. For this purpose, we extracted the panoramas and used a combination of screen capture and semi-automated spins and turns.

All the video assets, along with voiceovers and a soundtrack, were edited (on Adobe Premiere Pro) for brevity and pace, and strategically placed black dissolves were added to allow for the next stage. The resulting virtual tour, rich with action and interaction, was created without leaving the laptop. Finally, we used H5P Interactive Video to make a dynamic video by adding interactive links. This allowed us the additional benefit of exporting the project on a platform that is supported by LMS/Canvas sites (used by most tertiary education institutions) and that could be easily embedded into these student portals.

3.3. Project 2: *La Spedizione dei Mille* (The Expedition of the Thousand)

The second project consists of an immersive VR 3D journey accessible with both Oculus Quest headsets or as a 3D video watchable on computers or tablets. This virtual project is designed as a historical re-enactment of part of the journey undertaken by the volunteers participating in the 'Expedition of the Thousand' in Italy in 1860–61, which was fundamental to the unification of the nation.

The virtual project comprises two parts: first, a voyage by sea from Quarto (Genoa), in the north-west of Italy, to Marsala (Sicily) aboard the historical steamships *Lombardo* and *Piemonte*. The first part of the voyage is mostly seen through the sailing of the two vessels; on board are a group of volunteers, headed by Giuseppe Garibaldi, engaged in an expedition to liberate the Kingdom of the two Sicilies and other occupied states, to achieve Italy's unification (Figure 9.3). Once the steamships reach Sicily, the second part of the voyage follows the disembarkation of the troops and then moves through military battles and fights on land. The expedition continues from the south of Italy to Naples, and finally to Teano (near Rome) where the famous encounter between Garibaldi and King Victor Emanuel II took place, symbolically establishing the new Kingdom of Italy.

Figure 9.3. The voyage by sea of the two steamships, *Piemonte* and *Lombardo* (Project 2)
Source: Authors.

The VR expedition includes a voiceover narration of diary extracts compiled by three volunteers who participated in the expedition (Ippolito Nievo, Giuseppe Bandi and Giuseppe Cesare Abba). A carefully chosen selection of diary entries was used to create the narrative of the expedition throughout the whole virtual journey, giving the re-enactment a realistic and authentic tone. Additionally, along the journey, viewers are transported into a virtual exhibition space where they can see a display of images—ranging from paintings, maps and military relics to artefacts of the period—and a video installation chronicling the events of the journey (Figures 9.4, 9.5 and 9.6). The visual aspect, and specifically the use of paintings and other artefacts, is fundamental to the narration and representation of an event that has otherwise largely been depicted in official portraiture and patriotic propaganda. The narrative device of the voices of the three volunteers reading their diaries gives additional context and coherence to the series of 360° vignettes.

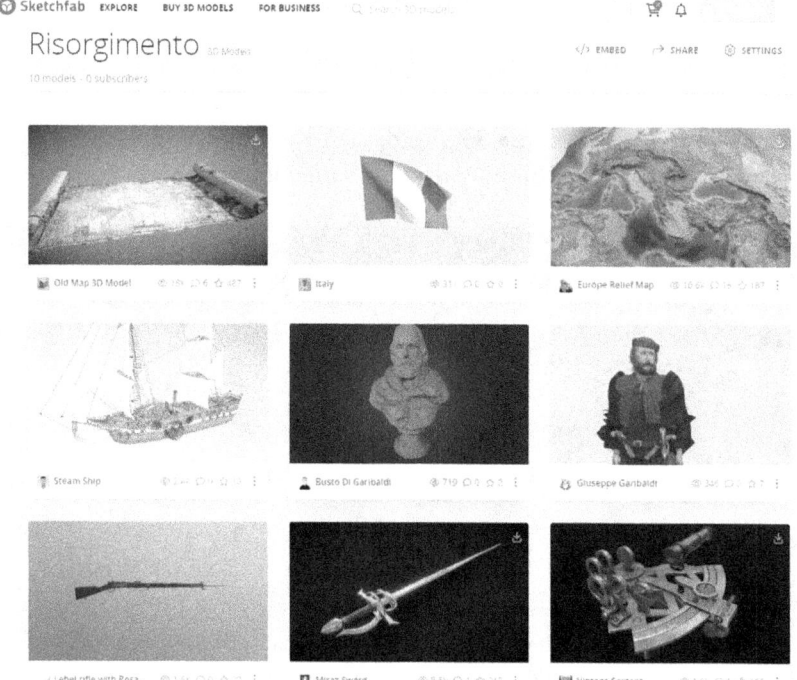

Figure 9.4. 3D models of the expedition artefacts created with Sketchfab (Project 2)
Source: Authors.

9. NO TICKETS REQUIRED!

Figure 9.5. Virtual gallery of the three diarist-volunteers (Project 2)
Source: Authors.

Figure 9.6. Video installation (Project 2)
Source: Authors.

213

Much like the previously presented virtual tour, the aim of the second project is to foster engagement in the study of the historical period while also providing an immersive experience through a historical reconstruction offered in an innovative way.

The project is produced in two versions, one with an Italian voiceover (for all students), and one in English, offered as an option to students enrolled in the post-beginner stream to facilitate comprehension. Students accessing the VR project in Italian benefit from the possibility of improving linguistic and comprehension skills.

This project was undertaken and completed in the post-pandemic context, once we were able to return to in-person teaching and had regained access to the required specialist equipment. Unlike our experience of the more linear 2D video production process, we spent a long time experimenting with the various production tools before the script and the storyline eventually came together. Our intention was not to construct a literal retelling of the expedition, but, rather, to generate evocative immersion in the places and the depictions of the expedition.

The project was realised through the use of both production hardware and software. For the production hardware, we used:

- Oculus Rift S VR headset and a high-powered gaming PC (handpainted 3D scenes)
- MacBook laptop (360° video production and virtual drone/satellite animation)
- Meta Quest 1 headset (360° video drafts and classroom immersive viewing).

For the production software we used:

- Google Earth Studio
- Adobe Premiere Pro
- Open Brush
- Google image search
- Sketchfab.com 3D model platform.

The production process comprises five types of 360° video shots that were devised using the following:

1. Google Earth Studio was used for virtual drone and low-orbit satellite shots that were animated to portray the geographical movement along the Italian coastline, across Sicily and southern Italy.
2. Adobe Premiere Pro was used to cut and remix battle scene re-enactments from existing documentaries and films into a 360° video to simulate the confusion and mayhem of combat.
3. Adobe Premiere Pro was also used for scenes of some of the locations that were edited for pace and brevity and converted to appear as rectangular 2D videos within 360° videos.
4. The VR painting and modelling tool Open Brush was used to compose 360° scenes moving through a virtual gallery. Special focus and attention were given to particular artworks that coincided with the voiceover narration.
5. Open Brush was also used for the virtual 360° camera shots depicting the writing desks and small possessions of the diarists to create short vignettes.

The screening and viewing of the final output was realised as two 360° videos (approximate running time is seven to eight minutes each), presented in class in two different formats through either Oculus Quest headsets or tablets/computers.

3.4. Pedagogical considerations, curriculum structure and implementation of the projects

Research demonstrates that the role of teachers and the development of learner-centred activities are central to achieving successful language learning outcomes in the use of VR (Bhattacharjee, 2015; Lan, 2020). These premises were conceptually central in the design and implementation of the two projects, ensuring the pedagogically meaningful, rather than tokenistic and poorly integrated, use of VR.

The two projects were conceived with a curriculum-centred focus and integrated to complement the material studied throughout the semester by students. One of the central premises in the choice of materials was diversification of text types to expose students to a broad array of styles and genres. Additionally, pedagogical consideration was given to the way a series of lectures could be used to create a coherent and contextual narrative of the historical period to facilitate understanding and assimilation of themes studied (French & Kennedy, 2017).

For the first project (From the Roman Forum to the Foro Italico), students are asked to watch the tour in their own time (preferably on a big screen) and to engage with the interactive material at their discretion to foster independent learning. Following this independent work, students are asked to complete a structured series of activities and questions in Italian that are then used during seminar discussions. Activities and questions are organised on two different levels:

1. Some informal learning activities and conversational prompts (for example, students are asked to indicate a location or building of preference and to comment on their general knowledge of the city; they are also required to take a virtual selfie in front of one of the locations virtually visited, post it on a Padlet wall and explain their choice to their fellow students).
2. An in-depth analysis of at least two interactive resources available in the virtual video, which is then shared with the rest of the class during the seminar, leading to a discussion on the role of architecture in the context of Fascist propaganda and its enduring impact on the contemporary Italian landscape.

For the second project (The Expedition of the Thousand), students are required to complete some pre-VR tour work to fully understand the historical context. This work includes an analysis of the diaries of volunteers participating in the unification expedition and of images of paintings and artefacts from the historical period.

Students then watch the full immersion virtual tour in class via Oculus Quest headsets or tablets/computers. They are then asked to comment, in Italian, on both their experience of the historical re-enactment and their personal immersive experience. Padlet walls are created to allow students to record impressions observed during their immersive experience, and they are prompted to consider which elements differ or are new in comparison to their previous traditional analysis. Group discussion, in Italian, is then structured around themes related to personal recollection, historical memories and ideas of national identity and representation. Additionally, for one of the subjects, students are asked, as a collaborative project-based task, to create a virtual exhibition of their own, in line with the themes and findings analysed during the semester.

The use of group work for assessment and other class activities allows students to share personal impressions gained through the use of the immersive VR experience and apply learning outcomes acquired. Group activity, as a methodological tool, has been identified in pedagogical literature as an effective strategy to improve learning outcomes and help in the development of additional skills (Burke, 2011). Asking students to work as a group in collaborative teams means they are able to share outputs and develop skills related to project-based learning, thus decentring a traditional form of assessment linked to individual outputs.

4. Preliminary findings and potential skills acquisition

At the time of writing, the two projects discussed had only recently been completed. The formal results of students' learning experiences will inform future research publications, in which both qualitative and quantitative data will be collected and analysed. However, a preliminary, informal, in-class survey conducted for Project 1 (From the Roman Forum to the Foro Italico), aimed at gauging students' reception and interest, shows that the virtual tour was received by all students as an engaging and immersive resource. Students expressed enthusiasm and a desire to have additional resources of this kind embedded into their subject curriculum. Additionally, this informal survey showed that the project represented a break from traditional subject delivery by giving students access to material in a new and engaging style. Students commented on their enjoyment in experiencing a sense of the 'reality' of the place and a sense of 'being there in real life'. During class discussion it was noted that the VR tour helped to spatially visualise some of the spaces and concepts analysed. One interesting aspect that emerged during these discussions was a series of observations that had never been raised by students in previous years (when students had accessed similar material via traditional PowerPoint images). With the new VR format, students specifically commented on the spatial distances between the two areas of Rome and the centre of the city, geographical location, size of the area, and dimensions of buildings and statues. All comments indicated a much better appreciation of aspects that are usually connected to 'real' site visits. It was clear that the virtual tour had given students an additional 'dimension', so to speak, to analyse and reflect upon.

For the second project, a class discussion carried out after the immersive VR experience (through the use of Oculus Quest) highlighted the initial 'enjoyable' and 'immersive' aspect of the tool. Beyond this initial impression of novelty, students commented on the fact that the project helped in understanding and unpacking a complex historical period, bringing to life the ideas and concepts studied. Students also noted that the VR experience helped them to understand sentiments of national belonging, patriotism, and the tropes and metaphors that are central in the Risorgimento discourse.

These informal preliminary comments are, in fact, in line with theoretical literature on the reception of VR and reinforce the importance of innovative and diverse class formats. Additionally, these kinds of projects allow students to build on their language skills, fostering listening and comprehension, and facilitating vocabulary retention. Although listening and speaking skills have been the major focus of research on VR tools and affordances (Bahari, 2022; Dhimolea et al., 2022), it is important to note a range of additional skills gained by students through the use of VR with a focus on visual arts. Skills related to digital literacy, understanding of online virtual digital platforms and digitisation of images constitute essential skills that are easily transferable to other sectors (for example, museum curatorship, digital production, etc.).

5. Conclusion

In this chapter we have reviewed some of the current literature on the use and implementation of VR and VLE in the education context. Scholarly research highlights the beneficial use of VR as an educational tool, due to its variety of applications and ability to foster active, experiential learning through immersion and interaction (Lan, 2020; Schwienhorst, 2002).

The two VR projects presented show a diverse pedagogical approach centred on innovation and immersion and the use of multimodal delivery styles. The projects, initially conceived during the disruption caused by COVID-19, try to capitalise on the circumstances that emerged through the pandemic period, which forced most teachers in the educational system to adapt their teaching and learning practices to the online/dual delivery format.

With these projects, we seek to build from the newly decentred teaching methodologies and diversified subject delivery methods of the post-pandemic period, using available VR resources to promote student engagement and experiential learning. The two projects—which have been incorporated into the curricula of two Italian subjects, offered to post-beginners and second-year advanced students, respectively—show, in their distinct use of non-immersive VR and fully immersive VR, the wide-ranging scope and adoption that can be achieved with readily available VR tools. Designed to deepen students' understanding of two historical periods, the projects form part of the multimodal approach conceived for the two subjects. Through immersion, engagement and project-based activities, they aim at developing a wide range of skills related to language and culture learning outcomes, as well as transferable skills for other work and study sectors.

This chapter has provided a detailed description of the implementation and use of the projects within two Italian subjects and offered some preliminary informal findings. A further study on VR application in the classroom environment, and an analysis of qualitative and quantitative data collected from students, will be the subject of future research.

A key benefit to emerge from the two projects was the ability to create virtual material that did not necessitate costly additional resourcing or activities, such as on-location filming. This demonstrates how available technology allows us to create innovative content in a sustainable way. In fact, although the projects required lengthy preparation time, they use resources that can be accessed in class, necessitating minimal updates. While showing how VR tools can be adopted and adapted in the teaching of language and culture, this study also presents an example of the potential application of VR in other teaching and learning sectors and disciplines.

References

Amara, K., Zenati, N., Djekoune, O., Anane, M., Aissaoui, I. K. & Rahma Bedla, H. (2023). I-DERASSA: e-learning platform based on augmented and virtual reality interaction for education and training. In *2021 International Conference on Artificial Intelligence for Cyber Security Systems and Privacy* (pp. 1–9). IEEE. doi.org/10.1109/AI-CSP52968.2021.9671151.

Bahari, A. (2022). Affordances and challenges of teaching languages skills by virtual reality: A systematic review (2010–2020). *E-Learning and Digital Media, 19*(2), 163–188. doi.org/10.1177/20427530211036583.

Berti, M. (2019). Italian open education: Virtual reality immersions for the language classroom. In A. Comas-Quinn, A. Beaven & B. Sawhill (Eds.), *New case studies of openness in and beyond the language classroom* (pp. 37–47). Research-publishing. net. doi.org/10.14705/rpnet.2019.37.965.

Bhattacharjee, J. (2015). Constructivist approach to learning—an effective approach of teaching learning. *International Research Journal of Interdisciplinary & Multidisciplinary Studies, 1*(6), 65–74.

Bonwell, C. & Eison, J. (1991). *Active learning: Creating excitement in the classroom.* ASHE-ERIC Higher Education Report Nr 1. Jossey-Bass.

Burke, A. (2011). Group work: How to use groups effectively. *The Journal of Effective Teaching, 11*(2), 87–95.

Chen, Y.-L. (2016). The effects of virtual reality learning environment on student cognitive and linguistic development. *Asia-Pacific Education Researcher, 25*(4), 637–646. doi.org/10.1007/s40299-016-0293-2.

Chittaro, L. & Ranon, R. (2007). Web3D technologies in learning, education and training: Motivations, issues, opportunities. *Computers and Education, 49*(1), 3–18. doi.org/10.1016/j.compedu.2005.06.002.

Coppola, D. (2016). The use 3D virtual worlds in language learning. *EL.LE, 5*(3). doi.org/10.14277/2280-6792/ELLE-5-3-1.

Dhimolea, T. K., Kaplan-Rakowski, R. & Lin, L. (2022). A systematic review of research on high-immersion virtual reality for language learning. *TechTrends, 66*, 810–824. doi.org/10.1007/s11528-022-00717-w.

Figueroa, R. B., Palma Gil, F. A. & Taniguchi, H. (2022). Piloting virtual reality photo-based tours among students of a Filipino language class: A case of emergency remote teaching in Japan. AVANT, *13*(2). doi.org/10.26913/avant.202208.

French, S. & Kennedy, G. (2017). Reassessing the value of university lectures. *Teaching in Higher Education, 22*(6), 639–654. doi.org/10.1080/13562517.2016.1273213.

Jackson, D. (2015). Employability skill development in work-integrated learning: Barriers and best practice. *Studies in Higher Education, 40*(2), 350–367. doi.org/10.1080/03075079.2013.842221.

Kolb, D. (1984). *Experiential learning: Experience as the source of learning and development.* Prentice Hall.

Lan, Y. J. (2016). *The essential components of game design in 3D virtual worlds: From a language perspective.* Springer. doi.org/10.1007/978-3-319-17461-7_24.

Lan, Y. J. (2020). Immersion, interaction and experience-oriented learning: Bringing virtual reality into FL learning. *Language Learning & Technology, 24*(1), 1–15. hdl.handle.net/10125/44704.

Lave, J. (1988). *Cognition in practice: Mind, mathematics, and culture in everyday life.* Cambridge University Press.

Lave, J. & Wenger, E. (1991). *Situated learning: Legitimate peripheral participation.* Cambridge University Press.

Lin, T. J. & Lan, Y. J. (2015). Language learning in virtual reality environments: Past, present, and future. *Educational Technology & Society, 18*(4), 486–497. jstor.org/stable/jeductechsoci.18.4.486.

Magnusson, P. & Godhe, A.-L. (2019). Multimodality in language education—implications for teaching. *Designs for Learning, 11*(1), 127–137. designsforlearning.nu/articles/10.16993/dfl.127.

Palaima, T. (2014, 11 September). The lost art of listening. *Times Higher Education.*

Panichi, L. & Deutschmann, M. (2009). Instructional design, teacher practice and learner autonomy. In J. Molka-Danielsen & M. Deutschmann (Eds.), *Learning and teaching in the virtual world of Second Life* (pp. 27–43). Tapir Academic Press.

Panichi, L. & Deutschmann, M. (2012). Language learning in virtual worlds: Research issues and methods. In M. Dooly & R. O'Dowd (Eds.), *Researching online foreign language interaction and exchange: Theories, methods and challenges* (pp. 205–232). Peter Lang.

Pilgrim, J. M. & Pilgrim, J. (2016). The use of virtual reality tools in the reading-language arts classroom. *Texas Journal of Literacy Education, 4*(2), 90–97.

Repetto, C. (2014). The use of virtual reality for language investigation and learning. *Frontiers in Psychology, 5*, 1280. doi.org/10.3389/fpsyg.2014.01280.

Schott, C. & Marshall, S. (2018). Virtual and situated experiential education: A conceptualization and exploratory trial. *Journal of Computer Assisted Learning, 34*(6), 843–852. doi.org/10.1111/jcal.12293.

Schwienhorst, K. (2002). Why virtual, why environments? Implementing virtual reality concepts in computer-assisted language learning. *Simulation & Gaming, 33*(2), 196–209. doi.org/10.1177/1046878102332008.

10

Loosening the reins of teacher control: Empowering student writers through web-based tools

Ana Maria Ducasse

1. Introduction

Written communication as a learning outcome is fundamental to tertiary education because of its requirement in many professional fields (Moore & Morton, 2017). However, learners of foreign, second or additional languages (AL) find it difficult to express their ideas accurately in writing. As a result, they often have recourse to online tools readily available on devices such as computers, tablets and smartphones. Despite the frequent use of online tools, they are not typically encouraged by teachers as the primary means of support for learners to express themselves in an AL (Groves & Mundt, 2015). However, these tools offer possibilities to drive learning and to develop learner agency, empowering students as authors and editors of their own work.

Task design, content, feedback and editing/correcting have traditionally been in the hands of teacher-assessors; however, in higher education, disruptive and decentring waves impacting the roles of teachers and students, particularly those related to web-based (WB) tools, have led to new ways of viewing writing in the AL class. This study critically engages with the theme of decentring, specifically, the shift in thinking that sees online tools as potential sources of epistemological authority rather than the teacher being the sole expert when it comes to producing written outputs in the AL. While the particular study presented in this chapter was a response to emergency online teaching during pandemic lockdowns, the questions raised about student use of WB tools in written production remain critically relevant. Applications including, but not limited to, ChatGPT, DeepL, Google Translate, Microsoft Editor and Grammarly have now forced learning and teaching committees, university management and other stakeholders to reflect on teachers' and students' practices and experiences and to consider how artificial intelligence (AI) applications can positively or negatively impact learning. It is therefore propitious to explore teacher implementation of a guided feedback protocol that takes advantage of digital resources and seeks to engage students with them productively.

This chapter explores the pedagogical implications of opening up teaching and assessment practices to include guided student use of online tools as sources of knowledge. Using the author's reflections as an action researcher in an Australian tertiary setting, it presents and evaluates a project on technology-enhanced writing in an AL context, using a specific feedback protocol that avoids direct correction in favour of encouragement of student agency, including individualised consultation of online tools such as dictionaries, concordances, grammar checkers and machine translation (MT).

The paper is structured following an action research cycle of observation, reflection, planning and action. The first section describes the context in which the project is carried out and the problem requiring critical attention (observation). The second discusses the principles important to the design of the feedback protocol (reflection). This protocol is then presented (planning), followed by a description of its implementation (action). Data from a cohort of students using the protocol are presented as a second observation section, leading to further reflections. The paper concludes with recommendations for educators and students planning their own teaching and learning.

2. Observation (i): Pen and paper meet emergency remote teaching

The case study presented is both specific to the context and an example of a local disruption that reflects more generalised shifts in paradigms. The feedback protocol was developed in reaction to emergency remote teaching (ERT) during the pandemic, when it was impossible to maintain the previous regime of weekly pen and paper writing tasks performed in class, under supervision and with no use of additional resources, either paper-based or online. There was an urgent need to adapt pen and paper assessments for online delivery during the period of COVID-induced ERT. In addition, there were concerns about academic integrity (Ducasse, 2022), since all in-class assessments were, by necessity, conducted online, and students were able to consult MT tools without teachers noticing.

In ERT conditions, there were no specific guidelines or policies for the use of technological tools in assessment for Spanish at the author's institution, which meant she was free to develop her own strategies. She devised an evolving feedback practice intended to provide AL learners with individual, sustainable input to their writing (Ducasse & Hill, 2019) that supported learners' use of online translators, dictionaries and corpora for improving their writing. It seemed easier to adapt to and adopt the available technology, rather than to shut the door on its possibilities and pretend students were not using it.

The author's positionality in the participatory action research undertaken was actively and proactively critical. The interrogation of teaching practices was driven by what Kemmis et al. (2014, p. 6) describe as:

> dissatisfactions, or issues, that lead ... towards felt concerns ... in the way we think, in the way we do things, and in our responses to the conditions in which we live and work.

As a multilingual speaker and writer, the author considers it surprising that AL teachers often do not accept student use of digital tools, even though they themselves unavoidably use them when texting or writing on a phone or computer for their daily written communication needs.

During COVID-19, the author was supporting students to be successful language learners, while personally learning how to teach, assess and provide online feedback. She sought to draw on her teaching experience to extend her innovative teaching practice efficiently—that is, by placing less emphasis on surface errors and a greater focus on content by offering students the opportunity to redraft until their texts communicated their content clearly with the support of MT and WB tools. The author hoped that lifting the guilt of 'cheating' or challenging academic integrity would encourage learners to spot and edit mistakes and revise already written texts, which, as Wallwork (2016) underlines, is as important as teaching learners to write texts. This approach permitted students to use all available WB tools to learn from and engage with, while enabling them to be as accurate as possible through their own endeavours.

3. Reflection (i): Principles for use of WB tools in additional languages teaching and assessment

The following discussion engages with scholarly literature on the use of technology in teaching and learning to present important principles that guided the initial response and its subsequent iterations.

3.1. 'Sustaining' and 'disruptive' technologies

In the field of pedagogy, a longstanding distinction has been made between 'disruptive' and 'sustaining' uses of technology. For example, a disruptive technology 'lead[s] to possibilities beyond those previously envisaged' (Chalhoub-Deville, 2002, p. 472), which is where twenty-first-century learning and teaching currently stands with chatbot technology and AI. In contrast, a 'sustaining technology' makes it easy to continue current practices. This is exemplified by the now ubiquitous learning management systems (LMS) that are often used without any reflection on teaching innovation—for example, as a filing cabinet in the sky, or simply as a platform allowing for WB assessment to stand for pen- and paper-based tasks.

Behind the apparent preference of many teachers for 'sustaining' technologies may lie an unwillingness to embrace digital disruption, which is seen as leading to the relinquishment of teacher power and prestige in favour of technology. Thus, to avoid such a usurpation, some educators may resist moving away from the teacher-controlled environment of pen and paper assessment and feedback (see Shahzadi & Ducasse, 2022). However, as Crossley (2018) has suggested with specific reference to MT, disruption transcends the university language classroom; it has moved to a digital space where potential language students can, rightly or wrongly, rely on MT applications for their communication needs rather than learning a language. Even those who do engage in language learning can see WB MT as their go-to technology. More broadly, if the use of technological tools, from spellcheckers to translators, is an everyday practice in the world, even for experienced language users (including teachers), why limit students' use of these tools in educational fora?

Many WB tools are available to improve written communication, offering particular benefits to adult AL learners frustrated by the simplification involved in writing at beginner levels. An early study suggests that embracing WB editing tools also supports L2 learning (Milton, 2006). It is imperative, therefore, to encourage learners to experiment with technologies to complete AL writing tasks, but with guidance and teacher feedback (Hyland & Hyland, 2006).

3.2. Technology-mediated language assessment and target language use

As a precursor to developing the new writing task, feedback protocol and marking rubric, the author considered various Bachman and Palmer's (2010, pp. 127–130) questions on the design of language assessment. Particularly relevant and reassuring was the question: 'To what extent and in what ways do TMLA [technology-mediated language assessment] tasks correspond to TLU [target language use] tasks?' Not only were pencil and paper tasks impossible to run in lockdown, but they were also deemed no longer authentic or related to target language usage in the real world. In contrast, the revised WB assessment tasks were completely relevant: 'writing tasks with access to online resources are situationally authentic for today's language learners' (Shin et al., 2021, p. 19). By motivating learners to use WB tools to produce and edit their L2 written texts, educators help them prepare for the digital world of work (Kivunja, 2015) in the twenty-first century. Such work mirrors current decentring perspectives in teaching and learning realities, moving away from teacher-focused feedback to encourage students to become proactive.

3.3. Translation

Research has shown that learners using MT access language they would have difficulty retrieving independently, allowing for improved construction of their AL text. Further, translation can foster understanding of connections between L1 and L2 structures (Roehr-Brackin, 2018) in addition to helping students understand the many options that exist to create their intended meaning (Vold, 2018). Teachers can train learners at all levels to improve accuracy and to discern mistranslations while using MT (Chung & Ahn, 2021).

3.4. Rich materials reflecting multilingual reality

The use of online resources, beyond textbooks and grammar books, can support intercultural learning as expressed in the revised Common European Framework of Reference (Council of Europe, 2020), which recognises learners as plurilingual subjects. As Canagarajah (2005, pp. 196–197) writes of English:

> we readily recognise that teaching literacy in a single language (English or vernacular) or a single dialect of that language (standard English or native varieties of English) fails to equip our students for real-world needs.

Opening up the classroom to online resources builds on this real-world idea: students of Spanish as an AL, based in Australia, move between different Spanish or English varieties as they explore WB resources and make strategic choices about their own use. This leads to a reflection on authentic communication.

3.5. Engagement with resources and feedback

While students may have access to WB tools, this does not mean that they necessarily know of them or how to best use them; nor does it mean that, having such knowledge, they will act on it. In the past, much research on revisions in language learning focused on the correction of errors in written products following pedagogic interventions. Few studies focused on student *processes* of writing and revision.

However, some studies have examined student engagement with feedback. In Attali's (2004) study, over two-thirds of the students involved did not produce a second draft after automated writing evaluation (AWE) feedback.

In Grimes's (2005) research, students engaged only superficially with AWE feedback, while half of the students in El Ebyary and Windeatt's (2010) study failed to redraft essays after such feedback. From early on, it was thought that 'tools and approaches ... providing frequent, individualised feedback on student writing ought to be considered, but not without keeping a critical eye turned onto carefully designed research' (Warschauer & Ware, 2006, p. 176). The trend of AWE studies showing limited benefits to students points to the need for a more complex chain of interaction with WB tools. In 2018, Zhang and Hyland put out an urgent call for studies examining how individual students engaged with feedback—either automated or from their teachers—in their redrafting. Both Man et al. (2022) and Ducasse and Hill (2019) used training activities and found that students were more proactive in the feedback process. A shift from feedback as information to processes that focus on learners' and teachers' perception of feedback helps students revise and improve their writing skills (Chong, 2022) and understanding of feedback processes (Ducasse et al., 2024).

Student feedback literacy has evolved as a student-centric concept (see definition in Yu et al., 2022) concerning students' approach, use and evaluation of feedback while managing their emotions. Building on this premise, Yu et al. (2022) developed and validated a scale for feedback on L2 writing assessment. Affect, one of the dimensions on the scale, interacts with student willingness to engage with the feedback process. Wu et al. (2023) underline the importance of developing students' feedback literacy to ensure they are emotionally ready for the feedback process, which may include discussing their work with teachers. To (2022) explores how learner-centred feedback design promotes engagement with feedback by increasing learner responsibility; feelings of psychological safety; and evaluative judgement, being the 'capability to make decisions about the quality of work of oneself and others' (Tai et al., 2018, p. 5).

3.6. Assessment for learning framework

An assessment for learning (AfL) framework places students at the centre of a class, with student agency made explicit (see Larsen-Freeman, 2019). This framework was selected because it embodies the author's aspirations and intentions. AfL is a framework in which:

> students become more metacognitively aware—that is, they learn about themselves as learners and become more aware of their own thought processes. They become more reflective as they engage

> in peer and self-assessment, set goals, reflect on their learning, and decide their next learning goals (with the teacher's help)—and hence develop self-regulated learning skills and boost their motivation. They also become more autonomous as they take greater responsibility for learning.
>
> (Lee, 2016, p. 272)

Five strategies are the mainstays of AfL (Wiliam & Thompson, 2017): clarifying success, eliciting evidence of student progress via assessment, peer-assessment and feedback, developing student self-assessment, and encouraging self-regulation. Feedback is one of the key strategies for this case study, as it is central for improvements in student learning using a combination of the remaining strategies.

4. Planning (i): Task design and feedback protocol

Previously, before COVID-19, language students typically wrote a paragraph at the end of each class to hand in for feedback at the next lesson. To facilitate autonomy during the lockdowns, and with students no longer in a classroom setting, assessment was implemented in iterative cycles across two semesters with a tightly designed feedback protocol. The task shifted from a face-to-face, closed-book restrictive teacher-controlled task ('How well can you write on a topic with pen and paper within a time-limit with no resources and only one attempt?') to an open-browser free-for-all ('How well can you write on a topic online with the help of WB tools, for example, dictionaries, conjugators, thesaurus, text editors, language keyboard etc. in your own time with drafting processes guided by teacher feedback?'). In response to the lack of teacher control over access to resources available online, a tool was designed to harness the use of WB tools. The resulting tool was intended to promote engagement and understanding of feedback, to improve student feedback literacy and their capacity to act on it (Ducasse & Hill, 2019). Students were supported to engage with, and be successful in, language learning because WB tools provided support beyond dictionary use: students could search for a single word, a phrase to be translated or check usage information for lexico-grammatical patterns (for example, use of prepositions or articles). Delimiting what was being assessed involved shifting sands, as power lay with the student to engage with language learning, editing and writing quite differently from previous semesters or their previous Spanish learning experience.

Over the semester, students wrote and submitted 10 short homework drafts and received feedback. The required number of words gradually increased, and each text covered a different genre. After producing a first draft with minimal use of WB tools, students received feedback from the teacher that, rather than correcting their work, pointed them towards online resources that could be used to improve their text. These assessments were called 'engagement tasks'. The engagement was with the class topic for homework and, more importantly, with the teacher's suggested edits (not corrections) on drafts. They received a percentage of the total 10 per cent engagement mark for each task. The engagement tasks were designed as sustainable, interactive formative assessment tools with individualised feedback. Students' voices were heard on the feedback coversheet and in weekly engagement task email exchanges. The teacher set a deadline within which students could address the feedback, make sense of it and act on it. Following this protocol, the teacher invited learners to demonstrate what feedback they were acting on, encouraging them to articulate how they used the feedback or not.

Until students took note of teacher feedback and made efforts to improve the text, referencing the resources used, no marks were awarded. They received a 10 per cent engagement mark for each task. The first draft submission was marked for the quality (grammar, vocabulary and communication of ideas) and the second, edited and improved with WB and other tools, was marked for accuracy through appropriate use of these aids.

Four drafts were submitted as summative assessments in weeks 4, 8, 10 and 12 of a 12-week semester: these end-of-topic summative WB tests were final drafts, completed in class. The summative language proficiency tasks were designed to build on previous formative tasks, and the links were made explicit because, as reported by Zimbardi et al. (2017), learners are then more likely to draw on feedback from previous tasks. The 10 per cent engagement mark was a formative practice for the summative tasks. While, ideally, formative assessment should not be marked, without marks, students do not complete them. Completing the extra 10 per cent could lift final grades to the next band (for example, distinction rather than credit), and students were meticulous in their drafting because they knew it was being marked. Anecdotally, the same task run as a pilot with no mark attached resulted in less than 10 per cent of the class actioning feedback. Adding the 10 per cent mark for drafts distributed the benefits of feedback across the class, as more students completed the task.

As mentioned, the final submission was not only a writing/editing practice but also part of a test. For these pieces, students were marked on how well they edited, using the rubric shown in Table 10.1. The first three rows refer to the writing criteria used to mark the final draft for cohesion and range of vocabulary and structures at the course level; therefore, the marking is course-content specific and criterion-referenced. Students were also marked for how efficiently they used tools to edit and the range of tools used. Since students were novices at using such tools, the greater number of tools used was to their advantage, because this gave them a range of inputs to choose from on the same question. This clearly advantaged students who had more mistakes. However, most beginner AL writers need considerable support to write accurately. In the grid, the typical usage for each level is determined from student self-reporting.

Table 10.1. Template grading rubric

	Below level <1	Pass 1.5	Credit 2	Distinction 2.5>	High distinction 3	/15
Original text						
Text flow Use of connectors and connected content						/3
Range and level of vocabulary						/3
Range and level of expression						/3
Edited text						
Edits marked up/in capitals edited correctly		>50%	>60%	>70%	>80%	/3
Tools used referenced in text	1 tool	2 tools	3 tools	4 tools	5 tools	/3
Tools (D) Online dictionary (OC) Online conjugator (OT) Online translator (CN/N) Class notes/notes (PPT) Class PowerPoint (M) Memory (A) Autocorrect (K) Keyboard						

Source: Author.

The feedback protocol facilitated learner agency through requiring a sustained effort to edit texts. Students gained marks from editing mistakes instead of losing marks for making them while trying to practise.

5. Action: Protocol in practice

This section presents examples of the draft, feedback and revision process, the design of which has been argued for and described above.

In an engagement task, students submitted Draft #1, written using only a WB dictionary referenced in the text as (D) to indicate where it had been consulted. They could request feedback on 'accuracy', 'expression variety', 'vocabulary' and 'flow and connectors'. The teacher marked up places in the text to carry out edits, listed suggested edits under the four criteria headings and marked Draft #1 for quality. (Note that the summative end-of-topic test gave much more weight to this criterion.) Learners then submitted Draft #2 for marking, having had the opportunity to follow their teacher's suggestions to use online tools to make edits. The edits were referenced just as a student normally would when writing an essay and borrowing words or ideas from another source, a concept that was easy for university students to grasp, since academic integrity is discussed in all subjects. Thus, the student submitted the text, listing all WB and other tools used. They were marked on the accuracy of edits to their original text (see Box 1).

Box 10.1 Example LMS summative assessment task

> **Semester 1 Spanish 3 A2**
> Draft 1 for feedback.
> Paste in Draft #1 here for feedback. It is your text written in response to the topic, with essential use of MT for single words only. Label in text with (D) for online dictionary if used.
> Paste in Teacher mark-up of Draft 1
> Paste the improved Draft #2 for assessment. Include the references in text to WB resources used to edit, as suggested by the teacher's mark-up.

An example of this process is presented below:
- *Student submission of Draft #1*: The task is to recount an important moment in history.

Box 10.2. Draft #1 — the original submitted text

En 2008 primer ministro, Kevin Rudd, se disculpó oficialmente a los pueblos indígenas de Australia, específicamente por la generación robada. Antes de la disculpa, no había reconocimiento gubernamental de malas acciones contra los pueblos indígenas en el pasado. En la sociedad en general, las personas no lo pensaban a menudo, o el tema era evitado porque las personas se sentían culpable, enojada o triste sobre la situación o desconectada de la situación completamente. Ahora todavía tenemos mucho que hacer para crear paz con nuestro pasado como un país, pero las actitudes sobre los pueblos indígenas están cambiando. Antes éramos muy separado, pero ahora hay algunas iniciativas para crear un futuro compartido.

- *Student feedback focus request*: This student ranks their priorities for teacher focus in feedback as: 1) accuracy, 2) expression variety, 3) vocabulary range, 4) flow and connectors (for discussion of L2 feedback requests, see Ducasse and Hill [2019]).
- *Teacher response to the feedback request*: For 'accuracy', the teacher uses symbols to mark up the text, pointing out edits that will earn marks (see Box 10.3). Accuracy mark-up key:
    - (): word is missing
    - ( ) around a group of words: group needs editing
    - * a single word has an error.

Box 10.3. Marked up student work — teacher insertions highlighted in yellow

En 2008 () primer ministro, Kevin Rudd, se disculpó oficialmente a los pueblos indígenas de Australia, específicamente por la generación robada. Antes de la disculpa, no había reconocimiento gubernamental de () malas acciones contra los pueblos indígenas en el pasado. En la sociedad en general, las personas no lo pensaban a menudo, o el tema era evitado porque las personas se sentían *culpable, * enojada o * triste sobre la situación o * desconectada de la situación completamente. Ahora todavía tenemos mucho que hacer para crear paz con nuestro pasado como un país, pero las actitudes sobre los pueblos indígenas están cambiando. Antes * éramos muy * separado, pero ahora hay algunas iniciativas para crear un futuro compartido.

- For 'expression variety', the teacher provides encouragement 'you are doing well', then suggests using a different structure to start each sentence: *Expression: vas bien. Piensa en empezar cada frase con una forma o estructura diferente.*
- For 'vocabulary range', the teacher suggests an online site for quick access to synonyms to provide variety: *150 palabras puedes usar sinónimos* www.lenguaje.com/herramientasV2/sinonimos.htm.[1]
- For 'flow and connectors', the teacher remarks that all is well for the student's level: *vas bien usas los marcadores de tiempo y algunos conectores que estudiamos.*
- *Student's submission of Draft #2.* The redraft includes in-text references to facilitate the teacher's cross-referencing of edits to the list of resources used: see Box 10.4, where the in-text references are highlighted.

Box 10.4. Draft #2 with in-text references highlighted

En 2008 *el* (OT) primer ministro, Kevin Rudd, se disculpó oficialmente a los pueblos indígenas de Australia, específicamente por la generación robada. Antes de la disculpa, no había reconocimiento gubernamental de *las* (OT) malas acciones contra los pueblos indígenas en el pasado. *En aquellos tiempos (N), en* la sociedad en general, las personas no lo pensaban a menudo, o el tema era evitado porque las personas se sentían *culpables* (A), *enojadas* (A) o *tristes* (A) sobre la situación o *desconectadas* (A) de la situación completamente. Ahora, *aunque* todavía tenemos *un largo camino para recorrer* (SpD) para crear paz con nuestro pasado como un país, las actitudes sobre los pueblos indígenas están cambiando. *Donde una vez* estábamos (N) separados (N), *hoy en día* (N) hay respeto entre las personas y hay *muchos más esfuerzos por ambas partes* para crear un futuro compartido.

Along with the draft, the student completes a record of the changes to demonstrate authorship of the edits and to indicate what tools were used.

---

1   Webpage discontinued.

Table 10.2. Student edits and sources table

Teacher edit number	Original teacher markup	Student tool for edits	Student edited text	Correct Yes/No
1	( ) primer ministro	OT	el primer ministro	Y
2	de ( ) malas acciones	OT	de las malas acciones	Y
3	*Culpable	Autocorrect Word	culpables	Y
4	*enojada	Autocorrect Word	enojadas	Y
5	o *triste	Autocorrect Word	o tristes	Y
6	*desconectada	Autocorrect Word	desconectadas	Y
Student edit	Antes	Linguee	Donde una vez	-
Student edit	Algunas iniciativas	Linguee	Muchos más esfuerzos por ambas partes	-
Student edit	Ahora	Notes	Hoy en día En aquellos tiempos	-
7	Ahora todavía tenemos mucho ( ) hacer	Spanish Dict.	Ahora, aunque todavía tenemos un largo camino para recorrer	Y
8	(un) país	-	Un país	N
9	*eramos muy	Notes	Estábamos muy	Y
10	*separado	Notes	separados	Y

Note: Online translator (OT).
Source: Author.

The intention was to encourage students to use online resources to demonstrate understanding of teacher feedback by making accurate choices in the resubmitted drafts. Such engagement could correlate positively with feelings of agency in using online tools to achieve and to demonstrate visible improvement (Zhang & Hyland, 2018), thus supporting a realisation of the value of ongoing effort. This fits with ideas expressed by psychologist Carol Dweck (Hopkins, 2005):

> When students fail, teachers should also give feedback about effort or strategies—what the student did wrong and what he or she could do now. We have shown that this is a key ingredient in creating mastery-oriented students.

In other words, teachers should help students value effort. Too many students think effort is only for the inept. Yet sustained effort over time is the key to outstanding achievement.

In addition, this process permitted the gathering of data on the online tools students were using to edit and improve texts.[2]

6. Observation (ii): Data collection on implementation of the protocol

Here I explore the specific teaching intervention put in place in response to the considerations outlined above. An exploration of student engagement with feedback and WB tools contributes to evolving knowledge about how CALL projects support learners to achieve language-related goals (Buendgens-Kosten, 2020) and develop agency, especially attributes such as judgement and self-reliance (Bridgstock, 2009).

6.1. Data collection tools

The following data will be discussed here: learning analytics from the Canvas LMS for learners who had given informed consent, and a content analysis of open-text anonymous comments harvested from the university-administered student evaluation of courses.

6.1.1. Participants and recruitment

LMS data were collected from intermediate Spanish language learners (n = 6) at an Australian university. They were predominantly enrolled in a Bachelor of International Studies (Global Studies) in which the focus of language learning is to understand the culture of the other. Students attended online workshops twice a week for two hours during the two 12-week semesters of 2020. In Semester 1, they took Spanish 3, CEFR level A1.2; in Semester 2, they took Spanish 4, CEFR level B1.1. This was the first time the course was taught synchronously using the Canvas Collaborate LMS. Ethical clearance was granted via approval for an international digital feedback project in various institutions. The student participants, after responding to email recruitment after the course was finished and the marks published, provided consent to quote from their assessments and feedback.

---

2   For discussion in relation to Spanish AL multimodal writing contexts, see Ducasse (2022).

6.2. Learner engagement

Table 10.3 presents LMS data for the six participating students.

Column 1 indicates those students who studied in the two semesters and volunteered to participate. Column 2 shows how many of the 10 drafts they submitted. Column 3 presents LMS analytics that rate the student participation online as low, moderate or high. Column 4 shows the students' rankings in their whole cohort (41 in first semester, 31 in second) in terms of number of page views. In column five appear the total marks for Spanish 3 and Spanish 4, which can be compared with the marks for drafts, presented in the remaining columns. Based on the criteria shown in Table 10.2, 0–5 is a poor mark, 5–10 is a mid-range mark and a good mark (in the top third) is between 10 and 15.

It is interesting to note that the number of page views does not correlate with how well the student fared by marks or the number of submissions made for drafting. High page viewers were likely to receive both high and low marks.

Table 10.3. Learner engagement as shown by LMS analytics

Students n = 6	Drafts submitted		LMS participation		LMS page views ranking		Final marks		LMS task Poor mark		LMS task Fair mark		LMS task Good mark	
	S1	S2	S1	S2	S1	S2	S1	S2	S1	S2	S1	S2	S1	S2
(M) CM_1	8	5	mod	high	13/41	03/31	81	77	0	1	1	3	7	2
(F) CB_2	9	8.5	mod	mod	04/41	04/31	90	83	0	0	0	0	8	6
(F) MB_3	8	7	high	high	09/41	06/31	75	75	1	0	3	3	4	3
(F) MF_4	9	8.5	mod	high	21/41	18/31	93	93	0	0	0	0	8	6
(F) HC_5	7	7	mod	high	14/41	9/31	71	75	2	1	3	1	3	4
(F) MG_6	5	6	high	mod	03/41	2/31	76	76	2	0	0	2	6	4

Source: Author.

6.3. Affective response and personal reflections

Further data on the students' response to the intervention come from the university-administered course evaluation exercise and the anonymous answers to open-ended questions. The teacher/author inferred from these that the use of the engagement task protocol facilitated learner empowerment and autonomy.

One question on the course evaluation asked how much feedback was provided. Earlier work in this area by Ducasse and Hill (2019) was provoked by the uninspiring responses from students who did not recognise the amount of work that went into providing feedback. With such an explicit feedback protocol as presented here, it was pleasing to read: 'She always makes sure to comment on your work' (Student Participant [SP]3, 2020). Another student wrote:

> The best aspect of this course was the paragraph writing that we sent and got feedback for. We then used online tools to make our paragraph better. I think I learnt the most out of that task.
>
> (SP3, 2020)

Another described the feedback as 'valuable', 'good', 'extremely helpful' (SP4 2020). Students also reflected on the impact the exercise had on their study habits: 'helps me to synthesise what I've learnt'; 'great for keeping me on track'; 'helps me refine my writing skills and also to practise my grammar + sentence structure' (SP3, 2020); and 'a great way to keep improving my writing' (SP4, 2020). One student reported 'lik[ing] the weekly writing tasks because they help me to synthesise what I've learnt while getting valuable feedback' (SP3, 2020). Another reflected on their level of personal effort: 'I really challenged myself and learnt lots this semester' (SP3, 2020). The feeling of empowerment that came from improving their own work autonomously using online tools was a driver for success, as students could observe their improvements from Draft #1 to Draft #2.

7. Reflection (ii): Supporting student agency

The data analysis shows that the engagement task protocol contributed to a culture in which language learners felt confident that their agency could help them to advance. It provided learners with strategies and insights into how they could improve their texts using WB tools and following their teacher's guidance. Confident that they understood the quality to aspire to and the rigour required in addressing teacher feedback, students were able to develop self-regulation techniques. The learning environment gave students ownership of their language learning, and both weaker and stronger students were motivated to take on the digital feedback tasks to improve learning and their marks.

Lecturers in Australian universities feel under threat of being replaced by technology, but there is compelling evidence that lecturer–student relationships enhance student outcomes (Farr-Wharton et al., 2018). The findings presented here show that technology, utilised appropriately with teacher guidance, is a motivator of students. Learners oriented positively to individualised feedback, responded well to editing their texts digitally and benefitted from observing the transformation from the first draft to the final text.

By emphasising shifts in the conceptualisation of learner agency, the innovative feedback protocol in the study contributes to AL education across private and public material and digital social contexts in a multilingual world (Douglas Fir Group, 2016, p. 20). It is clear that online tools can be sources of epistemological authority in instructed second language acquisition, rather than the teacher being the sole authority. That said, it is also the case that using WB tools exposes students to a greater variety of language than normally available through a teacher's editorial or proofreading input, requiring them to exercise discernment as they critically evaluate the worth of the information gathered. Decentring the teacher as editor promotes awareness that learners have the agency to lead their own learning and be 'the first editor' of their work (Ducasse & Hill, 2019), promoting the development and application of evaluative judgement.

8. Planning (ii): Practical implications

Numerous practical implications can be drawn from this protocol for teachers and students. For teachers:

- Focus on learning processes by providing formative feedback, developing students' ability to lead their own learning and complete diverse tasks in the target language

- Offer digital tools and enable students to use an open browser to accelerate learning by making use of individualised tools to develop their writing
- Do not ban or ignore digital tools and but discuss their use
- Take a position on web-based tools and develop policies for their use (Barrot, 2023)
- Train students if, how and when to use tools selectively and effectively.

For students:

- Become aware of their agency to lead their own learning
- Be 'the first editor' of their work before submitting assessments
- Find ways of determining for themselves 'the extent of the benefit' of self-correction for individual language learning.

In brief, what is necessary is a change in the positioning of digital tools so that they are seen as a means of helping students to do their work rather than simply fixing it (Brooks et al., 2021). Helpful here is Hattie's (2008) idea of visible learning, in which students are taught to see their work through the eyes of teachers, then plan the next steps with teachers to see what is needed for them to learn. In the case of this project, this support comes from well-used online tools.

Future research might include an analysis of which WB tools learners use the most for editing purposes and their uptake over time. Close scrutiny of weekly submitted writing tasks may offer evidence of the latter. It would also be instructive to analyse the reactions of teachers and students to the permitted use of online tools in assessment. Teachers may find it challenging to support students in executing technology-enhanced writing in tertiary AL classrooms. Nevertheless, the findings have practical implications for teachers to focus on learning by providing all types of formative feedback that develop learners' ability to lead their learning and, thus, their capacity to complete diverse tasks in the target language. More than ever since the arrival of ChatGPT, teachers should take a position and develop policies for using WB tools. This should include training students how and when to use WB tools selectively and effectively to drive their own learning and outputs.

Ethics approval

RMIT University ethics approval #2020-23688-13090.

Acknowledgements

This chapter is situated within the research project Inter_ECODAL: Interculturality and Inter-Comprehension Assessing Plurilingual Discourse Competence: Digital Student Feedback Literacy (grant number PID2020-113796RB-I00), co-funded by the Spanish Ministry of Science and Innovation and the *Agencia Estatal de Investigación*.

References

Attali, Y. (2004). Exploring the feedback and revision features of Criterion. *Journal of Second Language Writing 14*(3), 191–205.

Bachman, L. F. & Palmer, A. S. (2010). *Language assessment in practice: Developing language assessments and justifying their use in the real world*. Oxford University Press.

Barrot, J. S. (2023). Using ChatGPT for second language writing: Pitfalls and potentials. *Assessing Writing, 57*, 100745. doi.org/10.1016/j.asw.2023.100745.

Bridgstock, R. (2009). The graduate attributes we've overlooked: Enhancing graduate employability through career management skills. *Higher Education Research & Development, 28*(1), 31–44. doi.org/10.1080/07294360802444347.

Brooks, C., Burton, R., van der Kleij, F., Carroll, A., Olave, K. & Hattie, J. (2021). From fixing the work to improving the learner: An initial evaluation of a professional learning intervention using a new student-centred feedback model. *Studies in Educational Evaluation, 68*, 100943. doi.org/10.1016/j.stueduc.2020.100943.

Buendgens-Kosten, J. (2020). The monolingual problem of computer-assisted language learning. *ReCALL, 32*(3), 307–322. doi.org/10.1017/S095834402000004X.

Canagarajah, S. (2005). Critical pedagogy in L2 learning and teaching. In E. Hinkel (Ed.), *Handbook of research in second language teaching and learning* (pp. 931–949). Routledge.

Chalhoub-Deville, M. (2002). Technology in standardized language assessments. In R. Kaplan (Ed.), *Oxford handbook of applied linguistics* (pp. 471–484). Oxford University Press. doi.org/10.1093/oxfordhb/9780195384253.013.0035.

Chong, S. W. (2022). The role of feedback literacy in written corrective feedback research: From feedback information to feedback ecology. *Cogent Education, 9*(1) 2082120. doi.org/10.1080/2331186X.2022.2082120.

Chung, E. S. & Ahn, S. (2021). The effect of using machine translation on linguistic features in L2 writing across proficiency levels and text genres. *Computer Assisted Language Learning, 35*(9), 2239–2264. doi.org/10.1080/09588221.2020.187 1029.

Council of Europe. (2020). *Common European Framework of Reference for Languages: Learning, teaching, assessment—companion volume.* Council of Europe Publishing.

Crossley, S. A. (2018). Technological disruption in foreign language teaching: The rise of simultaneous machine translation. *Language Teaching, 51*(4), 541–552. doi.org/10.1017/S0261444818000253.

Douglas Fir Group. (2016). A transdisciplinary framework for SLA in a multilingual world. *Modern Language Journal, 100*(S1), 19–47. doi.org/10.1111/modl.12301.

Ducasse, A. M. (2022). Oral reflection tasks: Advanced Spanish L2 learner insights on emergency remote teaching assessment practices in a higher education context. *Languages, 7*(1), 26. doi.org/10.3390/languages7010026.

Ducasse, A. M. & Hill, K. (2019). Developing student feedback literacy using educational technology and the reflective feedback conversation. *Practitioner Research in Higher Education, 12*(1), 24–37.

Ducasse, A. M., Hill, K., Mullan, K., Qi, J., Ni, J., Yoshida, M. and Fujioka, M. (2024) The tangle in the feedback loop: Learner agency through a feedback loop activity across four university language programs. *Practitioner Research in Higher Education Journal*, 82–102.

El Ebyary, K. & Windeatt, S. (2010). The impact of computer-based feedback on learners' written work. *International Journal of English Studies, 10*(2), 121–142. doi.org/10.6018/ijes/2010/2/119231.

Farr-Wharton, B., Charles, M., Keast, R., Woolcott, G. & Chamberlain, D. (2018). Why lecturers still matter: The impact of lecturer-student exchange on student engagement and intention to leave university prematurely. *Higher Education, 75,* 167–185. doi.org/10.1007/s10734-017-0190-5.

Grimes, D. (2005). Assessing automated assessment: Essay evaluation software in the classroom. In *Proceedings of the Computers and Writing Conference, Stanford, CA.*

Groves, M. & Mundt, K. (2015). Friend or foe? Google Translate in language for academic purposes. *English for Specific Purposes*, *37*, 112–121. doi.org/10.1016/j.esp.2014.09.001.

Hattie, J. (2008). *Visible learning: A synthesis of over 800 meta-analyses relating to achievement*. Routledge.

Hopkins, G. (2005). How can teachers develop students' motivation—and success? Interview with Carol S. Dweck. *Education World*. educationworld.com/a_issues/chat/chat010.shtml.

Hyland, K. & Hyland, F. (2006). Feedback on second language learners' writing. *Language Teaching*, *39*(2), 83–101. doi.org/10.1017/S0261444806003399.

Kemmis, S., McTaggart, R. & Nixon, R. (2014). *The action research planner: Doing critical participatory action research*. Springer.

Kivunja, C. (2015). Teaching students to learn and to work well with 21st century skills: Unpacking the career and life skills domain of the new learning paradigm. *International Journal of Higher Education*, *4*(1), 1–11. doi.org/10.5430/ijhe.v4n1p1.

Larsen-Freeman, D. (2019). On language learner agency: A complex dynamic systems theory perspective. *The Modern Language Journal*, *103*(S1), 61–79. doi.org/10.1111/modl.12536.

Lee, I. (2016). Putting students at the centre of classroom L2 writing assessment. *Canadian Modern Language Review*, *72*(2), 258–280. doi.org/10.3138/cmlr.2802.

Man, D., Kong, B. & Chau, M. H. (2022). Developing student feedback literacy through peer review training. *RELC Journal*, *55*(2). doi.org/10.1177/00336882221078380.

Milton, J. (2006). Resource-rich web-based feedback: Helping learners become independent writers. In K. Hyland and F. Hyland (Eds.), *Feedback in second language writing: Contexts and issues* (pp. 123–139). Cambridge University Press. doi.org/10.1017/CBO9781139524742.009.

Moore, T. & Morton, J. (2017). The myth of job readiness? Written communication, employability, and the 'skills gap' in higher education. *Studies in Higher Education*, *42*(3), 591–609. doi.org/10.1080/03075079.2015.1067602.

Roehr-Brackin, K. (2018). *Metalinguistic awareness and second language acquisition*. Routledge.

Shahzadi, A. & Ducasse, A. M. (2022). Language assessment literacy of teachers in an English medium of instruction university: Implications for ELT training in Pakistan. *Studies in Language Assessment*, *11*(1), 92–218. doi.org/10.58379/BZWF5085.

Shin, D., Kwon, S. K. & Lee, Y. (2021). The effect of using online language-support resources on L2 writing performance. *Language Testing in Asia*, *11*(4), 1–23. doi.org/10.1186/s40468-021-00119-4.

Tai, J., Ajjawi, R., Boud, D., Dawson, P. & Panadero, E. (2018). Developing evaluative judgement: Enabling students to make decisions about the quality of work. *Higher Education*, *76*, 467–481. doi.org/10.1007/s10734-017-0220-3.

To, J. (2022). Using learner-centred feedback design to promote students' engagement with feedback. *Higher Education Research and Development*, *41*(4), 1309–1324. doi.org/10.1080/07294360.2021.1882403.

Vold, E. T. (2018). Using machine-translated texts to generate L3 learners' metalinguistic talk. In Å, Haukås, C. Bjørke & M. Dypedahl (Eds.) *Metacognition in language learning and teaching* (pp. 67–97). Routledge. doi.org/10.4324/9781351049146-5.

Wallwork, A. (2016). *English for writing research papers.* Springer.

Warschauer, M. & Ware, P. (2006). Automated writing evaluation: Defining the classroom research agenda. *Language Teaching Research*, *10*(2), 157–180. doi.org/10.1191/1362168806lr190oa.

Wiliam, D. & Thompson, M. (2017). Integrating assessment with learning: What will it take to make it work? In C. A. Dwyer (Ed.), *The future of assessment: Shaping teaching and learning* (pp. 53–82). Routledge. doi.org/10.4324/9781315086545-3.

Wu, S., Yu, S. & Luo, Y. (2023). The development of teacher feedback literacy in situ: EFL writing teachers' endeavor to human-computer-AWE integral feedback innovation [sic]. *Assessing Writing*, *57*, 100739. doi.org/10.1016/j.asw.2023.100739.

Yu, S., Di Zhang, E. & Liu, C. (2022). Assessing L2 student writing feedback literacy: A scale development and validation study. *Assessing Writing*, *53*, 100643. doi.org/10.1016/j.asw.2022.100643.

Zhang, Z. V. & Hyland, K. (2018). Learner engagement with teacher and automated feedback on L2 writing. *Assessing Writing, 36*, 90–102. doi.org/10.1016/j.asw.2018.02.004.

Zimbardi, K., Colthorpe, K., Dekker, A., Engstrom, C., Bugarcic, A., Worthy, P., Victor, R., Chunduri, P., Lluka, L. & Long, P. (2017). Are they using my feedback? The extent of students' feedback use has a large impact on subsequent academic performance. *Assessment & Evaluation in Higher Education*, *42*(4), 625–644. doi.org/10.1080/02602938.2016.1174187.

Index

Note: Page numbers with 'n' indicate footnotes.

Aboriginal English (AE) 9, 20, 22–23, 26, 28, 30, 32–33, 36
  see also Indigenous languages
Aboriginal Education Strategy 2019 to 2029 (SA) 50, 55
Aboriginal Languages Framework see Australian Indigenous Languages Framework
Aboriginal languages see Indigenous languages
Aboriginal students see Indigenous students
academic integrity 225, 226, 233
active citizenship 121–122, 126, 129, 133
active learning 13, 126, 206
Adnyamathanha 42, 47–48, 52
agency
  student 4, 13, 101, 119, 126, 181, 223–224, 229, 233, 236–241
  teacher 4, 13, 150
  human 14, 169
  definition 14
Amery, Rob 43, 46–47, 49
anxiety 12, 106, 179–180, 183–186, 194–197
artificial intelligence (AI) 14, 15, 170, 224, 226
assessment for learning (AfL) 229–230
authentic
  activities 24, 27, 180, 182, 227

communication/interaction 116, 133, 182, 192, 212, 228
  selves 21
  texts/sources 13, 65, 96–97, 124, 181, 201, 206–207
authenticity 32, 209
Australian Indigenous Languages Framework (AILF) 46, 49, 52, 54, 56, 59
Australian Kriol 22
Australian Skills Quality Authority (ASQA) 44–45

Bain, Kira 47n5
Batchelor Institute (College) 20, 22–24, 28, 34, 35, 46
bilingual/ism 23, 31, 50, 129
'black look' 33
Blake, Barry 47
blended learning 118–119, 149
Boandik 42, 47–48
both-ways learning/teaching 20–26, 28, 30–31, 36
brave spaces 98–99, 105
Buckskin, Jack Kanya 46, 47n5, 49
Burbules, Nicholas C. 117–118
Byram, Michael 120–121

Canvas 207, 210, 237
  see also LMS
catcalling 129, 132, 134, 140
Charles Darwin University 28, 35

ChatGPT 224, 241
Chinese language 153, 155–156, 158–161, 163–164
cisgender/ism 91, 94, 95, 99, 100, 103, 107
communicative event 64–76, 80–81
comprehension 65, 73, 79, 94, 165–166, 180, 182–183, 201, 214, 218
computer-assisted language learning (CALL) 149–151, 153, 154, 168, 203, 237
computer-mediated communication (CMC) 149
corpus linguistics 70
COVID-19 11, 13, 77, 89, 115, 144, 182, 186, 191, 202
   disruption, 1, 13, 148, 218
   emergency online/remote teaching 7, 150, 224–225
   lockdown 116, 146, 190, 224, 227, 230
   post-pandemic 13, 118, 151, 214, 218
critical language education 80
cultural safety 26, 28, 36
curriculum-centred 215

decolonisation 5
digital communications technology 10, 63, 64, 75, 80
de l'Horizon, Kim 101
design for learning 148–149, 151–154, 156, 161, 168–170
design pattern/s 12, 149, 153–158, 160, 163, 166–170
design-based research (DBR) 154
dual delivery 202
digital literacy 204, 218
digital tools *see* web-based tools
disruptive technology 15, 226
disruption
   assumptions 80
   concept 2–4, 6, 8–9
   COVID-19 1, 13, 148, 218

digital technology 149, 226
   historical 42
   idealisations 79, 81
   ideology 64, 75, 81
   pedagogical practices 118
   virtual reality 13
decentring
   blended learning 119
   cis-heteronormative language 107
   concept 4–5, 6, 8–9
   digital communications technology 64
   online tools 223–224
   pedagogical practices 2, 80, 89, 180–181, 196, 217, 227, 240
   power and control 41
diversification
   concept 5–6, 7, 8–9
   design 156, 163, 167–168
   pedagogical practices 116, 118, 136, 148, 179–180, 202, 205, 208, 215

Eckert, Paul 48
e-learning 153
emergency online/remote teaching *see* COVID-19
empathy 15
English language teaching 4, 90
experiential learning 13, 204–205, 218–219
expert knowers 68–69, 81

feminist 92–95, 101
Flip 116, 128–129
formality 11, 74, 101, 102, 103, 133

Gale, Mary-Anne 44, 45, 47–48
gender
   bias 92, 95
   binary 91, 97, 102, 103
   equality 124, 134, 140, 141
   just/justice 11, 89, 90, 92, 94–96, 98–99, 101, 103–106, 107

nonconforming 95–99, 105
stereotypes 92, 95–97, 99
studies 97
gendered language 94, 97, 103
Genki: An Integrated Course in Elementary Japanese 70, 97
German language 49, 90, 92–97, 100–101, 104–105, 107
German Language Association 94
global citizenship 11, 116, 117, 121, 123–126, 133, 139–146
global warming 128, 129
Google Earth 202, 210, 214, 215
grammar 45–46, 93, 100–101, 132, 149, 194, 207, 231
checkers 13, 224
dictionaries 91, 228
Grammarly 224
Gray, Mike 43, 46
guitar (metaphor) 9, 19, 26, 34–35

H5P Interactive Video 202, 207, 210
hashtags 10, 75–77
heteronormativity 11, 91, 102, 103, 106, 107
higher education 2, 15, 20, 29, 121, 147, 202, 223
homestay 72, 74, 123

idealisation 10, 64–70, 72, 74–77, 79–81
ideology 23, 64, 67, 68, 91
Indigenous
epistemologies 19
languages 5, 7, 10, 22, 41–59
literacies 24
standpoint 20, 21
students 9, 10, 20, 24, 35–36, 42, 47n5, 54
knowledge systems 10, 21, 25, 31
immersion 117–118, 201, 203–204, 206, 214, 216, 218–219
in-country exchange 11–12, 123, 136
see also study abroad

Indigenist research 26
Instagram 10, 75, 76
interactive technologies 75, 119
see also social media; videoconferencing
instructional designers 12, 149, 153–158, 162, 163, 165–170
intercultural citizenship 11, 120–122, 125–126
intercultural competence 120–121, 126
Italian
colloquial 181, 192, 196
community/presence 192–193
culture 124, 126, 182, 207
language courses 13, 123, 129, 201–202, 205–208, 214, 216, 219
language learners 11, 116, 190–193
licei students 115–116, 133–135, 142
podcasting project 12, 192–193
speakers 12, 193, 197
studies 123, 127, 180–181

Japanese language 10, 65, 69–81, 90–91, 94–97, 101–107, 139
Japanese men's language (JML) 91, 102
Japanese women's language (JWL) 91, 102–103

kapati (metaphor) 9, 19, 26, 28–30, 34–35
Kaurna 42–43, 45–50, 52, 54, 57
Kaurna Plains School 46–47
knowledge building 10, 119

learning environment 5, 14, 31, 105, 107, 116, 119, 155, 162, 240
see also virtual learning environment
lockdown *see* COVID-19
Learnline 35

language learning textbooks *see* textbooks
L2 *see* second language
LGBTQIA+ 89–91, 96, 98, 100, 103–107, 129
Lang, Birgit 106
learner-centred teaching 13, 180, 204–205, 215, 229
learning management systems 11, 13, 106, 124–125, 207, 210, 226, 233, 237–238
linguistic repertoire/s 9, 20, 23–24, 27, 30–31, 35–37, 67, 72, 106, 122–123

machine translation 13, 224–228, 233
Maree, Claire 104
McHughes, Eileen 44, 45, 47
Mercurio, Tony 49
metaphor 4, 6, 218
    Indigenous use 9, 19, 24–26, 29–30, 34–35, 37
Mickan, Peter 44
Microsoft Flip *see* Flip
Miller, Gladys 44
Mission Australia Youth Survey Report 89, 100
Monaghan, Paul 44
monolingualism 50, 90, 106
Moon, David 47
motivation 122, 126, 179–191, 194, 201, 230
    extrinsic 184
    intrinsic 12, 184, 191, 196
multicultural/ism 7, 9, 14, 23, 134, 139, 141, 155
multilingual/ism 7, 9, 14, 23, 31, 50, 90, 105–107, 121, 155, 225, 240
multimodality 13, 76, 105, 125, 150, 156, 169, 205, 218–219
Murray Bridge 44, 45, 47

Narungga 42, 43, 47–48, 52
neopronouns 92–93, 97, 100
New Zealand 97, 150, 153
Ngarrindjeri 42, 44–45, 47–48, 52
non-binary 92, 95, 98, 101
non-verbal communication 33
    'the look'/'black look' 33–34
normalisation 16, 35
NVivo 186

O'Dowd, R. 116, 121, 126
O'Loughlin, Kevin (Dookie) 43
object-based learning (OBL) 205, 207
Oculus headset 13, 202, 207, 211, 214–216, 218
online tools *see* web-based tools
oral assessment/presentation 179, 180, 184–186, 194–196, 207
overseas exchange *see* in-country exchange; study abroad

pandemic *see* COVID-19
pedagogic device 64, 67
pedagogisation 68, 73, 80
Pitjantjatjara 42, 43, 48, 50, 54
place (concept) 12, 117–118, 156, 168
plurilingualism 228
podcasts 12, 180–184, 186, 189–197
politeness 91, 101, 103
project-based learning (PBL) 149–150, 180–181, 185, 190, 197, 217
pronouns 11, 73, 90–94, 100–106
    see also neopronouns
pronunciation 93, 132, 182, 183, 206
propaganda 202, 212, 216
Pusch, Luise F. 92, 100

queer pedagogy 90, 98, 104, 107
queering 90–91

readability 94
robot-assisted language learning (RALL) 149, 154–157, 159, 167–170
robots 12, 155–156, 159–167, 170, 176–177
Rome 202, 208, 210, 211, 217

safe/safe(r) spaces 98–99, 100, 103, 105, 106–107
see also brave spaces
SBS Italian 12, 180
second language 12, 66, 179–185, 188, 190n1, 192n2, 196, 227–229, 240
Second Life 203
semiotic choice 69–70, 72
sexism 94–95
sexuality 64, 89, 91, 97, 100, 102–103, 106
sign languages 5
slipping and sliding (metaphor) 9, 19, 26, 29–32, 35–36
social justice 6, 15, 50, 98, 99
social media 75, 76, 77, 80, 105, 126, 165–166
socialisation 10
SOGIESC (sexual orientation, gender identity and expression, and sex characteristics) 11, 89–91, 96, 105, 107
Spanish language 13, 79, 123, 225, 228, 231, 237
spatial-temporal language learning 169
speech community 22, 64–65, 67–68, 71, 74–77, 79–81
Standard Australian English (SAE) 22, 23, 30–32, 34, 35, 50
student-generated content (SGC) 180–181, 193, 194, 197
study abroad 70, 75, 103, 115, 118
sustaining technology 226

Tauondi Aboriginal Community College 42–47, 57
teacher-centred 180, 185
see also learner-centred
teacher education 9, 19–20, 25, 28, 31–32, 66, 149
teachers-as-designers 149, 152, 156–157, 161, 163, 165, 168–1169
technology
  digital 10, 147, 149–151
  disruptive 226
  mobile 148
  sustaining 226
  virtual reality 203
technology-enhanced language learning (TELL) 149–151, 153, 154, 168
see also computer-assisted language learning
technology, pedagogy and content knowledge (TPACK) 152
telecollaboration *see* virtual exchange
textbooks 10–11, 63–75, 79, 91–92, 96–98, 101, 103, 188, 228
Timaepatua, Berna 25
trans-affirming pedagogy 90, 98, 104, 107
translanguaging 31, 72, 106, 122, 123
translation 101, 104, 159, 228
see also machine translation

University of Adelaide 43, 44, 46, 54, 54n12
University of Melbourne 13, 96, 106, 116, 123, 127, 142, 179, 181–182, 201, 206
University of South Australia (UniSA) 48, 54
Usinger, Johanna 93

Varcoe, Nelson 43, 46
verbal memory 204
videoconferencing 75, 77

virtual
 exchange 11–12, 77, 115–129, 132, 136
 learning environment (VLE) 201, 203, 205–206, 218
 reality 13, 148–149, 201–202, 204–212, 214–219
 space 117, 122, 203
 tour 202, 208–210, 214, 216–217
vocabulary 132

Warriparinga 43, 46
Watkins, Cherie 43, 46, 49
web-based (WB) tools, 13, 223–231, 233, 236–237, 239–241
welcome to country 45–47
WhatsApp 126
 see also social media
Wirangu 42, 44, 48

Yandell, Julia 44
yarning 26
 see also kapati
Yolngu 25
YouTube 81, 208

Zoom 129, 144, 165, 207

www.ingramcontent.com/pod-product-compliance
Lightning Source LLC
Chambersburg PA
CBHW052048220426
43663CB00012B/2482